# CHESS STRATEGY

BY

EDWARD LASKER

TRANSLATED BY

J. DU MONT

DOVER PUBLICATIONS, INC.

NEW YORK

Published in Canada by General Publishing Company, Ltd., 30 Lesmill Road, Don Mills, Toronto, Ontario.
Published in the United Kingdom by Constable and Company, Ltd., 10 Orange Street, London WC 2.

This Dover edition, first published in 1959, is an unabridged republication of the second revised (1915) edition originally published by G. Bell & Sons, Ltd. This edition contains a new Preface by the author.

*Standard Book Number: 486-20528-2*
*Library of Congress Catalog Card Number: 59-4183*

Manufactured in the United States of America
Dover Publications, Inc.
180 Varick Street
New York, N.Y. 10014

# CONTENTS

# PART II

## ILLUSTRATIVE GAMES FROM MASTER TOURNAMENTS

# CONTENTS

# PREFACE TO DOVER EDITION

I was pleased and flattered by Dover Publications' offer to reprint this book that I wrote as a young student in Europe fifty years ago. It had run up a pleasantly large number of editions when the flames of Hitlerite fanaticism consumed the German version, and the British plates — in the publishers' words — were "destroyed by enemy action".

In a way, the book's success reflected the rapid growth of chess popularity everywhere. But I believe it owed that success mainly to the idea that had prompted me to write it: to teach chess on the basis of general strategic principles rather than widely diversified analyses. This method unquestionably appealed to the great majority of chess students.

The chess master must thoroughly know the published analyses of openings, and he must keep up with their ever-increasing depth, or else he loses too much time in analyzing an unfamiliar variation over the board. In tournament chess where the player's time is limited, this would place him at a great disadvantage. The amateur, however, has no such problems. His opponents are fairly certain to be as unfamiliar with opening analyses as he is himself. The player who better understands the characteristics that distinguish a good move from a bad one will win the majority of the games, often against adversaries of much longer practical experience.

These positional characteristics are based on a few strategic principles which are sufficiently general to make them applicable to almost any situation that may arise. Valid· general principles are not apt to change; properly applied, they rule chess strategy today as they did fifty years ago.

It was most gratifying to learn from a number of famous Chess Grandmasters, among them Paul Keres and Reuben Fine, that they received their first chess instruction from my book and that it guided their chess thinking in the right direction. Not every reader is likely to become a Keres or a Fine, but I hope the book will continue to provide a solid basis from which to develop considerable playing strength without spending too much time and effort.

*New York, 1960*

EDWARD LASKER

# TRANSLATOR'S PREFACE

As the first edition of Edward Lasker's *Chess Strategy* was exhausted within a comparatively short time of its appearance, the author set himself the task of altering and improving the work to such an extent that it became to all intents and purposes a new book. I had the privilege of co-operating with him to a slight degree on that second edition, and was in consequence able to appreciate the tremendous amount of work he voluntarily took upon himself to do ; I say voluntarily, because his publishers, anxious to supply the strong demand for the book, wished to reprint it as it stood.

A little later I undertook to translate this second edition into English for Messrs. Bell & Sons. Only a few months had elapsed, the tournaments at Petrograd, Chester, and Mannheim had taken place, several new discoveries had been made, and it is the greatest testimony to Edward Lasker's indefatigable devotion to the Art of Chess that I am able to say that this is not a translation of the second edition, but of what is practically a new book. It contains a new preface, a chapter for beginners, a new introduction, new variations. Furthermore, a large number of new games have taken the place of old ones.

I have no doubt that any chess player who will take the trouble to study *Chess Strategy* will spend many a pleasurable hour. Incidentally new vistas will be opened to him, and his playing strength increased to a surprising degree.

The author says in his preface that he appeals to the intelligence and not the memory of his readers. In my opinion, too, the student should above all try to improve his judgment of position.

Than the playing over of games contested by experts I can hardly imagine a greater or purer form of enjoyment. Yet I must at the outset sound a note of warning against its being done superficially, and with a feverish expectation of something happening. Every move or combination of moves should be carefully weighed, and the student should draw his own conclusions and compare them with what actually happens in the game under examination.

This applies particularly to some of the critical positions set out in diagrams in the course of the exposition of the several games.

The reader would derive the greatest possible benefit from a prolonged study of such positions before seeking to know how the games proceed. After having formed his own opinion about the merits of a particular position, he should compare the result with the sequel in the game in question, and thus find out where his judgment has been at fault.

The deeper study of the theory of the openings is of course a necessity to the student who wishes to become an expert, but the development of his judgment must precede it. To him Griffith & White's admirable book, *Modern Chess Openings*, will be a perfect mine of information. There are thousands of variations, and in most of them the actual game in which they were first tried by masters is named, thus adding to the interest and value of the work.

I must not omit to mention the invaluable help afforded me by my friend Mr. John Hart, to whom my warmest thanks are due.

                              JULIUS DU MONT.

# AUTHOR'S PREFACE

THE large majority of chess players who would like to improve their game, have not the necessary opportunity of pitting themselves against players of master-strength, or at least of obtaining the desired instruction from personal intercourse with them. It is for such players that the present work is intended. The books on which the learner has to rely hardly ever serve his purpose, being mostly little more than a disjointed tabulation of numberless opening variations, which cannot be understood without preliminary studies, and consequently only make for confusion. In the end the connection between the various lines of play may become clear, after the student has made an exhaustive study of the subject, but very few would have either the time or the inclination for such prolonged labour.

Therefore another shorter and less empirical way must be found in which to acquire the understanding of sound play. My system of teaching differs from the usual ones, in that it sets down at the outset definite elementary principles of chess strategy by which any move can be gauged at its true value, thus enabling the learner to form his own judgment as to the manœuvres under consideration. In my opinion it is absolutely *essential* to follow such strategical principles, and I go so far as to assert that such principles are in themselves *sufficient* for the development and conduct of a correct game of chess.

Even though instruction in chess is possible on very general lines alone, yet I think it advisable and indeed necessary to explain the application of such principles to the various phases of each game of chess. Otherwise the learner might unduly delay his progress, and lose valuable time in finding out for himself certain essentials that could more profitably be pointed out to him.

With regard to the way in which I have arranged my subject and the form of its exposition in detail, I have thought out the following plan.

After discussing at length the leading principles underlying sound play, I have first treated of the *openings*, in which such principles are of even more deciding influence than in any other stage of the game, as far as could be done on broad lines without having to pay attention to middle and end-game considerations.

I proceeded as follows, by taking as my starting-point the "pawn skeleton" which is formed in the opening, and round which the pieces should group themselves in logical fashion. As a consequence of the pawns having so little mobility, this "pawn skeleton" often preserves its shape right into the end-game. Applying the general strategical principles to the formation of the pawn skeleton, the learner acquires the understanding of the leading idea underlying each opening without having to burden his memory. Not only that, he will also be able to find a correct plan of development when confronted with unusual forms of opening.

The most important result of this system of teaching is that the learner does not lose his way in a maze of detail, but has in view at the very outset, the goal which the many possible variations of the openings are intended to reach.

Before I could proceed to the discussion of the middle game, I found it necessary to treat of the principles governing the *end-game*. For in most cases play in the middle game is influenced by end-game considerations. Here also it has been my endeavour as far as possible to reduce my subject to such principles as are generally applicable.

Finally, as regards the *middle game*, to which the whole of Part II is devoted, I have again made the handling of *pawns*, the hardest of all problems of strategy, the starting-point for my deliberations. I have shown at length how the various plans initiated by the various openings should be developed further. To ensure a thorough understanding of the middle game, I have given a large number of games taken from master play, with numerous and extensive notes. Thus the student has not to rely only on examples taken haphazard from their context, but he will at the same time see how middle-game positions, which give opportunities for special forms of attack, are evolved from the opening.

It has been my desire to make the subject easily understandable and at the same time entertaining, and to appeal less to the memory of my readers than to their common sense and intelligence. I hope in that way not to have strayed too far from the ideal I had in mind when writing this book, namely, to apply to chess the only method of teaching which has proved productive in all branches of science and art, that is, the education of individual thought.

If I have succeeded in this, I shall have the satisfaction of having contributed a little to the furthering, in the wide circles in which it is played, of the game which undoubtedly makes the strongest appeal to the intellect.

EDWARD LASKER.

# CHESS STRATEGY

## PART I

### CHAPTER 1

#### INTRODUCTORY

##### I. Rules of the Game

A GAME of chess is played by two opponents on a square board consisting of sixty-four White and Black squares arranged alternately. The forces on each side comprise sixteen units, namely a King, a Queen, two Rooks, two Bishops, two Knights, and eight Pawns. All units move according to different laws, and the difference in their mobility is the criterion of their relative value and of the fighting power they contribute towards achieving the ultimate aim, namely, the capture of the opposing King. Before I can explain what is meant by the capture of the King, I must set out the rules of the game in full.

Diagram I shows the position the forces take up for the contest. The board is so placed that there is a white square at the top left-hand corner. The Rooks take up their positions at the corner squares, and next to them the Knights. Next to those again are the Bishops, and in the centre the King and Queen, the White Queen on a White square, and the Black Queen on a Black square. The eight pawns occupy the ranks immediately in front of the pieces. From this initial position, White begins the game in which the players must move alternately.

The pieces move in the following way : The Rook can move from any square it happens to be on, to any other square which it can reach in a straight line, either perpendicularly or horizontally, unless there is another piece of the same colour in the way, in which case it can only move as far as the square immediately in front of that piece. If it is an opposing piece which blocks the way, he can move on to the square that piece occupies, thereby capturing it. The piece thus captured is removed from the board. The Bishop can operate along either of the diagonals of which the square on which he is standing forms part. A Bishop on a White square can therefore never get on to a Black one.

Diag. 1.

The Queen commands both the straight and the oblique lines which start from the square she stands on, and therefore unites the power of both Rook and Bishop in her movements.

The King has similar powers to the Queen, but curtailed, inasmuch as he can only move one step at a time. He therefore only controls one neighbouring square in any direction.

The Knight plays and captures alternately on White and Black squares, and only reaches such squares as are nearest to him without being immediately adjacent; his move is as it were composed of two steps, one square in a straight line, and one in an oblique direction. Diagram 2 will illustrate this.[1]

---

[1] I should like to quote my friend Mr. John Hart's clever definition of the Knight's move, though it may not be new. If one conceives a Knight as standing on a corner square of a rectangle three squares by two, he is able to move into the corner diagonally opposite.

The pawns only move straight forward, one square at a time, except at their first move, when they have the option of moving two squares. In contrast to the pieces, the pawns do not capture in the way they move. They move straight forward, but they capture diagonally to the right and left, again only one square, and only forward. Therefore a pawn can only capture such pieces or pawns as occupy squares of the same colour as the square on which it stands. If, in moving two squares, a pawn traverses a square on which it could have been captured by a hostile pawn, that pawn has the right to capture it, as if it had moved only one square. This is called capturing *en passant*. However, this capture can only

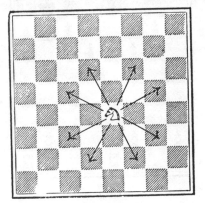

Diag. 2.

be effected on the very next move, otherwise the privilege of capturing *en passant* is lost.

If a player succeeds in reaching the eighth rank with one of his pawns he is entitled to call for any piece of higher grade, with the exception of the King, in place of such pawn.

Each move in a game of chess consists of the displacement of one piece only, with the exception of what is termed "castling," in which the King and either Rook can be moved simultaneously by either player once in a game. In castling, the King moves sideways to the next square but one, and the Rook to which the King is moved is placed on the square which the King has skipped over. Castling is only allowed if neither the King nor the Rook concerned have moved before, and if there is no piece between the Rook and King.

Diagram 3 shows a position in which White has castled on the Queen's side, and Black on the King's side. Castling is not permitted if the King in castling must pass over a square attacked by a hostile piece. A square (or a piece) is said to be " attacked " when the square (or the piece) is in the line of action of a hostile unit. A square (or a piece) is said to be covered or protected if an opposing piece occupying that square (or capturing the piece) could itself be captured.

When attacking the King it is customary to call " check," to notify the opponent of the fact ; for the attack on the King

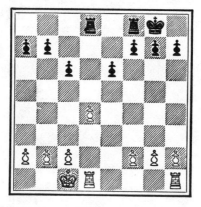

Diag. 3.

must be met in some way or other. This can be done by capturing the attacker or by interposing a piece (this is not possible in case of attack by a Knight or a pawn), or lastly by moving the King to a square which is not attacked. The latter must not be done by castling. If it is impossible by any of the three methods above mentioned to avoid the attack upon the King, the King is said to be checkmated, and the game is ended.

If a King is unable to move, though not attacked, and none of his remaining pieces can move, the King is said to be stalemated, and the game is drawn. A game is also drawn when neither side has sufficient material left to enforce a mate. (Compare page 63.)

If a player resigns his game before he is actually mated,

he acknowledges that in the end mate is unavoidable, and the game is counted as a loss to him.

A game is null and void if it is shown that a mistake was made in setting the board or men. The same applies when in the course of the game the position and number of pieces have been altered in a manner not in accordance with the proper course of play, and the latter cannot be reconstructed from the point where the error was made.

If a player having the move touches one of his pieces he is under compulsion to move it ; if he touches a hostile piece he must capture it, provided that the piece can be properly moved or captured in either case. This rule is of no effect if the piece so touched cannot be moved or captured, as the case may be. So long as the hand has not left the piece to be moved, the latter can be placed on any accessible square. If a player touches a piece with the sole object of adjusting its position, he must apprise his opponent of his intention by saying " J'adoube " beforehand. It is best to move the King first when castling. If the Rook is moved first, and unless the King is played almost simultaneously, a doubt might arise whether castling or a Rook's move only was intended.

If a player has castled illegally, Rook and King must be moved back, and the King must make another move, if there is a legal one. If not, any other move can be played. A player who makes an illegal move with a piece must retract that move, and make another one if possible with the same piece. If the mistake is only noticed later on, the game should be restarted from the position in which the error occurred.


## II. NOTATION

A special notation has been adopted to make the study of games and positions possible, and it is necessary for students of the game to become thoroughly conversant with it. The original and earliest notation is still in use in English, French, and Spanish speaking countries. It is derived from the original position in the game, in that the squares take the names of the pieces which occupy them. Thus the corner squares are called R 1 (Rook's square or Rook's first), and to distinguish them from one another Q R 1 or K R 1 (Queen's or King's Rook's square). The squares immediately in front are called Q R 2 or K R 2. A distinction is made between White and Black, and White's R 1 is Black's R 8, Black's R 2 is White's R 7, White's K B 3 is Black's K B 6, and so on. K stands for King; Q for Queen; B for Bishop; Kt for Knight; R for Rook; and P for Pawn. In describing a capture, only the capturing and the captured pieces are mentioned, and not the squares.

When confusion is possible, it is customary to add whether King's side or Queen's side pieces are concerned, *e.g.* K R × Q Kt. In this notation it is necessary to bear in mind which Kt is the Q Kt, which R is the K R. This becomes increasingly difficult as the game goes on and pieces change their places. Many sets of chessmen have one Rook and one Knight stamped with a special sign, to show they are King's side pieces. This is not necessary in the case of Bishops: a white K B is always on white squares, a white Q B on black squares.

A more modern notation is the algebraic notation, which has been adopted in most countries. It has the advantage of being unmistakably clear, and also more concise. Here the perpendicular lines of squares (called files) are named with the letters a–h, from left to right, always from the point of view of White, and the horizontal lines of squares (called ranks) with numbers 1–8 as before, only with the distinction that the rank on which the White pieces stand is always called the first; thus the square we named White's Q B 2 or Black's Q B 7 is now called c 2 in both cases. Black's Q B 2 (White's Q B 7) is always c 7. In capturing, the square on which the capture takes place and not the piece captured is noted, for the sake of uniformity. In the case of pawn moves, the squares only are noted.

O—O stands for castles on the King's side; O—O—O stands for castles on the Queen's side; : or × stands for captures; + for check.

In the following opening moves, both notations are used for the purpose of comparison:

| | | | |
|---|---|---|---|
| 1. P—Q 4 | P—Q 4 | 1. d 4 | d 5 |
| 2. P—Q B 4 | P—K 3 | 2. c 4 | e 6 |

| 3. Kt—Q B 3 | P—Q B 4 | 3. Kt c 3 | c 5 |
| 4. P×Q P | K P×P | 4. cd : | ed : |
| 5. P—K 4 | Q P×P | 5. e 4 | de : |
| 6. P—Q 5 | Kt—K B 3 | 6. d 5 | Ktf 6 |
| 7. B—K Kt 5 | B—K 2 | 7. Bg 5 | Be 7 |
| 8. K Kt—K 2 | Castles | 8. Ktg e 2 | O—O |

In most books in which the algebraic notation is used, both squares of a move are written out for the benefit of the student. The moves above would then look like this :

| 1. d 2—d 4 | d 7—d 5 |
| 2. c 2—c 4 | e 7—e 6 |
| 3. Ktb 1—c 3 | c 7—c 5 |
| 4. c 4×d 5 | e 6×d 5 |
| 5. e 2—e 4 | d 5×e 4 |
| 6. d 4—d 5 | Ktg 8—f 6 |
| 7. Bc 1—g 5 | Bf 8—e 7 |
| 8. Ktg 1—e 2 | O—O |

To conclude : I will give the denomination of the pieces in various languages :

| English . . . | K | Q | R | B | Kt | P | Castles |
| French . . . | R | D | T | F | C | P | Roq |
| Spanish . . . | R | D | T | A | C | P | Enrog |
| German and Austrian | K | D | T | L | S | | O—O (O) |
| Italian . . . | R | D | T | A | C | | O—O (O) |
| Russian . . . | KP | Φ | L | C | K | | O—O (O) |
| Dutch . . . | K | D | T | L | P | | O—O (O) |
| Scandinavian . . | K | D | T | L | S | | O—O (O) |
| Bohemian . . | K | D | V | S | J | | O—O (O) |
| Hungarian . ; | K | V | B | F | H | | O—O (O) |

# CHAPTER II

## HINTS FOR BEGINNERS—ELEMENTARY COMBINATIONS

THE mental development of the chess player is a gradual struggle from a state of chaos to a clear conception of the game. The period required for such development largely depends upon the special gifts the learner may possess, but in the main the question of methods predominates. Most beginners do not trouble very much about any particular plan in their study of chess, but as soon as they have learnt the moves, rush into the turmoil of practical play. It is self-evident that their prospects under such conditions cannot be very bright. The play of a beginner is planless, because he has too many plans, and the capacity for subordinating all his combinations to one leading idea is non-existent. Yet it cannot be denied upon investigation that a certain kind of method is to be found in the play of all beginners, and seems to come to them quite naturally. At first the pawns are pushed forward frantically, because there is no appreciation of the power and value of the pieces. Conscious of the inferiority of the pawns, the beginner does not conclude that it must be advantageous to employ the greater power of the pieces, but is chiefly concerned with attacking the opposing pieces with his pawns in the hope of capturing them. His aim is not to develop his own forces, but to weaken those of his opponent. His combinations are made in the hope that his adversary may not see through them, nor does he trouble much about his opponent's intentions. When most of his pawns are gone, then only do his pieces get their chance. He has a great liking for the Queen and the Knight, the former because of her tremendous mobility, the latter on account of his peculiar step, which seems particularly adapted to take the enemy by surprise. When watching beginners you will frequently observe numberless moves by a peripatetic Queen, reckless incursions by a Knight into the enemy's camp, and when the other pieces join in the fray, combination follows combination in bewildering sequence and fantastic chaos. Captures of pieces are planned, mating nets are woven, perhaps with two pieces, against a King's position, where five pieces are available for defence. This unsteadiness in the first childish stages of development makes it very difficult for the beginner to get a general view of the board. Yet the surprises which each move brings afford him great enjoyment.

A few dozen such games are by no means wasted. After certain particular dispositions of pieces have proved his undoing, the beginner will develop the perception of threats. He sees dangers one or two moves ahead, and thereby reaches the second stage in his development.

His combinations will become more and more sound, he will learn to value his forces more correctly, and therefore to husband his pieces and even his pawns with greater care. In this second stage his strength will increase steadily, but, and this is the drawback, only as far as his power of combination is concerned. Unless a player be exceptionally gifted, he will only learn after years of practice, if at all, what may be termed " positional play." For that, it is necessary to know how to open a game so as to lay the foundation for a favourable middle game, and how to treat a middle game, without losing sight of the possibilities of the end-game. It is hopeless to try to memorise the various openings which analysis have proved correct, for this empirical method fails as soon as the opponent swerves from the recognised lines of play. One must learn to recognise the characteristics of sound play. They apply to all and any position, and the underlying principles must be propounded in a manner generally applicable. And this brings me to the substance of my subject, round which I will endeavour to build up a system compatible with common sense and logic.

Before I proceed to develop my theme, I shall set down a number of elementary rules which will facilitate the understanding of such simple combinations as occur at every step in chess.

---

If we ignore the comparatively small proportion of games in which the mating of the opponent's King is accomplished on a full board, we can describe a normal, average game of chess in the following way. Both sides will employ their available forces more or less advantageously to execute attacking and defensive manœuvres which should gradually lead to exchanges. If one side or the other emerges from the conflict with some material gain, it will generally be possible to force a mate in the end-game, whilst if both sides have succeeded by careful play to preserve equality of material, a draw will generally ensue.

It will be found a little later that a single pawn may suffice, with some few exceptions, to achieve a victory, and we shall adopt the following leading principle for all combinations,

viz. loss of material must be avoided, even if only a pawn
It is a good habit to look upon every pawn as a prospective
Queen. This has a sobering influence on premature and im-
petuous plans of attack.

On the other hand, victory is often brought about by a
timely sacrifice of material.

But in such cases the sacrificing of material has its compensation in some particular advantage of position. As
principles of position are difficult for beginners to grasp, I propose to defer their consideration for the present and to devote
my attention first to such combinations as involve questions
of material. Let us master a simple device that makes most
combinations easy both for attack and defence. It amounts
merely to a matter of elementary arithmetic, and if the beginner neglects it, he will soon be at a material disadvantage.

Diagram 4 may serve as an example :

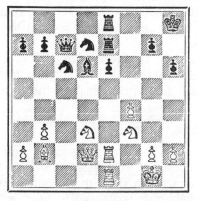

Diag. 4.

It is Black's move, and we will suppose he wishes to play
P—K 4. A beginner will probably calculate thus : I push on
my pawn, he takes with his pawn, my Knight takes, so does
his, then my Bishop takes, and so on. This is quite wrong, and
means waste of time and energy.

When the beginner considers a third or fourth move in such
a combination, he will already have forgotten which pieces
he intended to play in the first moves. The calculation is
perfectly simple upon the following lines : I play P—K 4.

then my pawn is attacked by a pawn and two Knights, a Bishop and two Rooks, six times in all. It is supported by a Bishop, two Knights, two Rooks and a Queen, six times in all. Therefore I can play P—K 4, provided the six units captured at K 4 are not of greater value than the six white units which are recaptured. In the present instance both sides lose a pawn, two Knights, two Rooks, and a Bishop, and there is no material loss. This established, he can embark on the advance of the K P without any fear.

Therefore: in any combination which includes a number of exchanges on one square, all you have to do is to count the number of attacking and defending units, and to compare their relative values; the latter must never be forgotten. If Black were to play Kt × P in the following position, because the pawn at K 5 is attacked three times, and only supported twice, it would be an obvious miscalculation, for the value of the defending pieces is smaller.[1]

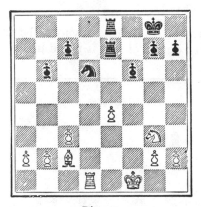

Diag. 5.

Chess would be an easy game if all combinations could be tested and probed exhaustively by the mathematical process just shown. But we shall find that the complications met

[1] It is difficult to compare the relative value of the different pieces, as so much depends on the peculiarities of each position, but, generally speaking, minor pieces, Bishop and Knight, are reckoned as equal; the Rook as equal to a minor piece and one or two pawns (to have a Rook against a minor piece, is to be the "exchange" ahead). The Queen is equal to two Rooks or three minor pieces.

with are extremely varied. To give the beginner an idea of this, I will mention a few of the more frequent examples. It will be seen that the calculation may be, and very frequently

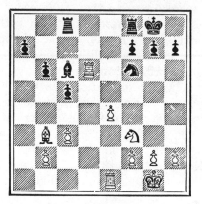

Diag. 6.

is, upset by one of the pieces involved being exchanged or sacrificed. An example of this is found in Diagram 6; Kt × P

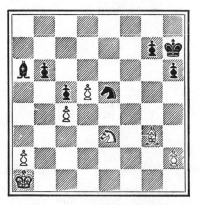

Diag. 7.

fails on account of R × B; this leaves the Knight unprotected, and White wins two pieces for his Rook. Neither can the Bishop capture on K 5 because of R × Kt, leaving the Bishop unprotected, after which B×Kt does not retrieve the situation because the Rook recaptures from B 6.

A second important case, in which our simple calculation is of no avail, occurs in a position where one of the defending pieces is forced away by a threat, the evasion of which is more important than the capture of the unit it defends. In Diagram 7, for instance, Black may not play Kt×P, because White, by playing P—Q 6, would force the Bishop to Kt 4 or B 1, to prevent the pawn from Queening and the Knight would be lost. A further example of the same type is given in Diagram 8. Here a peculiar mating threat, which occurs not

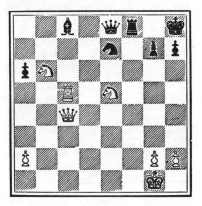

Diag. 8.

infrequently in practical play, keeps the Black Queen tied to her K B 2 and unavailable for the protection of the B at B 1.

White wins as follows :

1 Kt×B, Kt×Kt ; 2 R×Kt, Q×R ; 3 Kt—B 7, ch K—Kt 1 ; 4 Kt—R 6 double ch, K—R 1 ; 5 Q—Kt 8 ch, R×Q ; 6 Kt—B 7 mate.

We will now go a step further and turn from "acute" combinations to such combinations as are, as it were, impending. Here, too, I urgently recommend beginners (advanced players do it as a matter of course) to proceed by way of simple arithmetical calculations, but, instead of enumerating the attacking and defending pieces, to count the number of possibilities of attack and defence.

Let us consider a few typical examples. In Diagram 9,
if Black plays P—Q 5, he must first have probed the position
in the following way. The pawn at Q 5 is attacked once and
supported once to start with, and can be attacked by three
more White units in three more moves (1 R—Q 1, 2 R (B 2)—Q 2,
3 B—B 2)   Black can also mobilise three more units for the
defence in the same number of moves (1 Kt—B 4 or K 3, 2 B—
Kt 2, 3 R—Q 1). There is, consequently, no immediate danger,
nor is there anything to fear for some time to come, as White has
no other piece which could attack the pawn for the fifth time.

Diag. 9.

It would be obviously wrong to move the pawn to Q 6 after
White's R—Q 1, because White could bring another two pieces
to bear on the P, the other Rook and the Knight, whilst Black
has only one more piece available for the defence, namely, his
Rook.

The following examples show typical positions, in which
simple calculation is complicated by side issues.

In Diagram 10, the point of attack, namely, the Black
Knight at K B 3, can be supported by as many Black units
as White can bring up for the attack, but the defensive efficiency of one of Black's pieces is illusory, because it can be
taken by a White piece. The plan would be as follows : White
threatens Black's Knight for the third time with Kt—K 4,
and Black must reply Q Kt—Q 2, because covering with

R—K 3 would cost the "" exchange," as will appear from a comparison of the value of the pieces concerned. The " exchange " is, however, lost for Black on the next move, because

Diag. 10.

White's further attack on the Knight by Q—B 3 forces the Rook to defend on K 3, where it gets into the diagonal of the Bishop, which at present is masked by White's Knight. The sequel would be 3 Q Kt × Kt ch, R × Kt (not B × Kt on account of B × R winning a whole Rook), 4 B × R, and so on.

A similar case is shown in Diagram 11.

Diag. 11.

Here, too, there is a flaw in the simple calculation, because the defending units are not secure.  Beginners should devote special attention to this position, which is in practice of frequent occurrence.

It can be easily perceived that the Bishop cannot capture the pawn at B 7 on account of P—Q R 3.  But to take with the Knight would also be an error, because Black would then keep chasing away the covering Bishop.

1 P—Kt 4 ; 2 B—Q 6, K—B 3 ; 3 Kt—K 8, B—B 2 ; and wins one of the pieces.

Finally, one more example, in which one of the defending pieces being pinned makes simple calculation impracticable.

In Diagram 12 it seems at first sight as if Black could play Kt × P : although White can pin the Knight with R—K 1

Diag. 12.

and then attack it once more with his Knight, Black would appear to have sufficient protection available, with his Kt and B.   White has no time to double Rooks, because if he does so, after his R—K 2 Black would play the King away from his file and allow the Knight to escape.

But White can, by a simple sacrifice, bring the slumbering R at R 1 into sudden action :

1...Kt × P ; 2 R—K 1, B—B 4 ; 3 Kt—B 3, Kt—Q 3 ; 4 R × Kt, Kt × R ; 5 R—K 1, and White wins two pieces for his Rook.

These illustrations will be sufficient to give the beginner an understanding of economy of calculation in all kinds of combinations. His power of combining will grow speedily on this basis, and thrive in the fire of practical experience. Where an opponent is missing, the gap must be filled by reference to such books as treat of the science of combination and give examples taken from actual play.

# CHAPTER III

## GENERAL PRINCIPLES OF CHESS STRATEGY

In bringing the teachings of this book under the collective heading " Chess Strategy," it was not in any way my intention to draw anything like an exact parallel between the manœuvres on the chess-board and military operations in actual warfare. In trying to seek such analogies there is great danger of being led astray, and little likelihood of gaining knowledge that might be of use in practical play. Plain common-sense will give us all we need, without our being influenced by those tactical and strategical considerations that have been found useful in war.

The following definition may not be out of place : Strategy sets down the whole of the problems which must be solved in war, in order to attain the ultimate result aimed at ; tactics solve such problems in various ways, and according to the conditions prevailing in the particular case. Sound strategy, when setting the task, must never lose sight of tactical practicability, and only a thorough knowledge of tactical resources makes correct strategy possible.

Now we shall not under any circumstances, as unfortunately even great chess masters have done, seek in outward similarities justification for transferring to chess the teachings of the strategy and tactics of war. It sounds pretty enough to say : Chess is a game of war—the various pieces represent the various kinds of forces : the pawns represent the infantry, the Knights take the place of cavalry, the Rooks do the work of heavy artillery, sweeping broad lines ; the different

ways in which the pieces move find a parallel in the topography
of the theatre of war, in that the various battle-fields are more
or less easy of access.   But it is quite unjustifiable to assign to
the Knights the functions of scouts, and to say that Rooks should
stay in the background, as heavy artillery, and so on.   Such
pronouncements would not have the slightest practical value.
What we take from the science of warfare is merely the
definition.   In each game the strategy of chess should set us
the tasks which must be accomplished (in order to mate the
opponent's King), and tactics point the way in which it is
possible to solve such problems.   Correct chess strategy will
only set such tasks as are tactically possible, and, if we wish
to expound the principles of chess strategy, we cannot exclude
chess tactics from the field of our observations.   If here and
there the results of our deliberations bear some analogy to actual
warfare, we may certainly give way to a kind of æsthetic satisfaction in that our own occupation has some parallel in real
life, but we must never fashion our principles in accordance
with such fortuitous circumstances.

Having surveyed the problems we have to solve, we can
now plunge into our subject.

In the first chapter, when considering special cases in elementary combinations, we have already noticed the important
part played in each skirmish by the balance between the attacking and defending units.   Speaking quite generally, common-
sense will tell us that, in all operations on the chess-board,
the main consideration for the defence will be to maintain that balance, and that there is only justification for an
attack when it is possible to concentrate more forces on the
strategic point than can be mustered by the defence. However,
one very important point must not be neglected, though I
did not touch upon it when discussing elementary combinations for fear of complicating matters for beginners :   the
balance between the contending forces is by no means established by their numerical equality.   A paramount factor is
the mobility of such forces, and as soon as it is no longer one
of the elementary cases of capture and recapture described
previously, this factor must be taken into account in order to
decide, on a general survey, whether there is a sufficient
defence to an impending attack, or whether one's own intended

attack is likely to prevail. That mobility is the first and foremost consideration should be self-evident, since the relative value of the pieces can only make itself felt by their greater or lesser mobility.

Except in certain positions, which are brought about by some particular array of the pieces, the intrinsic value of a Rook is greater than that of a Bishop, because it can command all the squares on the board, whilst a Bishop is tied to its own colour ; Knight and Bishop are considered equivalent, because the Knight's advantage in being able to act on all the squares of either colour is balanced by the fact that the Bishop can sweep long diagonals. Two Bishops are, generally speaking, of greater value than two Knights, because together they also act on all the squares, and their command of long diagonals is a clear advantage. The whole of this valuation, however, comes to nought when the pieces are hindered in their mobility by the peculiarity of any particular position.

We will consider one instance from end-game play, and one from the openings.

In Diagram 13, White derives no advantage from being

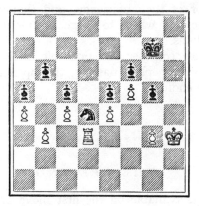

Diag. 13.

the exchange to the good, for the Rook has no file which could be used to break into the Black camp.

In Diagram 14, the numerical equality of forces will not save Black, because bad development reduces the mobility of his pieces to such an extent that he has no resources with which he can parry the impending attack.

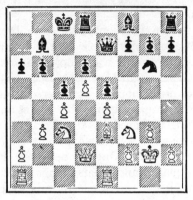

Diag. 14.

White will assail the Black King's position on the Queen side, and Black is unable to concentrate his forces quickly enough for the defence of the jeopardised entrenchments.   Let us therefore bear in mind that the mobility of the pieces is the deciding factor of their efficiency, and that mobility is the highest criterion by which to judge the merits (or demerits) of their operations.

We will now consider this principle in its application to the three stages of play, namely, the opening, the middle-game, and the ending.


# CHAPTER IV

## THE OPENING

THE only pieces available on the first move are the Knights. In order to develop other pieces as well, it is necessary to move pawns first, and such pawn moves will be best as give an outlet to as many pieces as possible.   For quick development is of the utmost importance, and he who succeeds first in placing all his pieces, from their initial awkward positions, to such places as give them command of the greatest possible number of

squares, has the better chance of concentrating a superior
force on some important point.

It follows that White, having the first move, is, so to speak,
always morally justified in attacking, whilst Black should
assume the defensive. It is a step in the right direction, to
appreciate the truth of this proposition. Unfortunately most
beginners fail to realise it, and so pave the way, from the first,
to the loss of the game.

There are not many developing pawn moves to choose from.
Apparently from the point of view of quick development only
P—K 4 and P—Q 4 need be considered, since they free both
Bishop and Queen, whilst other pawn moves liberate one
piece only. Generally speaking it is only required to move
two or three pawns to allow all pieces to be developed, and
it is good, on principle, to make only such pawn moves in the
opening, which are necessary for the development of pieces.
To play other pawns really means the loss of a move. To
" lose a move " means to make a move which is not essential
to the attainment of a desired position. Thus the " loss of a
move " results also from playing a piece to a given square
in more moves than necessary.

I shall now give a few games showing the far-reaching
consequences of losing moves. The first one is a typical
though glaring example, which is very instructive and came
to my notice some time ago :

| | | |
|---|---|---|
| 1. | P—K 4 | P—K 4 |
| 2. | P—Q 4 | P×P |
| 3. | Q×P | Kt—Q B 3 |
| 4. | Q—K 3 | Kt—B 3 |
| 5. | P—K R 3 ? | |

I will not discuss the system of development adopted by
White in his first four moves. The last move, however, can
at once be recognised as faulty. It is the loss of a move such
as occurs in the vast majority of games played by beginners.
It was unnecessary to prevent K Kt—Kt 5, since the Knight
could not hold that square permanently. In any case B—K 2
would have had the same effect, and developed a piece at the
same time.

| | | |
|---|---|---|
| 5. | ......... | B—K 2 |
| 6. | P—QR 3 ?? | |

This, of course, is very bad. The consequences ot this loss of a second move are swift and deadly.

| 6. ........ | Castles |
| 7. B—B 4 | |

At last a developing move.

| 7. ........ | R—K 1 |
| 8. Q—Q Kt 3 | |

Another Queen's move. The attack on the Bishop's Pawn may be very tempting, but must necessarily be incorrect—and why ? Because White is much behind with his development. It is useless to analyse any kind of attack in face of this fact. The beginner finds it hard to get used to this way of thinking. He prefers to try to unravel a long string of variations and combinations, in which he will mostly lose his bearings. Even stronger players obstruct their own powers by refusing to see the value of judging a position on general merits. They lose valuable time in thinking out endless variations, to maintain positions which could be proved valueless by general and logical deductions.

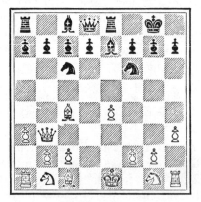

Diag. 15.

Then, as in the present position, retribution comes swiftly.

| 8. ........ | P—Q 4 |

White should have considered this move. It was obvious,

since the opening of the K file for the Rook is most dangerous, for the White King.

9. B × P          Kt × B

Black could have played Q × B at once.

10. Q × Kt          Q × Q
11. P × Q          B—Kt 5 double ch
12. K—Q 1          R—K 8 mate

A further example in which the loss of moves occurs, though not so glaringly, is the following famous game, which Morphy played against the Duke Karl of Brunswick and Count Isouard in the Royal box at the Paris opera-house.

1. P—K 4          P—K 4
2. Kt—K B 3          P—Q 3

According to the principles set out above, Kt—Q B 3 would have been better, since the text move shuts out the King's Bishop.

3. P—Q 4

Now the King's Pawn is attacked twice. It would be bad to support it with Kt—Q B 3, as White would exchange pawns and then Queens. Black would thus forfeit his chance of castling and lose much time in bringing the King into safety and the Rooks into play. P—K B 3, of course, is impossible, as it is not a developing move, and moreover blocks the natural development of the King's Knight. Protecting the pawn with the Queen would also block other pieces, and Q Kt—Q 2 cannot be good, as it blocks the Queen's Bishop.

Since it seems impossible to protect the King s Pawn, the only alternative would be to exchange it ; indeed it is on the whole the best course, although it allows a White piece to take up a dominating position in the centre. Wishing to avoid this, Black plays

3. ........          B—Kt 5

and, by pinning the opponent's Knight, indirectly protects the King's Pawn. This manœuvre is, however, ill-advised, as Black is forced to exchange the Bishop for the Knight

The Bishop will have moved twice, the Knight only once, therefore White will have gained a move for his development.

4. P×P        B×Kt

Should Black play P×P at once, White would exchange Queens, release the pin, and win the pawn.

5. Q×B        P×P
6. B—Q B 4

White has now two pieces more in play than Black, instead of only one, and the mobility of the White Queen, which Black himself has brought out, begins to have a threatening effect on Black's game.

6. ………        Kt—K B 3
7. Q—Q Kt 3        Q—K 2

Black cannot cover his King's Bishop's Pawn with Q—Q 2 because 8 Q×P wins the Rook, whilst now Black could play 8…Q—Kt 5 ch in reply, forcing the exchange of Queens. The text move, which is forced, blocks the Bishop, and at the same time prevents the development of the King's Rook, all of which is the direct consequence of the loss of one move.

8. Kt—B 3

White rightly disdains the gain of the Knight's Pawn, but prevents the exchange of Queens in developing a piece. He proves the superiority of his position much more convincingly in that way. Black must now lose yet another move to protect his Knight's Pawn.

8. ………        P—B 3
9. B—K Kt 5        P—Kt 4

Black must try to develop his Queen's Knight at last. He cannot play Q Kt—Q 2 at once, since his Knight's Pawn would again be unprotected; therefore he plays the move in the text, probably thinking that now White also must lose a move to withdraw his Bishop. But in view of the fact that Black's game is wholly undeveloped, and that he plays practically several pieces down, White sacrifices his Knight for two

pawns : he foresees the position which occurs a few moves·
later, when Black is hemmed in on all sides.

| | | |
|---|---|---|
| 10. | Kt × P | P × Kt |
| 11. | B × Kt P ch | Q Kt—Q 2 |
| 12. | Castles Q R | R—Q 1 |

This is the only piece available to cover Q 2, for the King's
Knight is pinned. White has another piece in reserve, his
King's Rook, and against this Black is defenceless.

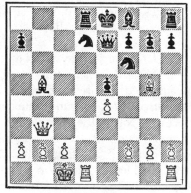

Diag. 16.

**13. R × Kt**
compare Diag. 12.

| | | |
|---|---|---|
| 13. | ......... | R × R |
| 14. | R—Q 1 | Q—K 3 |

This releases the King's Knight. Now White could win
by playing B × Kt and B × R ch, but he prefers to end up with
a magnificent sacrifice.

| | | |
|---|---|---|
| 15. | B × R ch | Kt × B |
| 16. | Q—Kt 8 ch ! ! | Kt × Q |
| 17. | R—Q 8 mate | |

The final position shows in a striking manner how a few
well-developed pieces can be worth more than many undeveloped ones, and the whole game is an example of the fatal
consequences which can follow the loss of a move, since it
often leads to the compulsory loss of further moves in the
course of the game.

" This is the curse of every evil deed
That propagating still it brings forth evil."

The logical sequence of the moves in this game, as pointed out in the commentaries to it, is borne out by the curious coincidence that I once had the opportunity of playing a game in exactly the same sequence of moves, against a player to whom Morphy's "brilliancy" was unknown.

---

The leading principle of all opening moves is made clear by the foregoing pages, namely, rapid development of pieces, and consequently the avoidance of the loss of a move in any shape or form.

Before treating of the various systems of openings, I will say a few words on the principles of *pawn play*.

Each opening is characterised by a well-defined pawn formation, and concurrently a certain method in the development of the pieces.  Naturally the formation of a pawn skeleton is not an independent factor, but must be evolved with a view to facilitating the favourable development of pieces.  But when considering the form of a pawn position and that of the pieces, we cannot shut our eyes to the fact that pawn formation must necessarily be the dominant consideration in our mind.  Pawn formation is of a more permanent character than that of the pieces, in consequence of the latter's greater mobility.  When we have made a rash move with a piece, to which our attacking disposition may have tempted us, we may still have a chance of retrieving the position by timely retreat.  Once a pawn has moved it cannot turn back, and only after the greatest deliberation should we embark on changes in our pawn formation in order not to disturb the balance of this " static element " of the game.  But we shall see that the pawn skeleton which was formed in the opening often weathers the storm and stress of the middle game, and frequently preserves its character right up to the end-game. I will therefore make pawn formation my starting-point in an attempt to show the way through the maze of the openings on the basis of general strategical principles.

If our pawn skeleton is to promote the freedom of all the pieces, we must not build it up with the narrow view of developing minor pieces only, but must consider from the very first in which way it will enable the Rooks to get into action. We can unite these tendencies in making the *centre of the board* the main field of action for all our forces. This means for both sides K 4 and Q 4, and also in a lesser degree Q B 4 and K B 4. We shall get a clear insight into the positional advantage of having command of the centre later on, when discussing the middle game. At present I will only touch the subject in a general way, explaining it in an elementary form, which will be sufficient to develop an understanding for pawn strategy in the opening. In the course of further deductions, after the grasp of this difficult stage of the game has become stronger, I will go into details which will allow the subject to be stated in a more precise form.

Placing the pieces in the centre is of value, because there they have more mobility than near the edge, which, of course, limits their range of action, and also because from the centre a concentration of forces on a given point can generally be effected in the quickest way.

In most cases two centre squares become inaccessible at once, through the opponent placing one of his pawns in the centre; therefore it would seem a good plan to lure that pawn away, and this is rendered feasible by playing P—K 4 or P—Q B 4 when the opponent has a pawn on his Q 4, and P—Q 4 or P—K B 4 when he has a pawn on K 4. In the following we will consider such manœuvres as could apply either to White or Black, from the point of view of White, to whom the initiative is, as pointed out above, a sort of birthright. Naturally, should White lose a move, as, for instance, 1 P—K 4, P—K 4; 2 Kt—K B 3, Kt—Q B 3; 3 P—Q R 3? the position is reversed, and Black is bound to obtain the initiative which is White's birthright.

The pawn moves mentioned above also have the tendency of giving the Rooks an opportunity for action. A Rook standing behind an advanced pawn may support its further advance, or, if the pawn should be exchanged, might get an open file.

The damage we wish to inflict on our opponent we must, of course, try to avoid ourselves. Thus we will not easily give up a centre pawn unless we can obtain some other advantage in doing so. This advantage may be, that in exchanging the centre pawn we open up lines of attack for our pieces, or that we are able to place one of our pieces in a commanding position in the centre of the board.

The following example may serve as an illustration. Supposing White plays after

| 1. P—Q 4 | P—Q 4 |
| 2. P—Q B 4 | |

His aim is to tempt Black's centre pawn away and to make his Q B 4 and K 4 accessible for his own forces. Black might be justified in taking the pawn, if he really could hold the pawn thus gained. We shall show later on that this is not so, and that White can win it back easily and advantageously. Therefore Black is more likely to play 2 P—K 3. Not 2...Kt—K B 3; for after 3 P×P, Kt×P; 4 P—K 4 would open White's game and drive the Knight away at once, gaining a move. Supposing, however, Black plays 2...B—B4; should White now think mechanically, " I will take his centre pawn and consequently have the better game," his deduction would be wrong. For after exchanging his Bishop for the Knight, which otherwise would drive his Queen away, Black brings the latter into a dominating square in the centre.

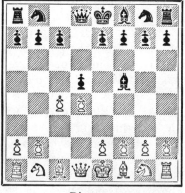

Diag. 17.

| 3. P×P | B×Kt |
| 4. R×B | Q×P |

Black's Queen cannot easily be driven away from her commanding position, particularly as White must lose a move

to save his Q R P.   Meanwhile Black gains time for concentrating his forces for an attack which wins the Queen's Pawn.

| 5. P—Q Kt 3 | Kt—Q B 3 |
| 6. P—K 3 | Castles Q R |
| 7. Kt—B 3 | P—K 4 |

and wins the Q P, or

| 5. P—Q R 3 | Kt—Q B 3 |
| 6. P—K 3 | Castles Q R |

and P—K 4 is again a threat hard for white to meet.

This position shows, that to bring one's opponent's centre
pawn away and to keep one's own, does not under all circumstances mean the command of the centre, but that the opening
up of files and diagonals for one's pieces towards the centre is
an important moment in the fight for positional advantage.

Considerations of this kind will help to improve our judgment in many of the various openings treated in the following
pages.

We will class the openings in this way :

A. White 1. P—K 4.
       (a) Black 1. P—K 4
       (b) Black 1. Any other move
B. White 1. P—Q 4.
       (a) Black 1. P—Q 4
       (b) Black 1. Any other move

C. White 1. Any other move

We shall find that openings classed under C generally lead
to positions treated under A and B.

---

A. We have already come to the conclusion that after 1 P—
K 4, P—K 4 White does well to try to force the exchange
of Black's centre pawn on Q 4 or K B 4, and that Black will try
to counteract this, unless by allowing the exchange he gets a
chance of exerting pressure in the centre by means of his pieces.

We will first see what happens when White undertakes the
advance in question on his second move.   Superficially the
difference between 2 P Q 4 and 2 P—K B 4 is that in the first
case the pawn thus advanced is covered, while in the second

it is not. An opening in which a pawn sacrifice is offered, is called a "gambit"; 2 P—K B 4 is therefore a gambit.

2 P—Q 4 is only a gambit if after 2...P×P White does not recapture the pawn. Nevertheless this opening has been called the " centre gambit," and though the denomination is not correct we will adhere to it, as it is in general use.

A very considerable difference between the centre gambit and the King's gambit lies in the fact that in the former acceptance is compulsory, whilst in the second it may be declined.

For : 2 P—Q 4 threatens to take the King's Pawn. To defend it by means of 2...P—Q 3 is unwise, since White exchanges pawns and then Queens, by which Black loses his chance of castling and impedes the development of his Rooks. 2...Kt—Q B 3 is also bad, since after 3 P×P, Kt×P; 4 P— K B 4, White drives the Knight away, gaining a strong hold on the centre, and Black has no compensation for giving up his centre pawn. It may be mentioned here that after 2...Kt—Q B 3, 3 P—Q 5 would be a useless move, as to begin with it would be inconsequent, since P—Q 4 was played in order to clear the centre, and moreover it would block up a diagonal which could be most useful to the King's Bishop.

We conclude now that Black cannot hold his pawn at K 4. He must relinquish the centre by 2...P×P. He will now either attempt to bring away White's King's Pawn by advancing his own Q P to Q 4, or try to utilise the King's file, which was opened by his second move, and operate against White's K P. The Rooks are indicated for this task. We shall refer to the execution of these plans later on.

In the King's gambit, White's attempt to bring away Black's King's Pawn may be safely ignored.

The move 2 P—K B 4 does not threaten to take the King's Pawn, as Black would win White's K P by Q—R 5 ch. Black can therefore develop in security with 2...B—B 4, and if then White prevents the Q check by Kt—K B 3, there is no objection to Black protecting his King's Pawn with P—Q 3, as the King's Bishop is already developed. After 4 B—B 4, Black has still no need to protect his K P with Kt—Q B 3, but can play Kt—K B 3 first, because after 5 P×P, P×P; 6 Kt×P would be answered by 6...Q—Q 5 winning a piece.

Black keeps the upper hand in these early encounters because he has made a developing move with a piece, whilst White has played a pawn move which is useless for the purpose of development.

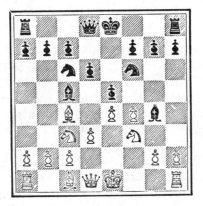

Diag. 18.

Diagram 18 shows the position which results from the following plausible moves :

|   |   |   |
|---|---|---|
| 2. | P—K B 4 | B—B 4 |
| 3. | Kt—K B 3 | P—Q 3 |
| 4. | B—B 4 | Kt—K B 3 |
| 5. | P—Q 3 | Kt—B 3 |
| 6. | Kt—B 3 | B—K Kt 5 |

If White wishes to castle on the K side, which must have been his intention when playing 2 P—K B 4, he will have to play Kt—Q R 4 and Kt × B.

Though this is of no disadvantage to Black, he could avoid the exchange of his K B by playing 6...P—Q R 3 instead of B—K Kt 5. If then White plays P—B 5 in order to hinder the development of Black's Q B and to bring out his own, the pressure on Black's K P is relieved permanently, and sooner or later Black will break through on the Q file, as his Q P is no longer needed at Q 3 for the support of the centre pawn.

A different pawn formation is the result if White enforces

the exchange of Black's centre pawn at once. This he can do by playing P—Q 4, *e.g* :

| 2. P—K B 4 | B—B 4 | or | 4. P—B 3 | Kt—K B 3 |
| 3. Kt—K B 3 | P—Q 3 | | 5. P—Q 4 | P×Q P |
| 4. P—Q 4 | P×Q P | | 6. P×P | B—Kt 3 |
| 5. Kt×P | | | | |

Here Black can get an early advantage by attacking White's K P, taking possession of the K file after castling on the K side.

All things considered, the student should in my opinion decline the gambit, as in doing so he can get an easy and satisfactory development. The treatment of the " King's Gambit accepted," which aims at holding the gambit pawn, is most difficult and leads early in the game to such complications as none but an expert can hope to master.[1] It is therefore unwise for the beginner to accept the gambit, unless there be a chance of compensation for the disappearance of his centre pawn, by forcing the exchange of White's centre pawn as well. The following line of play would fulfil this condition :

1 P—K 4, P—K 4 ; 2 P—K B 4, P×P ; 3 Kt—K B 3, Kt—K B 3 ; 4 Kt—B 3, P—Q 4 ! Black thereby abandons the gambit pawn.

On principle, and when he has the choice, the beginner should give preference to simple and clear development in the opening, rather than to the gain of a pawn, when this involves

---

[1] As an example of the difficult play which ensues when Black defends the pawn in the King's Gambit, I give the latest variation of an attack introduced by Professor I. L. Rice, and called the " Rice Gambit" :

1 P—K 4, P—K 4 ; 2 P—K B 4, P×P ; 3 Kt—K B 3, P—K Kt 4 ; 4 P—K R 4, P—Kt 5 ; 5 Kt—K 5, Kt—K B 3 ; 6 B—B 4, P—Q 4 ; 7 P×P, B—Q 3 ; 8 Castles ! B×Kt ; 9 R—K 1, Q—K 2 ; 10 P—B 3, Kt—R 4 ; 11 P—Q 4, Kt—Q 2 ; 12 P×B, Kt×F ; 13 P—Q Kt 3, Castles ; 14 B—R 3, Kt—B 6 ch ! ; 15 P×Kt, Q×P ; 16 R—K 5 ! B—B 4 ! ! ; 17 Kt—Q 2 ! Q—Kt 6 ch ; 18 K—B 1, Q—R 7 ; 19 B×R, P—Kt 6 ; 20 B—B 5, P—Kt 7 ch ; 21 K—K 1, Q—R 5 ch ; 22 K—K 2, Kt—Kt 6 ch ; 23 K—B 2, Kt—K 5 ch ; 24 K×P, B—R 6 ch ; 25 K—R 1, K—R 1 ; 26 Kt×Kt, R—K Kt 1, 27 R—Kt 5, with interesting possibilities.

Numberless interesting variations are possible, but their discussion does not lie within the scope of this work. They will be found in books treating of the analysis of the openings.

difficult and intricate play. This principle must also guide us in other openings.

A good example is to be found in the so-called " Danish gambit," [1] which will lead us back to those openings in which White plays P—Q 4 on his second move. After 2 P—Q 4, P×P, White has the option of sacrificing two pawns to obtain a very rapid development 3 P—Q B 3, P×P; 4 B—Q B 4, P×P; 5 Q B×P. It may now be just possible for Black to avoid the many threats which White can bring to bear with his beautifully placed forces, perhaps by giving back one or both of the pawns gained. But this question can only be of interest to us if there is no opportunity of adopting a simple line of development at the outset. As it is, this opportunity is not wanting. All that Black needs to do is to push on his Queen's Pawn as soon as possible, thus freeing his own Queen's Bishop.

| | | |
|---|---|---|
| 2. | P—Q 4 | P×P |
| 3. | P—Q B 3 | P—Q 4 |

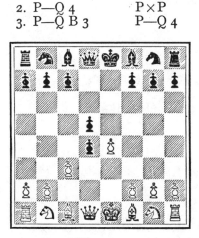

Diag. 19.

After 4 K P×P, Q×P, Black's position is at least as easy of development as White's. In the position set out in Diagram 19, White cannot play P—K 5, because Black wins a pawn by P×P without hindering his own development in the least.

[1] The names of the various openings, which I mention for the sake of completeness, are generally derived from towns or countries in which they were first extensively played and analysed.

The equalising power of Black's P—Q 4 in all K P openings where White has played P—Q 4 can be noticed in many variations. I shall now give a few typical examples, which will show the line of play that can be adopted in many similar cases, and which can often be evolved one from the other by altering the order of the moves.

### I. *Centre Gambit*

| | | |
|---|---|---|
| 2. | P—Q 4 | P×P |
| 3. | Q×P | Kt—Q B 3 |
| 4. | Q—K 3 | Kt—B 3 |
| 5. | Kt—Q B 3 | B—K 2 |
| 6. | B—Q 2 | P—Q 4 ! |

### II. *King's Bishop's Opening*

| | | |
|---|---|---|
| 2. | P—Q 4 | P×P |
| 3. | B—Q B 4 | Kt—K B 3 |
| 4. | P—K 5 | P—Q 4 ! |

### III. *Scotch Gambit*

| | | | | |
|---|---|---|---|---|
| 2. | Kt—K B 3 | Kt—Q B 3 | | |
| 3. | P—Q 4 | P×P | | |
| 4. | B—B 4 | Kt—B 3 | 4. P—B 3 | P—Q 4 ! |
| 5. | P—K 5 | P—Q 4 ! | | |

### IV. *Scotch Game*

| | | |
|---|---|---|
| 2. | Kt—K B 3 | Kt—Q B 3 |
| 3. | P—Q 4 | P×P |
| 4. | Kt×P | Kt—B 3 |
| 5. | Kt—Q B 3 | B—Kt 5 |
| 6. | Kt×Kt | Kt P×Kt |
| 7. | B—Q 3 | P—Q 4 ! |

In no case should Black forfeit his chance of playing P—Q 4. It is tempting after 2 P—Q 4, P×P ; 3 Kt—K B 3 to cover the pawn at Q 5 by P—Q B 4, but in that case White would sacrifice a pawn by P—Q B 3, by this means opening the Queen's file for himself, and so preventing Black from ever playing P—Q 4. Thus, for the loss of a pawn, White has a paramount advantage in position.

For after 4...P×P, 5 Kt×P (Diagram 20) White has developed both Knights, and his Bishops are free, whilst Black has none of his pieces out. P—Q 3 must also be played in order to mobilise the Queen's Bishop, leaving K 2 as the only square for the King's Bishop; finally the " backward " pawn [1] at Q 3 is open to constant attacks and is difficult to defend.

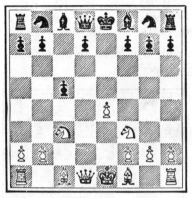

Diag. 20.

The best plan for Black is to decline the doubtful gift of the pawn and to bring about one of the positions, as sketched above, in which, by playing P—Q 4 early in the game, Black is sure of the free development of all his forces.

Black is able to play P—Q 4 early in all such openings, where White does not force the defensive move P—Q 3 by attacking Black's King's Pawn. For instance, in the King's gambit, since the move 2 P—K B 4 does not threaten P×P, Black can reply at once by 2...P—Q 4 (Falkbeer Counter Gambit). After 3 P×Q P, P—K 5 (to permit of Kt—K B 3, which at present is not feasible on account of 4 P×P); 4 P—Q 3, P×P; 5 Q×P, White is a pawn ahead, but his Queen obstructs his K B; therefore Black has better developing chances and should be able to win the pawn back at the very least.

A second example is the Vienna game, which proceeds as follows :

| 2. Kt—Q B 3 | Kt—K B 3 |
| 3. P—B 4 | P—Q 4 (Diagram 21) |

[1] A pawn is said to be " backward," when it cannot move into cover by another pawn.

If White plays 4 P × Q P, Black can play P—K 5, as in the Falkbeer gambit mentioned just now. In answer to 4 P × K P, on the other hand, Black can play Kt × P without having the slightest difficulty with his development. For instance,

| | |
|---|---|
| 5. Kt—K B 3 | B—K 2 |
| 6. P—Q 4 | P—K B 3 |
| 7. B—Q 3 | Kt × Kt |
| 8. P × Kt | Castles |
| 9. Castles | Kt—B 3 or B—K Kt 5 |

and Black also will soon have an open file for his Rook, with no disadvantage in position.

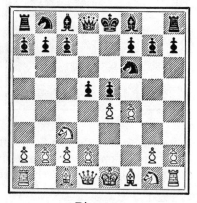

Diag. 21.

There is, however, one opening in which Black has the utmost difficulty in preventing White from getting a positional advantage in the centre. It is called the Ruy Lopez, and is held by many to be the strongest opening for White. The initial moves are : 1 P—K 4, P—K 4 ; 2 Kt—K B 3, Kt—Q B 3 ; 3 B—Kt 5. With this move White at once attacks the Black K P, though indirectly, by threatening to exchange the B for the Kt. To make the capture effective, however, White must first protect his own King's Pawn, which would otherwise be lost after 4 B × Kt, Q P × B ; 5 Kt × P, Q—Q 5 !. At first, therefore, Black need not provide against the threatened exchange.

I shall treat at some length the various defences from which Black can choose, and in studying this most important

King's side opening, we shall have occasion to note many points of general interest for operations in the centre.

Broadly speaking, two entirely different systems of defence can be distinguished : either Black will try to maintain his centre pawn, or else, giving up the centre, try to gain some other advantage as compensation.

Black can only maintain his centre pawn if he can prevent his Q Kt from being exchanged. As is readily seen, White can attack Black's K P a second time with P—Q 4, whilst after Black's P—Q 3 any other defensive move would hinder development. These considerations lead to the first main line of defence in which Black plays 3...P—Q R 3. After 4 B—R 4 Black has the option of releasing the pin by playing P—Q Kt 4 at some opportune moment. If White elects to exchange his Bishop for the Kt forthwith, he can remove the Black centre pawn after 4...Q P × B by playing 5 P—Q 4, but the exchange of the B for the Kt gives Black a free development and in consequence a good game. (Compare note to move 4 in Game No. 12.)

Diagram 22 reproduces a typical position in this defence. The more usual continuation for White is 4 B—R 4, Kt—B 3 ;

Diag. 22.

5 Castles ; he does not trouble to protect his K P as its capture would allow his Rook an open file on which to act against the opposing King (compare Games Nos. 14 and 17) 5...B—K 2. Now Black can capture the K P

without much risk, as the Bishop is on the King's file.   6 R—
K 1, White covers his pawn, and thereby threatens to win a
pawn by B × Kt.   Therefore Black must not delay playing
6...P—Q Kt 4.

After 7 B—Kt 3, P—Q 3 ; (Diagram 22) White cannot yet
execute the manœuvre which underlies the whole tendency of the
Ruy Lopez, namely P—Q 4, maintaining the pressure in the
centre, because after Kt × Q P, 9 Kt × Kt, P × Kt ;  10 Q × P ?
White loses a piece through 10...P—B 4, etc.   It is therefore
necessary to play P—Q B 3 first.    White could also obtain
a rapid development by Kt—B 3, P—Q 3, B—K 3 or
Kt 5, but this arrangement is not popular, because Black
can play Kt—Q R 4 and exchange the valuable K B.   The
pawn at Q B 3 supports an advance in the centre, and also
provides a retreat for the K B.   The Q Kt can be developed
in this way : Kt—Q 2—B 1—Kt 3 or K 3.   Black, however,
must try to round off his pawn position on the Queen's side,
by moving his Q B P into line.   Black's pawns at K 4 and
Q B 4 then exert a pressure on White's Q 4.   And this pressure
threatens to be reinforced by B—Kt 5.   From these considerations the following development seems to be natural :
8 P—B 3, Kt—Q R 4 ; 9 B—B 2, P—B 4 ; 10 P—Q 4, Q—B 2
(to support the K P) ; it leads to the position in Diagram 23.

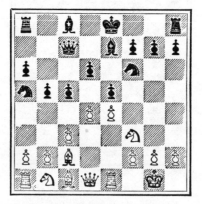

Diag. 23.

11. P—KR 3

One of the few instances in which this pawn move is justified.
It deprives Black's Q B of its only good square, and saves the
K Kt, the co-operation of which is urgently needed in the
centre.

This system of opening will receive more exhaustive treatment under the heading of " Middle Game." (Compare Game No. 12.)

In the second main line of defence, of which I shall treat now, Black renounces the maintenance of his K P, and makes an attempt to find compensation by attacking White's King's Pawn. The King's file, opened by the disappearance of the Black pawn, offers opportunities for that purpose. After the first few moves we arrive at the following position, which

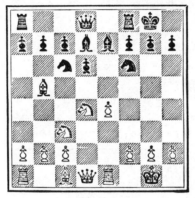

Diag. 24.

may be reached thus : 3 B—Kt 5, P—Q 3 ; 4 P—Q 4, B—Q 2 ; 5 Kt—B 3, Kt—B 3 ; 6 Castles, B—K 2 ; 7 R—K 1, P×P ; 8 Kt×P, Castles. The exchange on the seventh move is compulsory, because the loss of a pawn after B×Kt is in effect threatened, now that the White K P is supported by the Rook.

Black's intention of exerting pressure on the K P is now difficult of execution, because his pieces are very cramped and hinder one another in a restricted area. The K B in particular cannot be brought into action without great difficulty, for instance by : R—K 1, B—K B 1, P—K Kt 3, and B—Kt 2. It is therefore advisable for White to develop his Q B at Kt 2 instead of at Kt 5, in order not to give Black a chance of exchanging his troublesome Bishop. (In a game Bernstein-Emanuel Lasker, Moscow, 1914, there happened 9 B×Kt, P×B ; 10 B—Kt 5, P—K R 3 ; 11 B—R 4, Kt—R 2 ; 12 B×B, Q×B with a good game for Black.)

The defence has a totally different trend, if Black gives

up his own K P, but captures the White K P at once. I have already pointed out that White would not mind his K P being taken, in view of the attack on the open King's file. Let us now consider in which way this attack can be planned. There are two essentially different lines, according to whether Black interpolates P—Q R 3 or not.

After 3 B—Kt 5, Kt—B 3 ; 4 Castles, Kt×P ; 5 R—K 1, Black gets out of it comfortably by playing Kt—Q 3, B—K 2 and Castles, and White cannot permanently prevent Black's game from being freed by the advance of the Q P. P—Q 4 for White on the fifth move is therefore stronger. Black cannot very well exchange the pawns, leaving the King's file quite exposed, and must submit to White playing P×P, maintaining the pawn at K 5 and preventing Black's P—Q 4 for some time to come.

The opening might continue in this way : 5 P—Q 4, B—K 2 : 6 Q—K 2, Kt—Q 3 ; 7 B×Kt, Kt P×B (to make room for the Kt) ; 8 P×P, Kt—Kt 2 (Diagram 25).

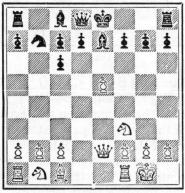

Diag. 25.

The whole of the manœuvres now centre round Black's endeavours to force his P—Q 4, and White's attempt to prevent it. Black ultimately gains his point, as will be seen, but at the expense of such disadvantages in the pawn position that it is questionable whether the whole variation (called the Rio de Janeiro Defence) is playable.

9 Kt—B 3, Castles ; 10 R—K 1, Kt—B 4 (the Knight is to be posted at K 3 to bring the White K Kt away from his

Q 4, whence he prevents the advance of Black's Q P by attacking Q B 6); 11 Kt—Q 4, Kt—K 3; 12 B—K 3, Kt×Kt; 13 B×Kt, P—B 4; 14 B—K 3, P—Q 4; 15 P×P *e.p.*, B×P. This is the critical position in the Rio de Janeiro defence. Black has succeeded in eliminating the White centre pawn, and sweeps long diagonals with his Bishops, but the advantage cannot be maintained. White exchanges the Bishop at Q 6, and there remains a backward pawn, which Black will hardly be able to hold permanently. In practice it has been shown that the end-game should be won by White in spite of Bishops of opposite colours, as Black's pawn at his Q B 4 is difficult to defend.

16 Kt—K 4, B—Kt 2; 17 Kt×B (not B×P because of B×B; 18 Kt×B, B×P followed by Q—Kt 4 ch), P×Kt; 18 Q R—Q 1 and P—Q B 4.

The game is much more favourable for Black if he first plays 3...P—Q R 3, and retains the option of driving the White K B away by P—Q Kt 4, after which P—Q 4 can be enforced very soon. 3 B—Kt 5, P—Q R 3; 4 B—R 4, Kt—B 3; 5 Castles, Kt×P; 6 P—Q 4, P—Q Kt 4; 7 B—Kt 3, P—Q 4; 8 P×P, B—K 3, 9 P—B 3.

Now Black's pieces are more mobile, and that is the reason why this system of defence is becoming more popular than any other.

On the other hand, it cannot be denied that Black's pawn formation on the Q side is weak, and that his centre is less secure. Whilst White has a pawn firmly posted in the centre, Black has a Knight there which will soon be driven away. White's Q 4, the basis of his centre, is entirely in his hands, whilst Black's Q 4 is exposed to a steady pressure by the White pieces. Finally Black's Q Kt is unfavourably placed, obstructing as it does the Q B P and preventing its falling into line with its fellows.

Diagram 26 shows the position after 9 P—B 3. The latter move prevents the exchange of the B after Black's Kt—R 4, an exchange which would allow Black to round up his pawn formation with P—Q B 4. The experts are not yet agreed as to the best continuation for Black in this critical position. To be considered are the moves B—Q B 4, B—K 2 and Kt—B 4. B—K 2 is preferred nowadays to B—Q B 4, as Q B 4 should be kept free for the K Kt in case the latter is driven from his dominating position, *e.g.* 10 R—K 1 and 11 Q Kt—Q 2. For if in that case Black exchanges the Knights, he only furthers White's development without doing anything towards strengthening his Q 4.

If Black covers the Knight with P—B 4, White plays P×P *e.p.* and Kt—-Kt 5, rids himself of Black's Q B, and thereby weakens Black's Q P still more.

Kt—B 4 would therefore seem to be the best choice, as the Q B becomes mobile again after White's B—B 2, nor can White

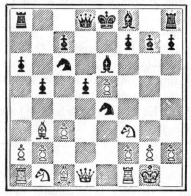

Diag. 26.

play P—Q 4 as yet. The position in the diagram therefore leads to the following variations :

A. 9...B—K 2 ; 10 R—K 1, Castles ; 11 Q Kt—Q 2, Kt—B 4 ; 12 B—B 2, B—K Kt 5. This manœuvre was introduced by Em. Lasker (Petrograd, 1909. For further particulars see Game No. 15).

B. 9...Kt—B 4 ; 10 Q Kt—Q 2, P—Q 5 (Capablanca-Em. Lasker, Petrograd, 1914) ; or 9...B—K 2 ; 10 R—K 1, Castles ; 11 Q Kt—Q 2, Kt—B 4 ; 12 B—B 2, P—Q 5 (Em. Lasker-Tarrasch, Petrograd, 1914).

Capablanca believes that the early advance of P—Q 5 can be refuted by Kt—K 4, *e.g.* 9...B—K 2 ; 10 Q Kt—Q 2, Kt—B 4 ; 11 B—B 2, P—Q 5 ; 12 Kt—K 4, P × P ; 13 Kt × Kt, B × Kt ; 14 B—K 4, Q—Q 2 ; 15 Q—B 2 or P × P.

The openings as sketched out up to this point give a sufficiently clear idea of the possibilities of combining sound development with an attempt to capture the centre after the opening moves 1 P—K 4, P—K 4. In most cases, Black's centre pawn being open to attack by White's P—Q 4, we find an early break-up of the centre, and concurrently the opening of the Ks or Qs file for the Rooks. That is why games opened in this fashion have been classed very generally as "open," whilst all the other openings are called "close games." Lately the distinction has been abandoned, and very rightly, since in the latter openings, too, the centre can be cleared occasionally.

We attain typical close positions when Black does not play 1...P—K 4 in answer to 1 P—K 4, but relinquishes all claim on his K 4 and takes possession of his Q 4 instead, leaving White the option of interlocking the pawns in the centre with P—K 5.

On principle it does not seem advisable for Black to play P—Q 4 on the first move in reply to 1 P—K 4. Although White's centre pawn disappears after 2 P×P, Q×P, Black loses a move through 3 Kt—Q B 3, and his Queen has no place from which it cannot be driven away very soon, unless it be at Q 1. This, however, would amount to an admission of the inferiority of the whole of Black's plan.

There are two moves which deserve consideration as a preliminary to P—Q 4, namely, 1...P—K 3 (French Defence)

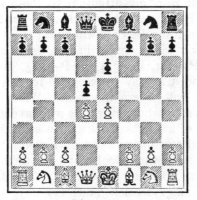

Diag. 27.

and P—Q B 3 (Caro-Kann defence). After 2 P—Q 4, P—Q 4, we attain the positions set out in the Diagrams 27 and 28, to which we must devote a good deal of attention.

These openings are worthy of study as being especially interesting examples of the struggle for the centre.

As early as the third move, White has to take an important decision. Is he to play P—K 5 and prevent the opening of

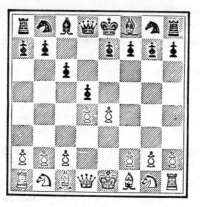

Diag. 28.

the K or Q file for a long time to come, or should he proceed to develop his pieces, and leave Black the option of anticipating the blocking of the centre by playing P × P himself ?

I shall first turn my attention to those games in which White plays P—K 5, starting with the French Defence, after which the Caro-Kann Defence will be easily understood.

The position which ensues in the centre after 1 P---K 4, P—K 3 ; 2 P—Q 4, P—Q 4 ; 3 P—K 5, divides the board diagonally, and it is easy to recognise roughly the main lines of play which will govern the game. White has more scope on the King's side, where his pieces will have greater mobility, and prospects of attack. Black's chances are on the Queen's side. Both sides will have to advance more pawns in order to obtain openings for their Rooks, and use them for the attack, since they have no future on the K and Q files, as was the case in the openings mentioned hitherto.

The obvious moves to this end are : for White the advance of the K B P, for Black that of the Q B P and sometimes even of the Q Kt P, that is when the Q B P has not been exchanged for the opposing Q P, but has pushed on to B 5.

In Diagrams 29 and 30 we see the chains of pawns formed by these manœuvres.

White's pawn attack is more dangerous than Black's,

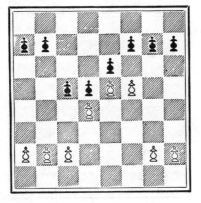

Diag. 29.

because it involves a direct assault on the King. And we shall see that Black will usually be compelled to suspend operations on the Queen's side temporarily, to ward off the storm by the

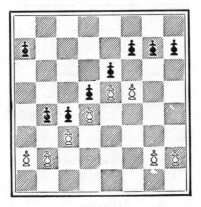

Diag. 30.

White Pawns on the King's side. He will attempt this either by P—K B 3 attacking White's centre or by P—K B 4 preventing White from playing P—B 5. In the latter case

White can only make a breach in the Black barrier by playing
P—K Kt 4 as well. These manœuvres result in the pawn
formations given in Diagrams 31 and 32.

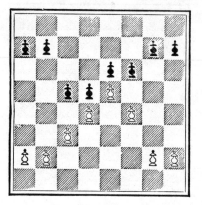

Diag. 31.

We must now turn to the development of the pieces corresponding to these pawn skeletons. If White plays P—K 5

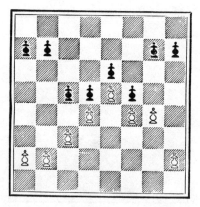

Diag. 32.

on his third move, he prevents the Black K Kt from reaching K B 3, whence he might have moved to Q 2. This is a
desirable position, from which he could support the advance of

P—Q B 4. But the Knight has other chances of development, to K R 3 and B 4, whence he can take his share in the attack on the White Pawn at Q 4. In consequence White must postpone P—K B 4 in order not to intercept the action of the Q B on R 6. Now, in that case White's Pawn at his K 5 has not sufficient support against the attack by Black's P—K B 3 (Diagram 31), and the latter move gives Black the advantage. The two main variations illustrative of these considerations are :

I

| 3. P—K 5 | P—Q B 4 |
|---|---|
| 4. P—Q B 3 | Kt—Q B 3 |
| 5. P—K B 4 | P × P |
| 6. P × P | Q—Kt 3 |
| 7. Kt—K B 3 | Kt—R 3 |

II

| 3. P—K 5 | P—Q B 4 |
|---|---|
| 4. P—Q B 3 | Kt—Q B 3 |
| 5. Kt—B 3 | P—B 3 |

In both cases the initiative falls to Black, in the first through the attack on White's Q 4, the mainstay of White's centre ; in the second through attack on White's K 5, the White centre itself. We must therefore consider White's advance of P—K 5 on the third move as premature. Let us now find out whether it is advantageous to effect the same subsequently. A developing move can be interpolated, *e.g.* 3 Kt—Q B 3, Kt—K B 3. If White plays P—K 5 now he gains time for his advance of P—K B 4, as Black's Knight must retreat. On the other hand he cannot now maintain his pawn at Q 4, as he has blocked his Q B P. We arrive at the following plan of development :

| 3. Kt—Q B 3 | Kt—K B 3 |
|---|---|
| 4. P—K 5 | K Kt—Q 2 |
| 5. P—B 4 | P—Q B 4 |
| 6. P × P | Kt—Q B 3 |

If Black were to play B×P at once, White could play
Q—Kt 4 with an attack on the Knight's Pawn. That is the
object of Black's waiting move. White must either play
7. Kt—B 3, which prevents his Q—Kt 4, or 7. B—Q 3,
after which Black would take the pawn on B 4 with his Knight,
getting rid of the White Bishop. 7. Q—Kt 4 at once would
be answered by P—B 4.

|       |           |           |
|-------|-----------|-----------|
| 7.    | Kt—B 3    | B × P     |
| 8.    | B—Q 3     | P—B 4     |

Black cannot castle yet, on account of the following threat,
which I give in full because it occurs frequently in practice:
8. ... Castles; 9. B×P ch, K×B; 10. Kt—Kt 5 ch, K—Kt 1:
11. Q—R 5, R—K 1; 12. Q×P ch; 13. Q—R 5 ch; 14. Q—
R 7 ch; 15. Q—R 8 ch; 16. Q×P mate.

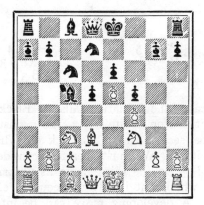

Diag. 33.

The position in the diagram seems favourable to Black
as White cannot castle for some time.

For that reason another line of play has come to the fore
in which White exchanges his inactive Q B for Black's troublesome K B.

|       |           |           |
|-------|-----------|-----------|
| 3.    | Kt—Q B 3  | Kt—K B 3  |
| 4.    | B—Kt 5    | B—K 2     |

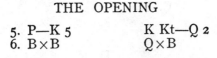

| 5. P—K 5 | K Kt—Q 2 |
| 6. B × B | Q × B |

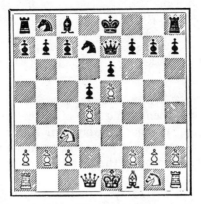

Diag. 34.

White has now the choice of two lines of development. He can either prepare for P—Q B 3 to support his Q P. or he can develop his King's side, holding the P at K 5 only

### I

| 7. Kt—Kt 5 | Kt—Kt 3 |
| 8. P—Q B 3 | P—Q R 3 |
| 9. Kt—Q R 3 | P—Q B 4 |
| 10. P—K B 4 | Kt—B 3 |
| 11. Kt—B 2 | Castles |
| 12. Kt—B 3 | B—Q 2 |
| 13. B—Q 3 | P—B 4 |

The sacrifice B × P ch, as mentioned above, was threatened.

| 14. Castles | Kt—R 5 |
| 15. R—Kt 1 | P—Q Kt 4 |

If White does not wish to lose so many moves with his Kt, he can effect the intended protection of his Q P as follows:

| 7. Q—Q 2 | P—Q R 3 |

not P—Q B 4 at once, because of Kt—Kt 5.

| 8. Kt—Q 1 | P—Q B 4 |
| 9. P—Q B 3 | |

II

| 7. P—B 4 | Castles |
| 8. Kt—B 3 | P—Q B 4 |
| 9. B—Q 3 | P—B 4 |
| 10. Castles | Kt—Q B 3 |

and so on.

In both cases White has an easy development, whilst Black has no convenient square for his Queen's Bishop.

To avoid this drawback Rubinstein has evolved the following variation, in which provision is made from the first for the freedom of action of the Queen's Bishop :

| 3. Kt—Q B 3 | Kt—K B 3 |
| 4. B—Kt 5 | P×P |

to open the diagonal for the Bishop at Q Kt 2, *e.g.* :

| 5. Kt×P | Q Kt—Q 2 |
| 6. Kt—K B 3 | B—K 2 |

followed by P—Q Kt 3 and B—Kt 2.

We will now leave the French defence and turn our attention to the Caro-Kann, of which the initial position was shown in Diagram 28. Here also we find two essentially different systems of development, according to whether White plays P—K 5 or gives Black the option of exchanging pawns by 3. Kt—Q B 3. In the first case a very noticeable difference from the French defence is, that Black can bring out his Queen's Bishop. Here the process of development may be :

| 3. P—K 5 | B—B 4 |
| 4. B—Q 3 | B×B |

Not B—Kt 3, because White could play P—K 6 ! and paralyse the whole of Black's game by preventing his playing the King's Pawn.

| 5. Q×B | P—K 3 |
| 6. Kt—K 2 or K R 3 | |

Through this the move P—K B 4, which fits into this pawn formation, is kept in reserve.

While White's development is easy and natural, Black has difficulty in finding good places for his King's side pieces. The game can proceed generally speaking on the lines of the French defence. Only Black can hardly attack White's centre with P—B 3, since the Pawn at K 3 would be weak in the absence of the Queen's Bishop. On the other hand, Black would be a move behind with an attack on the Queen's side, since to reach Q B 4 his pawn would have made two moves instead of one as in the French defence. A certain compensation lies in the fact that White's attacking King's Bishop has been exchanged.

In practical play it has nevertheless been shown that White's attack is more likely to succeed, and for this reason a variation introduced by Niemzowitsch has been tried several times; it aims at the exchange of Queens in order to weaken and retard White's threatened attack, and to gain time for Queen's side operations.

6. ......... Q—Kt 3
7. Castles Q—R 3 or Kt 4

But after 8 Kt—B 4, Q×Q; 9 Kt×Q, White is so much ahead with his development that Black's chance of equalising the game would seem questionable.

If White plays Kt—K R 3 on his sixth move, he foils at once Black's attempt of forcing an exchange of Queens, as he could play 8 Q—K Kt 3.

On the whole we can conclude that in the Caro-Kann defence White obtains a good game by 3 P—K 5.

A line of play which used to be in vogue, namely, 3 Kt—Q B 3, P×P; 4 Kt× P, Kt—B 3; 5 Kt×Kt ch, K P×Kt or Kt P × Kt, gives Black an even chance, for although he loses his centre pawn he obtains a good development, and later in the game he has opportunities of exercising pressure on White's Q P through his open Q file.

Except the French defence and the Caro-Kann, there is no game in which an irregular reply to White's 1 P—K 4 necessitates any special considerations either in development of pieces or pawn formation. In all such cases it is sufficient to maintain the pawn centre and to occupy such squares with the pieces, whence they cannot be driven away with the loss of a move. Just one example : If Black plays 1...P—Q B 4 (Sicilian defence), White will not play his King's Bishop to B 4, because Black can reply P—K 3, and gain a move by P—Q 4.

*B.* Let us now consider the openings in which the first move is 1 P—Q 4 on either side. Here the centre cannot be cleared as early as in the openings beginning with 1 P—K 4, P—K 4. The advance of a second centre pawn, which there led to a clearance, is not feasible in this case. White does not command his K 4, and for some time to come he will be unable to advance the K pawn beyond K 3. In consequence the K file does not seem a likely opening for the Rooks, and another file must be found for them. The conclusions arrived at for Black in the French defence hold good for both sides in the opening now under consideration, and accordingly the Q B file is that most advantageous for the Rooks. The advance of the Q B P strikes at the opposing centre, and, that being of paramount importance, the Queen's Knight must not be developed at B 3 before the Q B P has been pushed on. Another development might be conceivable for the Rooks ; viz. on the K B file, and also the K Kt or K R file ; here, as we shall see, an occasion may arise for storming the opposing King's side by a pawn attack. But in this case, too, although it seems unnecessary to play the Q B P, it is advisable to develop the Knight via Q 2, as there is a constant threat of the Q B file being forced open subsequently by the opposing forces.

We will start with the games in which the Q B Pawns are played in the earliest stages of the opening, so that the pawn skeleton in Diagram 35 forms the basis of development. The sequence of moves is of moment, because the advance of the K P, whether forced or not, determines the possibility of bringing out the Q Bishops. The simplest process of develop-

ment based on Diagram 35 is the following, in which both
sides block up the Q B.

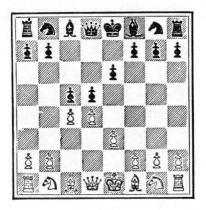

Diag. 35.

| 2. P—K 3 | P—K 3 |
|---|---|
| 3. Kt—K B 3 | Kt—K B 3 |
| 4. P—B 4 | P—B 4 |
| 5. Kt—B 3 | Kt—B 3 |
| 6. B—Q 3 | B—Q 3 |
| 7. Castles. | Castles |

The only useful square for the Q B's on either side is now at
Kt 2, and 8 P—Q Kt 3, P—Q Kt 3 are indicated. To play
P—Q Kt 3 before castling is very dangerous, because Black
can play P×Q P and pin the White Q Kt with B—Kt 5, forcing B—Q 2, when B—Kt 2 was the move intended, *e.g.*
6 P—Q Kt 3, B P×P; 7 K P×P, B—Kt 5; 8 B—Kt 2,
Kt—K 5; 9 Q—B 2, Q—R 4; 10 R—Q B 1, Q×P.

In order not to relinquish the square at Q Kt 4 to Black,
White can also try the following manœuvre:

| 6. P×B P | B×P |
|---|---|
| 7. P—Q R 3 | Castles |
| 8. P—Q Kt 4 | B—Q 3 |
| 9. B—Kt 2 | |

If Black imitates White's moves, viz. 9... P×P; 10 B×P,

P—Q R 3 ; 11 Castles, P—Q Kt 4 ; 12 B—Q 3, B—Kt 2, the result is the symmetrical position in Diagram 36.

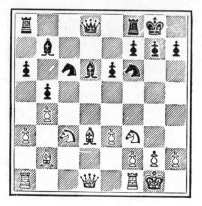

Diag. 36.

When treating of the middle game, we shall find that even in this apparently fully equalised position the influence of the first move is still at work.

In order to obtain a more thorough understanding of the Queen's Pawn game, we must now turn our attention very closely to the opening moves. Already on the second move White can play 2. P—Q B 4 and turn the game into a Queen's gambit, which Black can either accept or decline. Black would be justified in playing 2...P×P, and so furthering White's object of getting his (Black's) Queen's Pawn away, if he could permanently hold the gambit pawn, or if the giving up of the square at Q 4 fits into a reasoned system of development. The latter was, for instance, the case in the play leading to the position shown in the Diagram 36. But Black is well advised to wait until White has moved the King's Bishop before taking the pawn on his Q B 5. This forces the Bishop to move twice, and Black regains the move he lost in his development, when he played P×P.

It would be quite incorrect to try to hold the pawn by P—Q Kt 4 as follows :

|   |   |   |
|---|---|---|
| 2. | P—Q B 4 | P×P |
| 3. | Kt—K B 3 | Kt—K B 3 |

4. P—K 3          P—Q Kt 4
5. P—Q R 4

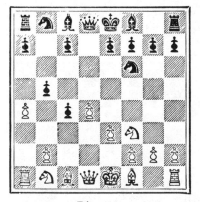

Diag. 37.

If now Black answers P × P, White simply plays B × P and the P at R 5 is lost very soon. If Black plays instead : 5...P—B 3, White wins back his pawn with 6 P—Q Kt 3, P × Kt P ; 7 P × P, P × P ; 8 B × P ch by Q × P, and moreover is much ahead with his development.

These considerations point to the conclusion that after 2 P—Q B 4 there is no inducement for Black to take the pawn. On the contrary, he will cover his centre pawn, which White wishes to tempt away, either with P—K 3 or P—Q B 3. The attempt to develop the Queen's Bishop before playing P—K 3 is not to be recommended, because the Q Kt's pawn remains unprotected and open to an immediate attack by 3 Q—Kt 3. Of the two remaining replies, 2...P—K 3 and 2...P—Q B 3, I will first discuss the former, as being the more natural of the two, since P—Q B 3 does not fit into the scheme for opening the Q B file for the Rooks. White, on the other hand, can bring out his Q B before playing P—K 3, in this way :

2 P—Q B 4, P—K 3 ; 3 Kt—Q B 3, Kt—K B 3 ; 4 B—Kt 5, and the game might proceed as follows : 4...Q Kt—Q 2. (Diagram 38.)

No fault can be found with this move, although it blocks the Bishop, since the latter can only be developed effectively at Kt 2. Moreover, the Knight at Q 2 supports the projected

P—B 4. White cannot win a pawn now with 5 P×P, P×P; 6 Kt×P, because of Kt×Kt; 7 B×Q, B—Kt 5 ch. Therefore 5 P—K 3 must be played first, and after B—K 2; 6 Kt—B 3, Castles; 7 R—B 1, P—Q Kt 3; 8 P×P, P×P; 9 B—Q 3, B—Kt 2, all the pieces have found rational development.

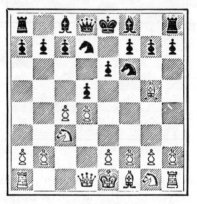

Diag. 38.

Quite a different system of opening ensues, when Black does not delay pushing the P to Q B 4 until after his pieces are developed, but makes the advance on his third move.

Here Black has the advantage of being able to avoid the pinning of his Knight by the opposing Q B.

|   |   |   |
|---|---|---|
| 2. | P—Q B 4 | P—K 3 |
| 3. | Kt—Q B 3 | P—Q B 4 |
| 4. | Kt—B 3 | Kt—Q B 3 ! |

Now Black threatens Q P×P with an attack on White's Queen's Pawn. If White plays P—K 3 we get the position mentioned in connection with Diagram 35. If he wishes to bring out his Q B first, he must anticipate Black's threat by B P×P.

After

5. B P×P          K P×P

the third of the typical main positions in the Queen's gambit ensues, and is given in Diagram 39.

Two continuations must now be considered. White can either develop his K B at Kt 2, and concentrate on the Black Q P, which is somewhat weak, or he can place the K B on one of the available squares between B 1 and R 6. In the first instance, the K P need not be played at all, and the Q B

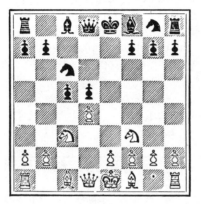

Diag. 39.

retains the option of developing at Kt 5, B 4, and even K 3. In the second, where the K P must make room for the K B, White must decide at once between B—B 4 or Kt 5, and only B 4 can be seriously considered on account of

6. B—Kt 5          B—K 2
7. B×B               Kt×B

which only furthers Black's development. White would only be justified in this course if he could now win a pawn with 8 P×P, but Black would win it back and have the superior game after

8. .........            P—Q 5
9. Kt—K 4        Castles

followed by B—B 4 and Q—R 4 ch. The correct move in this variation is consequently 6 B—B 4, and a possible continuation would be : Kt—K B 3 ; 7 P—K 3, B—K 3 ; 8 R—Q B 1 or B—Q Kt 5 or B—Q 3.

With this we will close the discussion of the variations initiated by 2 P—Q ·B 4, P—K 3, and study the reply 2...P—

Q B 3. The first question which arises in our mind is : Which file will Black be able to utilise for his Rooks ? An attempt to free the King's file through P—K 4 is conceivable. But White can prevent this by simply playing Kt—K B 3.

Two other possibilities present themselves : after playing P—K 3, Kt—B 3 and Q Kt—Q2, Black could steer into a line similar to the Queen's gambit accepted with P × P and P— Q B 4, or he could keep the centre closed with P—K B 4 and Kt—B 3, with the intention of playing Kt—K 5 and using the K B file for activating his Rook via K B 3. Diagram 40 gives the position reached after :

|  | 3. Kt—K B 3 | P—K 3 |
|---|---|---|
|  | 4. P—K 3 | P—K B 4 |
|  | 5. Kt—K 5 | Kt—B 3 |

Diag. 40.

White would not accomplish much with 6 P—K B 4. The more or less symmetrical lineup of the pieces would most likely lead to a draw after Black properly prepares freeing his hemmed-in Bishop with P—Q Kt 3 and B—Kt 2. A better plan would be 6 P—B 3, preventing Kt—K 5 and preparing the eventual advance of the King's Pawn to K 4. In reply to 6..., Q Kt—Q 2 White would then rather play 7 Kt—Q 3 than ex-change Knights, as after this exchange it would not be too diffi-cult for Black to bring his Bishop into play on the King's wing via K 1. Both of White's Bishops would be best placed on Kt 2. This "Stonewall" opening can also be played by White, who is then a move to the good in the variation just shown. But this opening has practically disappeared from modern tournament games, simply because the Q B cannot easily be brought into play.

The following variation is reminiscent of the " Stonewall " in the formation of the centre pawns. White develops his Queen's side just as Black did in the opening shown in connection with Diagram 38.

| | | |
|---|---|---|
| 2. | Kt—K B 3 | P—Q B 4 |
| 3. | P—K 3 | Kt—Q B 3 |
| 4. | B—Q 3 | Kt—B 3 |
| 5. | P—Q Kt 3 | P—K 3 |
| 6. | B—Kt 2 | B—Q 3 |
| 7. | Q Kt—Q 2 | P × P |
| 8. | P × P | Castles |

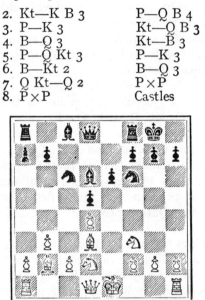

Diag. 41.

White can now settle his Knight at K 5, and initiate a violent King's side attack after castling, by P—K B 4, Q—B 3, which could be continued with P—K Kt 4, K—R 1, R—K Kt 1, and so on. Once the position in Diagram 41 has been reached, Black's resources against the dangerous onslaught of the White forces are scanty. Yet he can retaliate, not by making the simplest and most obvious developing moves, as mentioned before, but in the following way :

If White plays 5. P—Q Kt 3 before castling, Black exchanges pawns and checks with the Queen. Now White has the disagreeable choice between B—Q 2 and P—B 3.

The former must be bad, being contrary to the plan of development as intended by P—Q Kt 3. The latter blocks the very diagonal on which the Bishop was meant to operate. White can open up the diagonal by playing P—Q B 4 after castling, nor would it really imply the loss of a move to have played the B P twice, since Black must move his Queen again from R 4, where she has no future. But in any case there remains the disadvantage that White was forced to play the B P, whilst before he had the option of withholding its advance until a more opportune moment.

Another possible subtlety in Black's sequence of developing moves would be to withhold the advance of his K P until White has played P—Q Kt 3, and then to play the Q B to Kt 5. For, as I have already remarked, the objection to developing Black's Queen's Bishop lies in White's threat to attack Black's Q Kt P with Q—Kt 3. That possibility disappears after P—Q Kt 3.

Before bringing the discussion of the Queen's Pawn opening to a close, I may remark that in tournaments it has become usual for White not to play P—Q B 4 at once, but to play Kt—K B 3 as a preliminary, in order to avoid the complications of the Queen's counter gambit: 2 P—Q B 4, P—K 4.

If White plays 3 P×K P, Black's reply is P—Q 5, and the obvious move 4 P—K 3 fails on account of the following pretty combination : B—Kt 5 ch ; 5 B—Q 2, P×P ; 6 B×B, P×P ch ; 7 K—K 2, P×Kt ch ! ! ; 8 R×Kt, B—Kt 5 ch, etc.

Instead of 4 P—K 3, White should play P—K Kt 3 and develop his K B at Kt 2. Black could now try to regain his pawn with Kt—K 2—Kt 3, but he can also sacrifice a pawn by P—K B 3, with a view to rapid development.

It now only remains for us to discover whether Black has any other answer to P—Q 4 which would necessitate close analysis on White's part.

Here must be mentioned : 1...Kt—K B 3, 1...P—Q B 4, and 1...P—K B 4. The former move prepares P—Q 3, followed by P—K 4. In this opening there is no reason why White should play P—Q B 4, as there is no prospect of opening the Q B file for the Rooks. Furthermore, Black has relinquished the square Q 4 and made K 4 the basis of operations.

It will be more advisable to prevent Black from playing P—K 4 as far as this can be achieved in conformity with a logical development, *e.g.* 1 P—Q 4, Kt—K B 3 ; 2 Kt—K B 3. Not 2 Kt—Q B 3, because Black could then lead into the Queen's gambit by playing P—Q 4 and P—Q B 4, after which White has the disadvantage of not being able to open the Q B file. 2...P—Q 3 ; 3 B—B 4, Q Kt—Q 2 ; 4 P—K 3. Now Black can only enforce P—K 4 after P—B 3 and Q—B 2. Meanwhile White mobilises all his pieces, whilst Black's Q B remains blocked and the Kt must remain at Q 2 to cover the K P. If, on the other hand, Black exchanges pawns in order to free the Knight, there is no Black centre left.

With regard to the second irregular reply to 1 P—Q 4, namely, 1...P—Q B 4, two ways are open to White. One is to turn the opening into an ordinary Queen's gambit by play-ing P—K 3, on which Black can play P—Q 4. The second is to play 2 P—Q 5. Black will then develop his King's side with P—K Kt 3 and B—Kt 2. The Bishop is well posted here, and can frequently take up an attacking position at K 4 or Q 5. (See Game No. 45, Rubinstein *v.* Spielmann.)

If White plays 2 P × P, we have after 2...P—K 3 a Queen's gambit accepted by White, and, as pointed out before, this line of play is not commendable.

The last of the three irregular answers mentioned above : 1...P—K B 4 leads to two entirely different plans, according to the second move chosen by White.

White can confine himself to a simple development such as : Kt—K B 3, B—Kt 5, P—K3, Q Kt—Q 2 (Kt—B 3 would only be good if preceded by P—B 4, because Black would again lead into a Queen's gambit with P—Q 4 and P—Q B 4). The other possibility is the following : in view of the fact that 1...P—K B 4 does absolutely nothing to aid development, White can initiate a violent attack by giving up his King's Pawn (P—K 4) and thus accelerate his own development. The play might be as follows : 2...P × P ; 3 Kt—Q B 3, Kt—K B 3 ; 4 B—K Kt 5, P—B 3 (P—Q 4 ? 5 B × Kt followed by Q—R 5 ch) ; 5 P—B 3. If Black takes the pawn he lays himself open to an attack hard to meet. It seems best to play 5...P—K 6, which calls back the White Q B and leaves White's B P as a hindrance to the development of the K Kt.

IRREGULAR OPENINGS

Many openings in which neither P—K 4 nor P—Q 4 is the
first move lead to well-known positions by a simple transposition of moves. For instance, a Queen's gambit may well
have the following opening moves : 1 P—Q B 4, Kt—K B 3 ;
2 Kt—K B 3, P—K 3 ; 3 Kt—B 3, P—B 4 ; 4 P—K 3,
P—Q 4 ; 5 P—Q 4, or a French defence these : 1 Kt—Q B 3,
P—Q 4 ; 2 P—Q 4, Kt—K B 3 ; 3 B—Kt 5, P—K 3 ;
4 P—K 4.

There are, of course, systems of opening which deviate
absolutely from those which have been proved sound and are
in general use, and it is those openings that puzzle the beginner most of all. He says : What is the good of learning
correct openings, if my opponent plays incorrectly and wins
all the same ? This line of thought is wrong from its incep-
tion. The student is not supposed to " learn " openings by
heart, but to *understand* how the general principles of Chess
Strategy are applied to any opening. Such knowledge can
never be obtained from a tabulated analysis, but can only be
arrived at by the application of common sense. If a player
succeeds in winning in spite of an inferior opening, it only
proves that subsequently he has played a stronger game than
his opponent, who, after playing the opening according to
the book, did not know how to proceed further. And herein
lies the weakness, and not in the absence of knowledge of
the analysis of openings. The latter is rated far too highly.
Any player will hold his own in the opening, as soon as he has
grasped the real meaning of those principles which I cannot
repeat often enough, viz.: 1st, quick development of pieces
and avoidance of lost moves ; 2nd, the maintenance of a pawn
centre, hampering the development of the opposing forces,
and the avoidance of pawn moves that do not contribute to
the development of pieces.

How to conduct the middle game and end-game is not entirely a matter of deduction from such general rules. In order
to play the end-game correctly, one must know certain things
and positions which arise from and may be said to be peculiar
to the purely arbitrary rules of chess. The same applies to

the middle game, as in most cases it must be played with a view to the end-game which ensues, unless there be a chance of mating the opponent before. The student should have, therefore, a knowledge of the end-game before he can hope to be able to conduct the middle game efficiently. For this reason I have decided to treat of the end-game first.

## CHAPTER V

### THE END-GAME

JUST as it is difficult to state the exact point at which an opening ends, so is it equally difficult to say where the end-game may be said to commence. One of the main characteristics of end-games is the active part taken by the King. Clearly the King cannot venture out into the field of operations until there has been an exchange of the majority of the pieces, so that there can be no danger of his being mated. As soon as a player has attained some advantage in material which ensures the victory in the end-game, he will try to bring about the end-game by exchanging pieces, for there the lines on which to push home his advantage are clearly set out.

It is first necessary to know what surplus of forces is the minimum required in order to force a mate. The positions in which the mate can be forced may be shown by a few typical examples. But I shall lay stress mainly on one point. That is the ability to judge whether an end-game which could be brought about by exchanges is won or not ; in other words, whether it can be reduced to one of the typical positions referred to above.

It is obvious that the end-game is the particular demesne of pawn strategy. Nearly always one or more pawns survive the exchange of pieces, and the knowledge of the end-game will be invaluable for gauging the consequences of pawn moves in the course of the middle game. The latter represents probably the most difficult aspect of the strategy of chess.

In order to enable beginners to grasp the following chapters, I must again point out a few elementary considerations. Simple end-games, that is, end-games without pawns, are comparatively easy to understand. Let us first consider the case of a King denuded of all his troops. In order to force the mate it is necessary to obtain command of four squares, namely, those four squares which he controls after he has been driven into a corner. Supposing the Black King has been driven to Q R 1, the White King can prevent him from reaching two squares of different colour, namely, Q R 2 and Q Kt 2. Therefore it is necessary for White still to have such forces as can command two more squares of different colour, namely, Q R 1 and Q Kt 1. As can readily be seen, it will be essential to have at least the Queen or a Rook or two Bishops, or a Knight and Bishop, or two Knights.[1]

We shall see that in the latter case it is impossible to drive the King into a corner without bringing about a stalemate. The mates by a Queen or Rook are so simple that I only give an example of each for the sake of completeness.

Position 1—White : K at Q R 1, Q—K R 1
Black : K at K 4

1 K—Kt 2, K—Q 5 ; 2 K—Kt 3, K—K4 ; 3 K—B 4, K—Q 3 ; 4 Q—K 4, K—Q 2 ; 5 K—B 5, K—B 1 ; 6 K—B 6, K—Kt 1 ; 7 Q—Q R 4, or Kt 4 ch, or K 7, or R 7 and mate next move.

Position 2—White : K at Q Kt 3, R K R 2
Black : K at K 4

1 K—B 4, K—Q 3 ; 2 R—K 2, K—B 3 ; 3 R—K 6 ch, K—Q 2 ; 4 K—Q 5, K—B 2 ; 5 K—B 5, K—Q 2 ; 6 R—K 1, K—B 2 ; 7 R—K 7 ch, K—Q 1 ; 8 K—Q 6, K—B 1 ; 9 K—B 6, K—Kt 1 ; 10 R—K 1, K—R 7 ; 11 R—K 8, K—R 3 ; 12 R—R 8 mate.

Position 3—White : K at Q R sq, B at K Kt sq, B at K Kt 2
Black : K at K R sq

1 K—Kt 2, K—Kt 2 ; 2 K—B 3, K—B 3 ; 3 K—Q 4, K—K 3 ; 4 B—R 2, K—B 3 ; 5 K—Q 5, K—B 4 ; 6 B—K 5, K—Kt 4 ; 7 K—K 6, K—Kt 5 ; 8 B—Q R 8, K—Kt 4 ; 9 B—B 3, K—Kt 3 ; 10 B—K B 6, K—R 3 ; 11 K—B 7, K—R 2 ; 12 B—Kt 5, K—R 1 ; 13 B—Q 1, K—R 2 ; 14 B—B 2 ch, K—R 1 ; B—B 6 mate.

---

[1] How the King can be driven into a corner will be shown subsequently.

It is more difficult to mate with *Knight and Bishop*. It is only possible to mate on a corner square commanded by the Bishop, as the following argument shows clearly. A mating position in the corner which the Bishop does not command would have to be of the type set out in Diagram 42. Here the Bishop plays on White squares, and the Knight in order to checkmate must move on to a White square; in other words, he must come from a Black one. Therefore, when the Bishop checked on the previous move and drove the King away, the King had the option of two black squares, and had no need to go into the corner one. He is only mated in consequence of a wrong move.

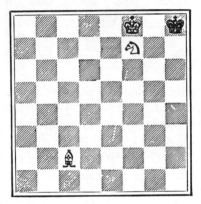

Diag. 42.

As stated above, however, it is possible in all cases to mate in the corner square which is of the same colour as the Bishop. The King is driven into the corner in this way: the Knight cuts him off such squares as the Bishop does not command. Diagram 43 will serve as an illustration.

1 K—Kt 2, K—Kt 2 ; 2 K—B 3, K—B 3 ; 3 K—Q 4, K—K 3 ; 4 Kt—Kt 3, K—B 3 ; 5 B—B 3, K—Kt 4 ; 6 K—K5, K—Kt 3 ; 7 Kt—K 4, K—Kt 2 ; 8 K—B 5, K—R 1 ; 9 K—B 6, K—Kt 1 ; 10 Kt—Kt 5, K—R 1 ; 11 Kt—B 7 ch, K—Kt 1 ; 12 B—K 4, K—B 1 ; 13 B—R 7, K—K 1 ; 14 Kt— K 5, K—Q 1 ; 15 Kt—B 4, K—B 2 ; 16 B—K 4, K—Q 2 ; 17 K—B 7, K—B 2 ; 18 K—K 7, K—B 1 ; 19 K—Q 6, K—Q 1 ; 20 B—Kt 6, K—B 1 ; 21 Kt—R 5, K—Q 1 ;

22 Kt—Kt 7 ch, K—B 1 ; 23 K—B 6, K—Kt 1 ; 24 K—Kt 6, K—B 1 ; 25 B—B 5 ch, K—Kt 1 ; 26 Kt—B 5, K—R 1 ; 27 B—K 6, K—Kt 1 ; 28 Kt—R 6 ch, K—R 1 ; 29 B—Q 5 mate.

Diag. 43.

It is impossible to force a mate with the *King and two Knights*. On the same grounds as given with respect to Diagram 42, the mate can only be attained through the opponent making a bad move. But a mate can be forced if the weaker side has a spare move which prevents the stalemate, *e.g.* Diagram 44.

Diag. 44.

1 Kt (K 3)—Q 5, K—Kt 2 ; 2 K—B 5, K—R 3 ; 3 K—Kt 4, K—Kt 2 ; 4 K—Kt 5, K—R 2 ; 5 Kt—B 7, K—Kt 2 ; 6 Kt (B 7)—K 8, K—R 2 ; 7 Kt—Q 6, K—Kt 1 ; 8 K—Kt 6.

K—R 1 ;  9 Kt—Q 7, P—B 4 ;  10 Kt—Kt 5, P—B 5 ;
11 Kt—B 7 mate.

Having decided as to the smallest amount of material
advantage with which it is possible to force a mate, we will
now turn our attention to simple game endings (still without
pawns).  To judge such endings correctly, it will only be
necessary to find out whether it is possible to obtain the
minimum advantage mentioned.  It is sufficient to discuss
cases in which a piece on the one side plays against a stronger
one on the other, because in endings where several pieces are
left on either side, fortuitous circumstances are generally the
deciding factors, and it would be impossible to characterise
and classify positions of that kind, by giving typical illustrations.  Besides, they are reduced sooner or later by exchanges
to such end-games as have been treated already, or are going
to be shown now.

The Queen wins against any other piece ; the Rook
alone may give trouble.  In Diagram 45 we illustrate a

Diag. 45.

position which is one of the most favourable to the weaker
side.

1 Q—R 6 leads to nothing, as R—B 2 ch follows, and after
2 K—Kt 6 Black forces a stalemate with R—B 3 ch.

It is necessary for White to gain a move in this position ;
in other words, White must try to transfer to the other side the
onus of having to move.  If then the Rook moves away from

the King, it gets lost after a few checks, or if Black's King plays to B 1, the Rook is equally lost through Q—R 6.

White plays therefore : 1 Q—K 5 ch, K—R 1 ; 2 Q—R 1 ch, K—Kt 1 ; 3 Q—R 5, and wins. For example, 3...R—B 2 ; 4 Q—K 5 ch, K—R 2 ; 5 Q—K 3 ch, K— R1 ; 6 Q—K 8 ch, and so on.

The Rook can win against a minor piece in exceptional cases only. In endings of *Rook against Bishop* the weaker King must take refuge in a corner square of different colour from that of his Bishop. For instance, Diagram 46 :

Diag. 46.

1 R—Q 5, B—B 5 (or R 2) ; 2 R—Q 8 ch, B—Kt 1, and Black is stalemate unless the Rook leaves the eighth Rank. Any outside square which is not of the same colour as that of the Bishop is dangerous for the King. Imagine the pieces in Diagram 46 shifted two squares towards the centre of the board, as in Diagram 47, and White wins with

|   |   |
|---|---|
| 1. R—Q Kt 5 | B—R 5 |
| 2. R—Kt 8 ch | B—K 1 |
| 3. R—R 8 |   |

The Bishop is lost, as it is Black's move.

In endings of *Rook against Knight*, the weaker side loses, where the Knight is cut off from his King.

For instance, in Diagram 48, 1 R—Q 5 ! In this " oblique opposition " the Rook takes four of the Knight's squares : 1...Kt—K 8 ; 2 K—B 5, Kt—B 7 ; 3 K—K 4, Kt—R 6 (Kt—

Kt 5 ? ; 4 R—Kt 5 ch ! wins the Knight). In this ending there is always a fatal check at some point, and the position in the

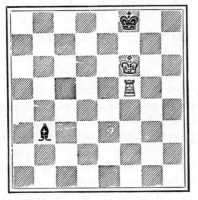

Diag. 47.

diagram is not in any way a chance win. 4 K—Q 3, K—B 2 ; 5 R—Q R 5, Kt—Kt 8 ; 6 R—R 1, and wins.

Diag. 48.

As soon as the Knight can obtain the King's support the game is drawn even when the King is already forced on to the edge of the board.

Position—White : K at K 6, R at K 5
Black : K at K 1, Kt at Q R 2

1 R—Q B 5, K—Q 1 ; 2 K—Q 6, Kt—B 1 ch ; 3 K—B 6,

Kt—K 2 ch, draw. In this case the King must avoid the corners, as the Knight would be bereft of his efficiency.

Position—White : K at K R 6, R at K R 4
Black : K at K R 1, Kt at K 2

1 R—K 4, Kt—Kt 1 ch ; 2 K—Kt 6 and wins.

---

We come now to the more interesting part of end-game play, namely, *pawn endings*. The best course will be first to study how to turn a material superiority in pawns to decisive advantage, after which we shall note particular positions, in which a win is possible with an equality or even an inferiority in pawns.

The ending of *King and pawn against King* is one of the simplest albeit one of the most important of elementary cases. The stronger side will evidently try to queen the pawn. But generally this is not possible if the adverse King has command of the queening square. One important condition, though, must be complied with : the weaker King must move into " opposition," and " opposition " is one of the characteristic and deciding factors in most pawn endings. It is absolutely necessary for the learner to understand fully the meaning of the term " opposition," and its value in elementary cases This knowledge is of far reaching influence in end-games.

Diag. 49.

In Diagram 49 White seeks to queen his pawn.

1 K—Q 4, K—K 2 ; 2 K—K 5

With this move White assumes the opposition. That is, he moves into the same rank or file, separated by one square only, so that both Kings stand on squares of the same colour. White has moved last, it is Black's turn to move ; it is said in this case that " White has the opposition." We shall soon see that Black is only able to draw the game, if he succeeds in assuming the opposition himself (which means that, having the move, he should step into opposition). 2...K—Q 2 ; 3 P— Q 6 (Diagram 50).

Diag. 50.

I propose now to recapitulate.

This is the critical moment, namely, when the pawn reaches the sixth rank. If now Black plays K—K 1 he is lost, for White playing K—K 6 has the opposition. After 4...K—Q 1, 5 P—Q 7, Black is forced to allow the White King to move to K 7, covering the queening square ; 5...K—B 2, 6 K—K 7, any ; 7 P queens. But Black has a draw in the position of Diagram 50, by playing 3...K—Q 1 ! ! (not K 1). Now after 4 K—K 6 he keeps the opposition himself with K—K 1 ; and after 5 P—Q 7 ch, K—Q 1 ; 6 K—Q 6, he is stalemated, or else wins the pawn if White plays differently on his sixth move. The King draws against King and pawn if he commands the queening square, and if he can retain the opposition on the first rank as soon as the pawn moves into his sixth.

It is of the utmost importance that the pawn should be

at his sixth; if the pawn is still further back, the opposition on the first rank is of no avail.

Diagram 51 will serve as an example. Having the move,

Diag. 51.

White would only draw with P—B 5, because Black's K—B 2 wins the pawn.

But White wins as follows: 1 K—Kt 6, K—B 1; 2 K—B 6, K—K 1; 3 K—K 6, K—Q 1; 4 K—Q 6, K—B sq:

Diag. 52.

5 P—B 5, K—Q sq. We see: Black has just assumed the opposition, but the pawn has not yet crossed to his sixth square, and White, by playing P—B 6, again forces Black to give up the opposition.

It might be more clear to put it in this way : with P—B 6 White wins the opposition, in that he brings about a position with Black to move. Therefore the game is won for White. Since the opposition on the outside rank is of no avail, when the pawn has not yet played to his sixth square, the weaker side must try to keep away the opposing King from the sixth rank until the pawn has reached that rank. This is possible in positions such as that in Diagram 53, where the stronger

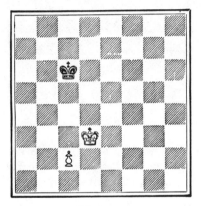

Diag. 53.

King is not more than one rank ahead of his pawn, and the weaker King can assume the opposition. In the position in Diagram 53 Black plays K—Q 4 and maintains the opposition until the pawn moves, after which a typical position, similar to the one treated in connection with Diagram 50 is brought about.

If White has the move, however, he wins easily by 1 K—B 4, thus :

| 1. ......... | K—Q 3 |
| 2. K—Kt 5 | K—B 2 |
| 3. K—B 5 | K—Kt 2 |
| 4. K—Q 6 | K—B 1 |
| 5. K—B 6 | |

and there is opposition on the eighth rank whilst the pawn has not reached the sixth.

If the King is more than one rank ahead of his pawn, as in Diagram 54, the end-game can always be won, for if Black

Diag. 54.

takes the opposition with K—Q 3, White deprives him of it again, winning a move by P—B 3, and the position is similar to that in Diagram 53, with White to move.

| 1. ......... | K—Q 3 |
| 2. P—B 3 | K—B 3 |
| 3. K—B 4 | and wins. |

This settles all typical end-games of King and pawn against King. There is, however, one exception to the rules set out, namely, when a *Rook's pawn* is concerned. Here the isolated King always succeeds in drawing if he can reach the corner where the pawn has to queen, for he cannot be driven out again. The Rook's pawn affords another opportunity for the weaker side to draw. Diagram 55 will illustrate this, and similar positions are of frequent occurrence in practice. Here Black draws with 1...K—B 5. As he threatens to capture the pawn, White must play 2 P—R 4. Then after the reply K—B 4, White is still unable to cut the opponent off from the corner with K—Kt 7, as the loss of the pawn is still threatened through K—Kt 5. And after 3 P—R 5 Black attains the position which is typical for this end-game, namely the opposition against the King on the Rook's file.

The latter cannot escape without giving up the contested corner, and the game is drawn.  3...K—B 3 ;  4 K—R 7, K—B 2 ;  5 K—R 8, K—B 1 ;  6 P—R 6, K—B 2 ;  7 P—R 7, K—B 1 ; and White is stalemated.

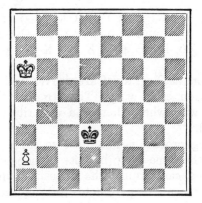

Diag. 55.

End-games with a majority of one pawn, when both sides still have pawns, are much more simple to manipulate.

Such games result in positions of which Diagram 56 is a

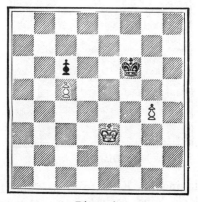

Diag. 56.

typical instance.   Here White does not even need to Queen his passed pawn.   The mere threat forces the win.   For the pawn at Kt 4 reduces the mobility of the Black King, in so far as the latter must at all times be ready to reach the queening square in as few moves as the pawn, or else the pawn would queen unmolested. The White King can therefore capture the opposing Bishop's pawn in peace and then queen his own.

1 K—K 4, K—K 3 ; 2 P—Kt 5, K—K 2 ; 3 K—K 5, K—B 2 ; 4 K—Q 6, and so on ; or 1...K—Kt 4 ; 2 K—K 5, K×P ; 3 K—Q 6, K—B 4 ; 4 K×P, K—K 3 ; 5 K—Kt 7, and so on.

Such positions as Diagram 56 are also reached when there are several pawns on each wing. The stronger side exchanges pawns on the wing where there is a majority until the extra pawn is passed.

The winning process is not quite so simple when all the pawns are on the same wing, because exchanges are of no use unless the King can assume the opposition in front of the last remaining pawn (compare notes to Diagram 53).

In Diagram 57, for instance, White must not play P—B 4. Therefore he can only win by gaining the Knight's Pawn,

Diag. 57.

that is, by bringing his King to B 5. This he achieves by forcing the Black King to relinquish the opposition with 1 P—B 3.

1...K—B 3 ; 2 K—K 5, K—Kt 2 ; 3 K—Q 6, K—Kt 3 ; 4 K—Q 5, K—Kt 2 ; 5 K—B 5, K—R 3 ; 6 K—B 6, and wins, as Black must abandon the pawn.

This position, being of frequent occurrence, is most important, and I recommend it as a valuable study in the use of the opposition.

Before I discuss positions of greater complexity, in which the only way to win is by sacrificing the extra pawn, I shall treat of end-games in which positional advantages ensure the victory although the pawns are equal. Here we shall find simple cases in which pawn manœuvres bring about the win, and more intricate ones in which King moves are the deciding factor.

Of the former the most important type is the end-game with the " distant passed pawn." A typical example is the position in Diagram 58, in which Black wins.

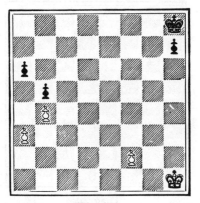

Diag. 58.

The King's moves are outlined by the necessity of capturing the opposing passed pawn, after which the Black King is two files nearer the battle-field (the Queen's side), so that the White pawns must fall.

1 K—Kt 2, K—Kt 2 ; 2 K—Kt 3, K—B 3 ; 3 K—Kt 4, K—K 4 ; 4 P—B 4 ch, K—B 3 ; 5 K—Kt 3, P—R 4 ; 6 K—R 4, K—B 4 ; 7 K×P, K×P ; 8 K—Kt 6, K—K 4, and so on.

For similar reasons the position in Diagram 59 is lost for Black. White obtains a passed pawn on the opposite wing to that of the King. He forces the Black King to abandon his King's side pawns, and these are lost. I give the moves in full, because this is another important example characteristic of the ever recurring necessity of applying our arithmetical rule. By simply enumerating the moves necessary for either player to queen his pawn—*separately* for White and Black—we can see the result of our intended manœuvres, however far ahead we have to extend our calculations.

1 P—R 4, K—K 3 ; 2 P—R 5, P×P ; 3 P×P, K—Q 3

Now the following calculations show that Black is lost. White needs ten moves in order to queen on the King's side, namely, five to capture the Black King's side pawns (K—K 4, B 5, Kt 6, R 6, Kt 5), one to free the way for his pawn, and four moves with the pawn. After ten moves, Black only

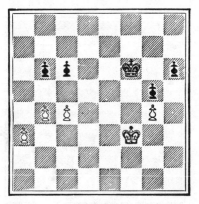

Diag. 59.

gets his pawn to B 6. He requires six moves to capture the White Queen's side pawns, one to make room for his pawn at B 3, and after three moves the pawn only gets to B 6. White then wins by means of many checks, forcing the Black King to block the way of his own pawn, thus gaining time for his King to approach. As we shall see later on (p. 97), if the pawn had already reached B 7, whilst under protection by his K, the game would be drawn.

It is necessary to make it a rule to examine positions in which each side has a passed pawn, by counting the moves in the way first shown. It is just because end-games can be calculated to a nicety, there being no moves of which the

consequences cannot be foreseen, that we note in contemporary
master play a tendency to simplify the middle-game by
exchanging pieces, as soon as there is an infinitesimal advantage in the pawn position (compare the game Charousek-
Heinrichsen, p. 108).

We will now turn our attention to positions in which the
pawns opposed on each wing are of equal number and no
passed pawn can be forced through. Everything depends on
the relative position of the Kings. The deciding factor in
valuing the King's position is whether pawn moves are possible,
or whether they are already entirely or nearly exhausted, so
that only manœuvres by the King are possible. The following illustrations make the position clear. We shall see that
the importance of getting the opposition is paramount.
Diagram 60 shows a simple instance in which there are no

Diag. 60.

more pawn moves. Whoever has the move wins by assuming
the opposition. The opposing King must then give the way
free to one of the pawns.

The state of affairs in Diagram 61 is similar to that in
Diagram 60. Having the move, White plays into opposition
and forces his way to Q 5, after which Black's Bishop's pawn is
lost.

1 K—K 4, K—Q 3; 2 K—B 5, K—Q 2; 3 K—K 5, K—B3;
4 K—K 6, K—B 2; 5 K—Q 5, K—Kt 3; 6 K—Q 6, and so
on (compare Diagram 57). If Black has the move he can only

draw, because the White Bishop's pawn is covered even though Black gains the square at Q 5.

1...K—K 4 ; 2 K—Q 3, K—B 5 ; 3 K—Q 2 ! ! and whatever Black plays White wins the opposition, so that the Black King's ingress is stopped ; 2 K—K 2 loses the game because of 3...K—K 5 ; 4 K—Q 2, K—Q 5 ; 5 K—B 2, K—K 6 ; 6 K—B 1, K—Q 6 ; 7 K—Kt 2, K—Q 7 ; 8 K—Kt 1, K—B 6 ; 9 K—R 2, K—B 7, and wins.

Diag. 61.

I shall take this opportunity of explaining what is called "distant opposition." In Diagram 62, White with the move wins by 1 K—K 2, thus assuming "distant opposition" (squares of the same colour ! !). If Black now enters his second rank, White immediately plays into opposition on his third rank, *e.g.* 1...K—Q 2 ; 2 K—Q 3, and still maintains it by 3. K—K 3 if Black plays a waiting move such as 2...K—K 2. Now Black has no further waiting moves, as White threatens to capture one of the pawns. But playing into the third rank is of no use, as White then assumes the direct opposition, and wins as in Diagram 60. Black must allow White access to one side or the other. He could not have remained on the first rank at the outset either, for after 1...K—Q 1, White advances through a square, to which Black cannot assume the opposition, namely, 2 K—B 3. If now Black wishes to answer the threat of K—B 4—Kt 5 and plays K—K 2, White answers 3. K—K 3 as before.

2. K—K 3 or K Q 3 would be wrong, as Black would then succeed in assuming the opposition at K 2 or Q 2, and would be able to maintain it. White would be unable to circumvent this or to attack the pawns.

Diag. 62.

In this position, too, there is ample scope for the study of the opposition.

If the pawns are still standing behind, the King who has the most advanced position has always the advantage, because he threatens to attack the opposing pawns should they leave their base. White has more pawn moves at his disposal, and will nearly always succeed in assuming the opposition. For instance, in Diagram 63, White, having the move, wins because his King gets first into the centre of the board.

1 K—K 3, K—Q 2 ; 2 K—B 4, K—K 2 ; 3 K—Kt 5 K—B 2 ; 4 K—R 6, K—Kt 1 ; 5 P—K B 4, K—R 1 ; 6 P—B 5, P×P ; 7 K—Kt 5, K—Kt 2 ; 8 K×P, K—B 2. Black has now the opposition but cannot maintain it, having no pawn moves available. The White King threatens to capture any pawn that ventures forward.

9 K—K 5, K—K 2 ; 10 K—Q 5, K—Q 2 ; 11 P—B 4, P—B 3 ch ; 12 K—K 5, K—K 2 ; 13 P—B 5, and wins, as Black will soon be compelled to play K—Q 2, after which a manœuvre shown previously gives White the Queen's Bishop's pawn.

13...P—K R 4 ; 14 P—K R 4, P—R 4 ; 15 P—R 4 ! K—Q 2 ; 16 K—B 6, K—Q 1 : 17 K—K 6, and so on.

If in Diagram 63 the King stood at Q 2 instead of B 1, he could just manage to draw. White takes eleven moves to capture the Black King's side pawns, and to queen one of

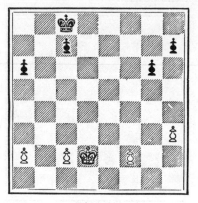

Diag. 63.

his own, as can be easily seen. In eleven moves Black captures the opposing Q B P and queens his own. We see here how the King's position can be counterbalanced by the weakness of a pawn, and lead to a draw. If the White Q B P was not isolated but standing, for instance, at Q Kt 2, Black would be lost, as calculation easily shows.

The strength or weakness of a pawn position, which, as we saw, had so deciding an influence in the end-game position just treated, is one of the most important factors in a game of chess, and should have full consideration in the middle game. A pawn, when isolated, is naturally weaker than when it is or can be protected by another. It may easily lead to the loss of a game, as the mobility of the King or a piece is reduced by having to protect the pawn (compare End-game, p. 102).

It is frequently and erroneously thought that *doubled* pawns as such are a weakness. Doubled pawns are weak when *isolated*, for they cannot support each other. But if doubled pawns can be supported by a pawn on the next file they need not by any means be at a disadvantage against three united single pawns on the opposite side. For instance, in Diagram 64, if Black had a pawn at Q Kt 3 instead of R 2,

White would have no winning chances. He could not attack the pawns, nor would any kind of manœuvres force a passed pawn through. In the diagram, however, White wins through

Diag. 64.

1 K—B 5 ; Black cannot then hold the pawn at B 3. 1...P—R 3 ; 2 P—Kt 4.

In this particular case the win is made easy by the fact that the White King is able to attack the Black pawn at once. But even without this advantage, the weakness of

Diag. 65.

doubled pawns usually entails the loss of the game. Diagram 65 may serve as an example.

1 K—Q 4, P—B 4 ch ; 2 K—B 4, K—B 3 ; 3 P—B 3 K—Kt 3 ; 4 K—Q 5, P—B 3 ch ; 5 K—B 4, and wins.

Doubled pawns are a drawback, even when not isolated, should there be no way of obtaining a passed pawn by exchanging them against a smaller number of single pawns. This is illustrated in Diagram 66, in which Black wins because the three pawns on the King's side hold up the four White pawns and the Black King can assail the White pawns from the rear,

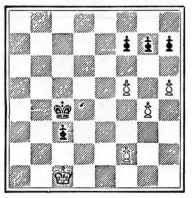

Diag. 66.

the White King being fettered by the necessity of capturing the Q B P. The proper formation for the Black pawns would be at B 3, Kt 2, R 3, after which White cannot force a pawn through by playing P—B 4 and P—Kt 5, as Black can refrain from making any exchange. Black could not afford to leave the pawns where they are, because even if there were no White pawn at B 2, White would, by playing P—Kt 5, threaten to win in the following way :

1 P—Kt 6, B P×P ; 2 P—R 6, and P—B 6, etc. ; or 1...
R P×P ; 2 P—B 6, with P—R 6, etc.   In a game Ed. Lasker-Moll (Berlin championship, 1904), from which the position is taken, Black played P—R 3 in order to obtain the formation mentioned above, and White resigned after 2 P—B 4 ? P—B 3, P—Kt 5, K—Q 5. There was, however, a pretty win after Black's P—R 3, namely : 2 P—B 6, P×P ; 3 P—B 4, K—Q 5 ; 4 P—Kt 5, B P×P ; 5 P×P, K—K 4 ; 6 P×P, K—B 6 ; 7 K—B 2 and Black is lost, because his own pawn obstructs the square B 2, and the King must release the square Kt 2, after which the White pawn queens.

This winning combination, however, is only an interesting exception to the rule that positions of this kind are generally won by the side which possesses the passed pawn. In this particular case Black could have made the position secure by obtaining the ideal position of B 3 Kt 2 R 3 for his pawns earlier, before the White pawns could advance so far. In the position of Diagram 66 Black could still have won by playing P—B 3. After 2 P—R 6, P×P; 3 P—B 4, K—Q 4; the Black King has time to overtake the passed pawn which results on the Bishop's file.

To conclude the study of pawn endings with an equal number of pawns on either side, we will discuss Diagram 67,

Diag. 67.

which illustrates a curious position occurring from time to time in practice. Whoever has the move wins by moving into distant opposition. White, therefore, should play K—K 5 K—Q 5 would lose, as Black would play K—Kt 5, protecting his pawn and attacking the White pawn, the protection of which White has to give up next move. In the same way Black with the move cannot play K—Kt 5 because White wins the pawn with K—Q 5. After 1 K—K 5 Black cannot avoid the loss of the game, e.g. K—R 3 ; 2 K—Q 5, K—Kt 3 ; 3 K—Q 6, and so on. Black with the move wins similarly with K—R 5.

We have still to consider end-games in which a draw results in spite of a majority of pawns, or where a win can only be achieved by the sacrifice of an extra pawn.

Diagram 68 shows the latter case. Here White can only win in the following manner : 1 P—Kt 4 ch, P × P ch ; 2 K—Kt 3, K any ; 3 K × P, and wins. Any other way would allow

Diag. 68.

Black to assume the opposition and to force the draw, *e.g.* 1 K—B 2, K—B 3 ! 2 K—Q 3, K—Q 4, etc.

Not 1 K—B 2, K—Kt 5 ? 2 K—Kt 2, K—B 4, 3 K—B 3, etc., as in Diagram 57.

Diag. 69.

A counterpart to this position is found in Diagram 69, which shows one of the few cases in which the possession of an extra pawn does not force a win. It seems at first sight as if White could win by simply assuming the opposition with

1 K—K 4 continued : ...K—K 2 ; 2 K—Q 5, K—Q 2 ; 3 P—B 5,
K—K 2 ; 4 K—B 6, etc. But Black would reply 1...P—
B 4 ch ! and after 2 P×P ch, K—B 3 followed by K×P
ensure the draw.

---

We come now to those end-games in which pieces as well
as pawns are left on the board.

As it is my aim to give typical examples, I shall confine
myself to positions where there is only one piece besides the
King. Most end-games with several pieces can be reduced
to that.

In nearly all end-games with pieces the King's manœuvres
used in pawn endings are of no avail, as far as opposition is
concerned, as the advantage of opposition means that the
opponent is forced to move his King, and as long as there
are pieces on the board, such " forced move " positions are
infrequent. However, the strength of the pawn position is of
the same importance as in pawn endings, just as the command
of as many squares as possible is essential for the King. A
third and very important factor is again the mobility of pieces.

A good example is found in Diagram 70, a position from a
game Post-Leonhardt (Berlin Jubilee Tournament, 1907).

Diag. 70.

Black's pawn position is weaker, because the White pawns,
being on Black squares, cannot be attacked by the Bishop,
whilst Black has two isolated pawns on White squares.
Furthermore the Black Bishop has less mobility than the

White one, and finally the Black King is tied to his Q 3, to prevent White's entry at B 5 or K 5. These drawbacks decide the issue. 1...B—R 2 ; 2 P—R 4, B—Kt 3 ; 3 B—B 2, P—R 4. (After B—R 2 White would command the square at Kt 6 through P—R 5) ; 4 B—Q 3, B—R 2 ; 5 B—B 1, and Black resigns, for White threatens to establish his Bishop at B 3, where the pawns at Q 5 and R 5 are both attacked, whilst the Black Bishop is at once forced to occupy the only square from which both pawns are covered, namely B 2. As this square must be abandoned in the next move, Black loses a pawn and the game.

5...B—Kt 1 ; 6 B—K 2, B—B 2; 7 B—B 3, and wins, or 5...B—Kt 3 ; 6 B—Kt 2, B—B 2 ; 7 B—B 3, and wins.

A corresponding instance of *Knight* v. *Bishop* is the endgame Blackburne-Schlechter (p. 102).

It is difficult to gauge the relative value of Bishop and Knight in the end-game. The Knight has the advantage of access to all squares ; against that the Bishop is able to fight at long range, and offers opportunities of gaining moves in certain positions where there is a " forced move " (compare p. 90).

As already stated, two Bishops are superior to two Knights because the limitation of the colour of squares ceases. A Rook generally wins against a Bishop or a Knight, sometimes even against a majority of one or two pawns, provided, of course, that there are still pawns on the Rook's side, and that their exchange cannot be forced. The following position (Diagram 71), from a game Moll-Post, shows how to proceed in such cases.

Here White can force a win in the following way :

1 R×P, P—Kt 6 ; 2 R—R 6, P×P ; 3 R×P, K—B 2 ; 4 R—B 2, B—Kt 5 ; 5 R—B 4, B—R 4 ; 6 P—B 4 ! The Black pawn position must first be torn up, if it is to be attacked successfully.

Now Black's defeat is inevitable, whether the pawn is taken or not. The sequel would be 6...P×P ; 7 R×P, after which the Rook goes to K R 5 and the Rook's pawn must fall, or : 6...K—Kt 3 ; 7 P×P, P×P · 8 R—B 6 ch, K—Kt 2 ; 9 R—B 5, and the Bishop's pawn is lost, unless Black gives up his passed pawn. In this case Black loses also : 9 R—B 5, B—Q 1 ; 10 K×P K—Kt 3 ; 11 K—Q 3, B—B 3 ; 12 R—B 6,

K—Kt 2 ; 13 K—K 4, K—Kt 3 ; 14 R—R 6, K—B 2 ;
15 K—B 5, B—Q 1 ; 16 R—K Kt 6, followed by R × P, etc.

The Queen against a minor piece wins so easily that it is not
necessary to give an example.   It only remains to discuss end-

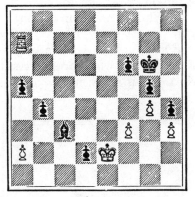

Diag. 71.

games of *Queen* v. *Queen, Rook* v. *Rook, and minor piece* v. *minor
piece*, in which one player has a majority of pawns, or an equal
number of pawns, one of which is passed.   As a rule the extra

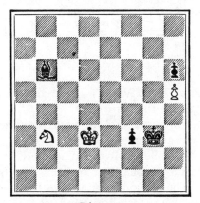

Diag. 72.

pawn leads to a win.   There are, however, exceptions frequently
recurring in practice to which I must refer specially.

Diagram 72 shows an end-game with a Rook's pawn and a
Bishop " of the wrong colour."

White draws with 1 Kt—Q 2, P—B 7; 2 Kt—K 4 ch, K—Kt 7; 3 Kt × P, and draws, as Black, in order to capture the White pawn, after K × Kt must give the White King access to the Rook's square, from which he could not be dislodged except by a Bishop on White squares.

In Diagram 73 White cannot win although his Bishop is of the "right colour" by 1 P—B 7, Kt × P; 2 B × Kt, and White cannot win the Rook's pawn. He can only attack the pawn from Kt 7 or Kt 8, both of which are inaccessible as the Black King gets to Kt 1. It is a stalemate position. If the White

Diag. 73.

pawn were still at R 5, White's King could attack the pawn from R 6 and secure the win.

In the position given, White could only win by keeping his passed pawn, and indeed it is possible to win by gaining a move with the Bishop. In the diagram it is White's move. Black with the move could not play K—B 2 because K—Q 6 would follow. The Knight would have to move, allowing the pawn to queen. Therefore White must try to bring about the same position with Black to move. He can do this, for instance, in the following way:

1 B—Kt 3, K—B 2 (now 2 K—Q 6 would be bad on account of Kt—Q 5, 3 P—B 7, Kt—Kt 5 ch, and Kt × P); 2 B—R 2, K—K 2; 3 B—K 5. Now White's plan has succeeded; the

same position has occurred, and it is Black's move. As mentioned before, the King must not move, but Knight's moves are of no avail. If 3...Kt—Kt 4; 4 B—B 6 ch, the Knight is lost, or alternatively the pawn queens. On 3...Kt—B 1, B—Q 6 ch decides, and on 3...Kt—Q 1; 4 B—B 6 ch, K—K1; 5 B x Kt would follow.

On this occasion I should like to point out that it is impossible to gain a move with a Knight, as a square which is accessible to him in an odd number of moves cannot be reached by him in an even number. A simple instance is Diagram 74.

Diag. 74.

White loses, having the move. 1 K—R 8, Kt—K 4; 2 K—R 2, Kt—Q 2; 3 K—R 8, Kt—B 1; 4 P—R 7, Kt—Kt 3 mate.

Black with the move cannot win, as he cannot bring about the same position with White to move.

In end-games of *Bishop* v. *Bishop*, of which we have already had an example in Diagram 70, an extra pawn wins in most cases if the Bishops are of the same colour. It is generally possible to force an exchange of Bishops and obtain one of the well-known pawn endings.

On the other hand an ending with Bishops of different colour leads mostly to a draw, frequently even against a majority of two pawns. The position in Diagram 75 is a draw, because it is impossible for the White King to get round his Kt pawn to drive off the Bishop.

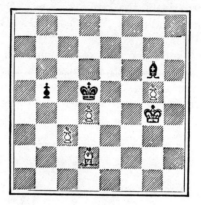

Diag. 75.

With two passed pawns distant from each other, a win can generally be forced, as in the folllowing position (Diagram 76).

Diag. 76

The King moves up to the pawn, the progress of which is barred by the Bishop (not the King). He thereby forces the sacrifice of the Bishop. If the Black King comes to the rescue of the Bishop, the other pawn proves Black's downfall.

1 K—K 4, K—K 2 ; 2 K—Q 5, K—Q 2 ; 3 B—K 4, B—K 2 ; 4 P—Kt 6, B—Q 1 ; 5 P—Kt 7, K—B 2 ; 6 K—K 6, and wins ; or 5...B—B 2 ; 6 P—B 6, B—R 7 ; 6 B—B 2, K—K 1 ; 8 K—K 6, B—Kt 1 ; 9 B—Kt 6 ch, K—B 1 ; 10 K—Q 7, and wins.

When the pawns are united, one should observe this rule : if they are attacked, they should, if possible, move to squares of the colour of the opposing Bishop.

Therefore in the position set out in Diagram 77 White should not play P—B 5, but P—K 5. After 1 P—B 5 there is no possible chance for White to assume the command of the Black squares, and in order to advance the pawns it is neces-

Diag. 77.

sary to force access to both White and Black squares. In the present instance play would proceed on these lines :

1 P—K 5, B—R 4 ; 2 K—K 3, K—B 2 ; 3 K—K 4, K—K 2 ; 4 P—B 5, B—Kt 5 ; 5 P—B 6 ch, K—B 1 ; 6 P—K 6, B—R 6 ; 7 B—R 4, B—Kt 5. White can only get through with the King's Pawn, as P—B 7 is unavailing on the grounds set out above. But in order to play P—K 7, the square K 7 must first be covered a second time, so that the Bishop cannot be given up for the two pawns. Therefore : 8 K—Q 5, B—R 6 (B—B 6 ; P—K 7 ch) ; 9 K—B 6, K—K 1 ; 10 K—B 7 ch, K—B 1 ; 11 K—Q 7, and wins.

In end-games with one Knight on each side, an extra

pawn usually decides the game much in the same way as in end-games with Bishops of the same colour; frequently even with equal pawns, the possession of a passed pawn is sufficient, as it keeps either the King or the Knight busy, so that there is only one piece available for the defence of the pawns. An instructive example is the end-game Ed. Lasker-Rotlevi on p. 100.

End-games with Rook against Rook are the most frequent, as well as the most difficult. Here the possession of an extra pawn is seldom sufficient for a win, unless the stronger side has also an advantage in the greater mobility of the Rook. Diagram 78 is typical of such cases, frequent in practice, in

Diag. 78.

which the greater mobility is the deciding factor. Although White has one pawn more, he can only win by reducing the mobility of the Black Rook through the following manœuvre : 1 R—B 2, R—Q 2 ; 2 R—R 2, R—R 2. Now the Black Rook has only one move left, whilst the White Rook has the freedom of the Rook's file. For instance, the Rook can be posted at R 5 and prevent the Black King from attacking White's King's side pawns, whilst the White King makes for the R at R 7 and effects its capture. If, on the other hand, the Black King tries to obstruct the way to the Queen's side, White penetrates into the Black pawn position. Black cannot maintain the opposition because the White Rook has spare moves, the Black Rook none. *e.g.* 3 K—B 3, K—Kt 3 ;

4 R—R 5, K—B 3 ; 5 K—K 4, K—K 3 ; 6 R—R 4, P—Kt 3 ; 7 R—R 5, K—Q 3 ; 8 K—Q 4, K—B 3 ; 9 K—K 5, and wins the pawns.

Having the move, Black would draw the game by : 1...R—Q 7 ch ; 2 K—R 3, R—R 7.  By placing his Rook behind the passed pawn he condemns the opposing Rook to inactivity, whilst his own is free to move on the Rook's file. If now the White King comes up, he will in the end force the sacrifice of the Black Rook for the pawn, but meanwhile the Black King captures the White pawns, and with passed pawns on the King's side might get winning chances.

When there is only one pawn left in endings of R against R, the weaker side maintains the draw, if the King can command the queening square.  Diagram 79 shows a position favourable to the stronger side, and which can mostly be obtained in this end-game.  But here, too, Black forces a draw with a pretty manœuvre : 1...R—B 2 ; 2 R—K Kt 2, R—Q 2 ch ; 3 P×R, and Black is stalemate.

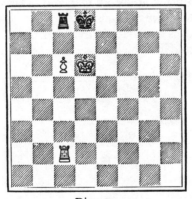

Diag. 79.

The chances of a draw are even greater in endings of Q against Q, as the King on the stronger side can seldom evade perpetual check.  For the sake of completeness I will show a few cases in which Q or R cannot win against an advanced pawn.

In Diagram 80 White can still draw, for in five moves the pawn reaches Kt 7, supported by the King at R 7, and in that time Black cannot come up with his King, so that he must give up the Rook for the pawn. Two passed pawns win, even when the King is away from them, if they have reached their sixth square. In Diagram 81, for instance, White is lost,

Diag. 80.

as Black gives up his Rook at Q 7 and plays P—Kt 6, after which one of the pawns queens.

The Queen wins against an advanced pawn, even when the latter is supported by the King ; only the R or B pawn can

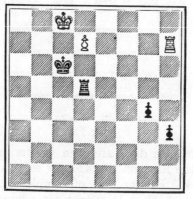

Diag. 81.

draw sometimes, when the pawn is on the seventh supported by the King, and the opposing Q cannot move to the queening square.

The following illustrates the three principal cases :

*A.* Position—White : K at Q Kt 8, P at Q R 7
Black : K at Q R 8, Q at Q B 3

Black must stop the pawn and plays Q—Kt 3 ch. White answers with K—R sq and is stalemate unless White lets the Kt's file free again. This end-game can only be won if the stronger King can assume the opposition in two moves. Therefore, if in the above example the Black King was standing at Q 5, Black would win as follows : 1...Q—K 1 ch ; 2 K—Kt 7, Q—K 2 ch ; 3 K—Kt 8, K—B 4 ; 4 P—R 8 = Q, K—Kt 3, and White cannot cover the mate.

*B.* Position—White : K at Q Kt 8, P at Q B 7
Black : K at Q 5, Q at Q B 3
White draws : 1...Q—Kt 3 ch ; 2 K—R 8, Q × P stalemate.

*C.* Position —White : K at Q Kt 8, P at Q Kt 7
Black : K at Q 5, Q at Q B 3
White loses.

1 K—R 7, Q—R 5 ch ; 2 K—Kt 6, Q—Kt 5 ch ; 3 K—B 7, Q—B 4 ch ; 4 K—Q 8, Q—Q 3 ch ; 5 K—B 8, Q—B 3 ch ; 6 K—Kt 8, K—B 4 ; 7 K—R 7, Q—R 5 ch ; 8 K—Kt 8, K—B 3 ; 9 K—B 8, Q—R 3, etc.

### END-GAMES FROM MASTER PLAY

In the following pages I give some instructive examples taken from tournament play. Step by step we will find how very important is the knowledge of the simple endings treated in the last chapter. We shall see that it is often necessary to consider many moves ahead to find the correct line, but that it is nearly always possible to foresee every consequence with unfailing certainty. Moreover, because of the reduction of forces there is no call to take very many variations into consideration. This explains why there is a tendency in modern master play to enforce the exchange of pieces, as soon as there is the slightest advantage sufficient to bring about one of the elementary end-game positions, in which the win can be forced.

I. *From a game Teichmann-Blackburne (Berlin, 1897).*

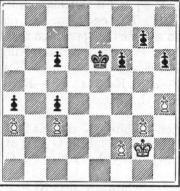

Diag. 82.

Black has an extra pawn on the Queen's side. But as it is doubled, the material superiority is of no account. A perceptible advantage, however, lies in the fact that White cannot bring about a "forced move" position, as Black has the move P—Q B 4 in reserve. White has also an infinitesimal weakness on the King's side, the Rook's pawn having advanced two squares and being therefore an easy mark. This disadvantage soon becomes apparent.

| | | |
|---|---|---|
| 1. | P—B 3 | K—B 4 |
| 2. | K—B 2 | P—R 4 |
| 3. | K—Kt 2 | P—Kt 4 |
| 4. | K—R 3 | K—K 4 |

With this move advantage is taken of one of White's weaknesses. White must exchange pawns. If the King moves, Black captures, freeing B 5 for his King, from where he can later on get to K 6 or Kt 6. But after the exchange at Kt 4, Black has the chance of obtaining a "distant passed pawn" on the Rook's file.

| | | |
|---|---|---|
| 5. | P×P | P×P |
| 6. | K—Kt 2 | K—B 4 |
| 7. | K—R 2 | K—B 3 |

If Black were to play P—R 5 at once, White would reply with 8 K—R 3, and after P×P, 9 K×P. Black would have to give up the spare move P—B 4, to gain the square at B 5 for his King. The game then would be drawn after 10 K—Kt 2 ! K—B 5, 11 K—B 2, because White maintains the opposition, and Black cannot get through at K 6 or Kt 6. Black therefore manœuvres his King first in such a way that the square at his B 4 is only reached when the White King is at Kt 3.

| | | |
|---|---|---|
| 8. | K—Kt 2 | K—Kt 3 |
| 9. | K—R 2 | P—R 5 |

Now neither P×P nor P—B 4 is of any use. In the first case Black obtains the distant passed pawn. In the second White obtains the distant passed pawn after 10 P—B 4, P×B P; 11 P×R P, but loses it again after K—R 4; 12 K—R 3, P—B 4.

| | | |
|---|---|---|
| 10. | K—R 3 | P×P |
| 11. | K×P | K—B 4 |

At last Black has captured the coveted square, whilst keeping the spare move in hand.

| | | |
|---|---|---|
| 12. | K—B 2 | K—B 5 |

The White King cannot move to Kt 2 now, because in that case Black would move the King to the White Q B P and queen in seven moves, and White, after seven moves, would only have the K B pawn at B 7.

| | | |
|---|---|---|
| 13. | K—K 2 | K—Kt 6 |
| 14. | K—K 3 | P—B 4 |

and wins, for White cannot hold the K B P now, but must capture the Kt P in exchange for it, after which the Black King reaches the Queen's side two moves ahead, e.g. :

| | | |
|---|---|---|
| 15. | K—K 2 | K—Kt 7 |
| 16. | K—K 3 | K—B 8 ! |
| 17. | K—K 4 | K—B 7 |
| 18. | K—B 5 | K×P |
| 19. | K×P | K—K 6, etc. |

Black would have forced a win also if White had played K—Kt 2 on his twelfth move thus : 12 K—Kt 2, K—B 5; 13 K—B 2.

Now White has the opposition, and after Black wrings it from him by playing the spare move P—B 4, he assumes it again with 14 K—K 2, K—Kt 6; 15 K—K 3. But he cannot maintain it after Black's K—R 6 because the square at Q 3 for distant opposition is not accessible. After 16 K—Q 2, K—R 7!; 17 K—K 3, K—Kt 6; 18 K—K 2, K—Kt 7; 19 K—K 3, K—B 8 we get the same result as before.

II. *From a game Ed. Lasker-Rotlevi (Hamburg, 1910).*

Diag. 83.

White has the advantage, because Black must keep either his King or his Knight permanently near the passed pawn, guarding against its advance, whilst both White's King and Knight can attack the Black pawns. As yet they stand so far in the rear that the White King cannot approach them Therefore White must first try to force their advance.

|   |   |   |   |
|---|---|---|---|
| 1. Kt—B 5 |   |   | P—Kt 3 |
| 2. Kt—Q 3 |   |   | P—R 4 |

This is now necessary, because the square B 3 is weak after P—Kt 3 and the White Knight threatens to win the Rook's pawn eventually with a check at B 6. For this reason Kt—Q 2, for instance, could not be played instead of the move in the text, because 3 Kt—K 5 would follow. Black now cannot exchange, of course, otherwise the position would resolve itself to an easy end game win similar to the one in

Diagram 56. There would be nothing left but Kt—Kt 1 to oppose the threat of Kt—B 6 ch, and this would get the Knight entirely out of play, so that White could queen the passed pawn easily after 4 K—Kt 6.

> 3. K—K 5        P—B 3

The King was threatening to enter via Q 5 and B 6.

> 4. K—B 5        Kt—K 3

If Black wishes to obviate the threat: Kt—K 5—B 4, and plays P—Kt 4, the White King goes to Q B 5 and wins all the pawns easily. Therefore Black endeavours to sacrifice a pawn in order to exchange the two others, after which a draw could be forced by exchanging the Knight for the remaining White pawn.

> 5. Kt—K 5        P—B 4
> 6. Kt—B 4        P—Kt 4
> 7. Kt×P          P—B 5

Diag. 84.

> 8. K—K 5        Kt—B 4
> 9. Kt—B 6 ch    K—B 1 !

Not K—B 2, because of 10 K—Q 4, Kt—Q 6 ; 11 Kt—K 5 ch.

> 10. Kt—R 7

Here White had only considered the following answer :
    Kt—Q 6 ch ; 11 K—Q 4, Kt×Kt P ; 12 Kt×P, Kt—Q 6 ; 13 P—B 5, Kt—Kt 5 ; 14 Kt—B 3, Kt—B 7 ch ; 15 K×P,

Kt—K 6 ch ; 16 K—B 5, Kt×P ; 17 P—R 4, Kt—K 2 ;
18 Kt—Q 5, Kt—B 1 ; 19 K—B 6, K—K 1 ; 20 K—B 7,
Kt—R 7 ; 21 K—Kt 7, and wins the Knight.

Black however draws, through a pretty combination :

| 10. ......... | P—Kt 5 |
|---|---|
| 11. K—Q 4 | P—B 6 |
| 12. P×P | Kt—K 3 ch |
| 13. K—B 4 | P×P |
| 14. K×P | Kt×P |

and White cannot prevent the ultimate exchange of Kt for P.
The last winning chance would have been : 10 K—Q 4 !,
Kt—Q 6 ; 11 K—B 3. This is in any case the more plausible
line, because now White can attack the pawns with both King
and Knight, as both the Black pieces are away from the field
of operations. The sequel could be : 11...Kt×B P ; 12 P—R 3
(Kt—R 7 would only draw : Kt—K 7 ch ; 13 K—Kt 4, Kt—B 8 ;
14 P—R 3, Kt—R 7 ch ; 15 K×P, P—B 6) ; 12...Kt—Q 4 ch ;
13 K—Q 4, Kt—B 5 ; 14 K—K 4 (Kt—R 7 ?, Kt—K 7 ch ! ! ;
15 K—K 3, P—B 6), Kt—Q 6 ; 15 P—Kt 4, Kt—Kt 7 ;
16 Kt—Q 4, and wins

III. *From a game Blackburne-Schlechter* (*Vienna*, 1898).

Diag. 85.

White has just played Q—B 4. P—B 5 is threatened, and
Black is forced to exchange Queens. The ensuing end-game,

however, is inferior for Black, because the Q P is weak and White threatens eventually to force his Queen's Pawn through.

| | |
|---|---|
| 1......... | Q—B 4 |
| 2. Q×Q | B×Q |
| 3. Kt—Q 4 | B—Kt 3 |
| 4. R×R | R×R |
| 5. R—K 1 | R×R |

If Black wants to avoid the exchange, he must yield up the King's file to White, and that would surely spell disaster, as the Black Rook would have no field of action, and would have to go to Q 1 to avoid the loss of a pawn through Kt—Kt 5 ch, after which the White Rook would take possession of the seventh rank, fettering the action of the Bishop into the bargain.

| | |
|---|---|
| 6. K×R | B—Q 6 |
| 7. P—Q Kt 3 | K—Q 2 |

Black is condemned to inactivity, and White can quietly set to work to force his pawn through.

| | |
|---|---|
| 8. K—Q 2 | B—K 5 |
| 9. P—Kt 3 | B—Kt 8 |
| 10. P—Q R 3 | B—K 5 |
| 11. K—K 3 | B—Kt 8 |
| 12. Kt—B 3 | |

In order to play P—Q Kt 4 and P—B 5, then to force Black to exchange at B 5, White must first have the opportunity of bearing a second time on Black's Queen's Pawn. Therefore he prepares the manœuvre Kt—B 3—Q 2—B 4.

| | |
|---|---|
| 12. ......... | K—K 2 |
| 13. P—Q Kt 4 | B—B 4 |
| 14. P—B 5 | B—Q 2 |
| 15. K—Q 4 | B—K 1 |
| 16. Kt—Q 2 | B—Q 2 |
| 17. Kt—B 4 | P×P ch |
| 18. P×P | P—B 3 |

It is not yet easy to materialise the advantage in position The advance P—Q 6 ch would be very bad, as B 6 and K 6 would be made accessible for Black. White starts by tempting

the pawns forward and thus systematically creates points of
attack.

|       |         |         |
|-------|---------|---------|
| 19.   | Kt—Kt 2 | B—B 4   |
| 20.   | P—Q R 4 | K—Q 2   |
| 21.   | P—R 5   | P—Q R 3 |

The Queen's side is paralysed. The text move is forced, as
P—R 6 would give White yet another passed pawn. Now
White turns his attention to the King's side.

|       |         |         |
|-------|---------|---------|
| 22.   | Kt—B 4  | K—B 2   |
| 23.   | Kt—Q 6  | B—Q 2   |
| 24.   | K—K 4   | B—R 5   |
| 25.   | P—Kt 4  | B—B 7 ch |
| 26.   | K—Q 4   | B—Kt 3  |

Black wishes to play P—R 4, in order to get a passed pawn
too, the only chance of saving the game.

|       |        |        |
|-------|--------|--------|
| 27.   | P—R 3  | K—Kt 1 |

Now P—R 4 would be countered by Kt—B 5, forcing the
exchange and leaving a backward pawn at Kt 2 and the Rook's
pawn would be bound to fall.

|       |        |        |
|-------|--------|--------|
| 28.   | Kt—B 5 | B×Kt   |
| 29.   | P×B    | K—B 2  |

Diag. 86.

It would now seem as if Black might have played P—K Kt 4
here, securing a passed pawn, and forcing a draw. After
30 P—R 4 Black would play P—R 3, and it is not evident
how White is to win. But 29...P—K Kt 4 is parried by
P×P *e.p.* The difference in the pawn positions, which decides

the issue for White, is found in the fact that the White passed pawn at Q 5 is unassailable because the support of the B P cannot be taken away by Black's P—Kt 3, whilst Black's passed pawn at his B 3 can be isolated at any time through P—R 4—R 5. White would take up a position on the Knight's file with the King, and push on the Rook's pawn. The isolated pawns are then an easy prey. On the text move White also pushes the Rook's pawn on to compel P—R 3 and reduce Black to moves by the King. The passed Queen's pawn decides the game.

|     | 30. | K—K 4     | K—Q 2     |
| --- | --- | --------- | --------- |
|     | 31. | K—B 4     | K—K 2     |
|     | 32. | K—Kt 4    | K—Q 2     |
|     | 33. | P—R 4     | K—B 1     |
|     | 34. | P—R 5     | P—R 3     |

Otherwise there follows : P—R 6, K—R 5, etc.

|     | 35. | K—B 4     | K—Q 2     |
| --- | --- | --------- | --------- |
|     | 36. | K—K 4     | K—B 2     |
|     | 37. | P—Q 6 ch  | K—B 1     |
|     | 38. | K—Q 5     | K—Q 2     |
|     | 39. | P—B 6 ch  | P × P ch  |
|     |     | (compare Diagram 68) |     |
|     | 40. | K—B 5     | Resigns   |

IV. *From a game Bird-Janowski.*

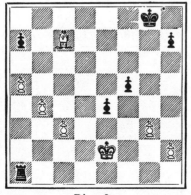

Diag. 87.

In spite of the preponderance of material, the win is not an easy one for Black, because of White's alarming pawn array

on the Queen's side. The King must first make use of his
great power as an end-game piece.

| 1. | ......... | K—B 2 |
| 2. | P—Kt 5 | K—K 3 |
| 3. | P—Kt 6 | P×P |
| 4. | P×P | K—Q 2 |
| 5. | B—K 5 | |

threatens P—Kt 7. But as White must first move his Bishop
to cover his pawn, the Rook's pawn is lost, and the manœuvre
therefore unsound. P—R 3 was indicated; it threatens the
break-up of the Black pawns by P—Kt 4 and their capture by
the King.

| 5. | ......... | K—B 3 |
| 6. | B—Q 4 | R—R 2 ch |
| 7. | K—K 3 | R×P |
| 8. | K—B 4 | R—Q 7 ! |
| 9. | P—Kt 4 | R×B |

Black reduces the position to an elementary ending, which is
theoretically a win. Whilst the two White passed pawns are
isolated and fall singly, Black obtains two passed pawns, which
are united and unassailable.

| 10. | P×R | P—K 6 |
| 11. | K×K P | P×P |
| 12. | K—B 4 | P—R 4 |
| 13. | P—Q 5 ch | K×Kt P |
| 14. | K—K 5 | K—B 2 |
| | Resigns. | |

**V.** *From a game Steiner-Forgacz* (*Székesfehervár*, 1907).

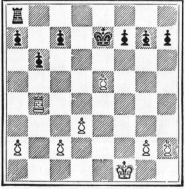

Diag. 88.

White has an advantage in the greater mobility of his Rook, and makes the most of it in an instructive fashion.

|  | 1. R—Kt 4 | P—Kt 3 |
|---|---|---|

White provokes this move in order to produce a weakness at K B 6.

|  | 2. K—K 2 | K—K 3 |
|---|---|---|
|  | 3. R—K B 4 | R—K B 1 |

Black naturally dare not allow the Rook to penetrate into the seventh.

|  | 4. P—Q 4 | P—Q B 4 |
|---|---|---|

This move would win the game, if the Rooks had been exchanged, because in that case the distant passed pawn which Black could obtain on the Q Kt file would decide the issue. But, supported by the mobile Rook, the centre pawns become irresistible. Instead of the text move, P—K B 4 was necessary in order to release the Rook.

|  | 5. P—B 3 | P×P |
|---|---|---|
|  | 6. P×P | P—K B 4 |

If it were not for the Rooks, the centre pawns would not help White, because Black would obtain a passed pawn on either wing.

|  | 7. K—Q 3 | P—K Kt 4 |
|---|---|---|
|  | 8. R—B 2 | R—B 1 |
|  | 9. P—Kt 4 | P—B 5 |

If P×P, 10 R—B 6 ch, K—K 2 ; 11 R—R 6 wins.

|  | 10. P—K R 4 | P—K R 3 |
|---|---|---|
|  | 11. P×P | P×P |
|  | 12. R—R 2 | R—B 1 |
|  | 13. R—R 6 ch | K—K 2 |
|  | 14. P—Q 5 | P—B 6 |
|  | 15. R—K 6 ch | K—Q 2 |
|  | 16. R—B 6 ! | Resigns. |

For after R×R, 17 P×R, White captures the B P, and still overtakes the passed pawn which Black obtains on the Queen's wing; the pawns at Q 5 and B 6 are unassailable (K—K 8, P—Q 6, K—B 7, P—Q 7, etc.). The consequences of 16 R—B 6 had to be calculated to a nicety. If, for instance, the Q Kt P were already at his fourth, White would lose. In four moves Black would have one of his pawns at his R 6, the other at Kt 5. In the meantime White would have taken the B P and come back to the Q file. Now Black would win with P—Kt 6, because after P×P the R P queens unmolested.

VI. *From a game Charousek-Heinrichsen (Cologne, 1898).*

Diag. 89.

White's position is superior; firstly, because the only open file on the board is his, and secondly, because the Black Queen's side pawns are advanced, and therefore weak for a King's ending. After exchanging the Queen and one Rook, the possession of the King's file ensures the advance of the King to K 4 and from there to Q 5. Then the weakness of Black's pawns decides the game.

| | |
|---|---|
| 1. Q×Q | R×Q |
| 2. R—K 8 ch | R×R |
| 3. R×R ch | K—R 2 |
| 4. K—R 2 | P—K Kt 3 |
| 5. K—Kt 3 | |

P×P is no threat, because White wins the pawn back at once

with R—K 5. By capturing, Black would only dislocate his
pawns.

| | |
|---|---|
| 5. ............. | K Kt 2 |
| 6. K—B 4 | K—B 3 |
| 7. R—K 5 | P—Kt 3 |
| 8. K—K 4 | R—Q 3 |
| 9. P—K B 4 | R—K 3 |

Black probably hopes for a counter chance by getting a distant
passed pawn on the K Rook's file.  But he underrates the
weakness of the Queen's side pawns, and even without the exchange of Rooks, White would win, by settling the King's side
first and then tearing up the Queen's side, as in the game:
10 P—K Kt 4, R—K 2 ; 11 P×P, P×P; 12 P—Kt 5 ch,
P×P ; 13 P×P ch.

| | |
|---|---|
| 10. P×P | P×P |
| 11. K—Q 5 | R×R |
| 12. P×R ch | K—K 2 |
| 13. P—Q Kt 4 | Resigns |

Black must capture, as he needs seven moves in which to exchange the Knight's pawn and queen his Rook's pawn, whilst
in that time White can win the Q P after P×P, and yet arrive
in time with his King to stop the pawn from queening.

After 13...P×P, however, there follows 14 K×P.  Then
White covers his passed pawn with P—Q 4, and his King,
having full freedom, captures all the Black pawns.


## CHAPTER VI

### THE MIDDLE GAME

#### GENERAL REMARKS

HAVING now a fair knowledge of the end-game, we should be
in a position to appreciate how the middle game should be
conducted.  We must throughout maintain a favourable
pawn formation, in view of the end-game which might be
forced on us by exchanges.  On the other hand, as soon as we
have gained an advantage sufficient to secure the victory in
the end-game, we must ourselves, by the exchange of pieces,

try to reduce the position to one of the typical elementary cases which we have discussed. Now it will invariably be found that beginners are unwilling to make these essential exchanges. This is explained by the attraction which combinations involving the action of many pieces have for them. They assume that exchanges, particularly of the Queens, make the games dull. Such ideas only prove that the beginner has not grasped the nature of chess, the essence of which is stern logic and uncompromising conclusions, and this demands the shortest and clearest way leading to a mate. To the strong player, able to play logically, logic will always be inseparable from beauty in chess.

To play logically means to subordinate all combinations to a leading plan of campaign, but there is difficulty in finding the latter. An unsound scheme, even if worked out to its logical conclusion, can of course be of no value. All the same it is better than no plan at all. And in time one gains by experience, and develops a sort of instinct for rejecting from the large number of possible operations all those which, properly countered, cannot bring any advantage.

Beside practical play, which is essential in order to gain this instinct, a methodical theoretical instruction is of inestimable value, and accelerates the development of the student's mind. Now the instruction I wish to give in the *theory* of chess will not take the form of an *analysis*, brought up right into the middle game, of the various openings, tested and found correct in master play. Such collections erroneously bear the title of " Theory of the Openings," and are, besides, quite useless at this stage, since they only embody the results of *analysis*.

It is first necessary to ascertain a few leading principles, which can be taught in a most simple manner, by the exercise of common sense, rather than by applying oneself to the study of long-winded analysis. The student will no longer need to discover time-worn maxims in the light of his own weary experience, and on the other hand, these principles will help him to understand analysis, and to keep clearly before his mind's eye the common and principal lines of play, of which he might easily lose sight in the labyrinth of suggested variations.

I propose to show the application of such principles to master play, and this will give us a further opportunity of deeper study, both of the rules set out in the first part for conducting the opening correctly, and of the end-game principles, which should be well considered.

---

I have made the pawn skeleton with its attendant grouping of pieces the main consideration in the study of the opening ; now in the investigation of the problems of the middle game, I will start from the *transformation* which the pawn skeleton has to undergo in the course of further operations. In my opinion this is the best starting-point for the choice of effective manœuvres of the different pieces.

Before we are able to evolve a practical scheme we must have under consideration the following important points : How do we know if an attack is likely to succeed ? In other words : On what point should I concentrate the attack ? It should be clear to all that it is of no possible use to direct an attack on anything that can move away. Yet beginners frequently infringe this obvious rule, and I have often witnessed manœuvres such as these (Diagram 90):

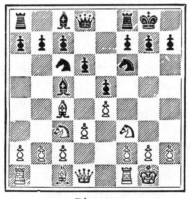

Diag. 90.

1 P—Q R 3, 2 P—Q Kt 4, and then, after the B has retired to his Kt 3 even, 3 R—Q Kt 1, 4 P—Q R 4, 5 P—R 5. Meanwhile Black will have played P—Q R 3, to make a loophole for his B at R 2, and what is the result ? The Black Bishop is as effectual at R 2 as at B 4, but White has advanced his pawns, and weakened them, as they are now more liable to

attack. Moreover, White has used up five moves to achieve
his aim, whilst Black only needed three. Therefore Black has
gained two moves, which he can use for the development of
his pieces.

Diagram 91 illustrates another mistake frequently made in
the choice of an objective, and one which can utterly spoil
the whole game, even in its earliest stage. Black has to

Diag. 91.

move, and his game is somewhat hindered by the dominating
position of the White Queen. The latter prevents the Bishop
from occupying a desirable square at his Q B 4, and also
makes the liberating move P—Q 4 impossible. Therefore it
would seem desirable to drive the Queen away. But this
should only be done if it is not attended by some further
disadvantage.

Now the average player is not particularly fastidious in
his methods. The Queen irritates him, therefore the Queen
must be repelled one way or the other. He would probably
try P—Q B 4. The result is that the Queen selects another good
square, for instance at K 3 or Q R 4, but Black has not improved matters, for he still can play neither B—B 4 nor P—Q 4.
On the other hand, irredeemable harm has been done, inasmuch
as the Black Q P now remains " backward." The attack
on the Queen by P—Q B 4 must consequently be rejected.
Sallies such as these, in which short-lived attacks are made by
pawns upon pieces, are always of doubtful value. They must

unquestionably be avoided if they break up the pawn skeleton, which is formed in the opening, and confine the mobility of the pieces.

Also with regard to manœuvres of *pieces*, intended solely to drive away an opposing piece, it is obviously essential that the attacking pieces in effecting their purpose should not be made to stray too far afield, lest they become out of play.

I shall delay dealing with the features underlying good forms of attack, both by pieces and pawns, until I have treated of the choice of an objective.

From what we have already expounded, it is clear that the subject of an attack should be incapable of evasion. Should it, in the course of attack, be desired to prevent a *piece* from being moved, that can only be effected by means of a "pin." A *pawn*, however, can be held in place either by occupying the square immediately in front of it, or by controlling the latter with more forces than the opponent can bring to bear upon it.

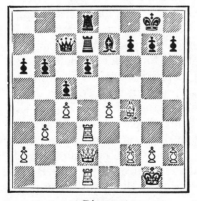

Diag. 92.

The last two diagrams exemplify this. If in Diagram 91 Black makes the mistake of playing P—Q B 4 as suggested, the backward Q P becomes a welcome objective for White's attack. White can keep that pawn back by playing P—Q B 4 as soon as it threatens to advance, after which he would develop quietly, double his Rooks, and bring the Q and Q B to bear in a concentrated attack on Q 6. A position not unlike that in Diagram 92 will result ultimately, in which Black defends the pawn as many times as it is attacked, but in which White can bring up his K P to the attack, as the Q P cannot move away, whilst Black has no further defensive move at his disposal. Play against a backward pawn nearly always develops on these lines, and is even easier when there is no defending B of the same colour as the pawn. (See p. 40, and Game No. 26.)

Such manœuvres, in the course of which pieces are pinned and attacked, are illustrated in Diagram 90. The most obvious move, which initiates an attack and at the same time completes the development of the minor pieces, is B—Kt 5. Attacks by means of such devices are so frequent and varied that it will be necessary to treat them at some length, which I now propose to do. I should also add that, with regard to Diagram 90, the student will derive lasting benefit from a thorough study of the position, and will thus improve his power to judge of the desirability, or otherwise, of obtaining open files, diagonals, doubled pawns, etc. After B—K Kt 5, the threat is to attack the Knight a second and third time with Kt—Q 5, and Q—B 3, after moving the K Kt away. As Black's K Kt is only supported twice, and there is no chance of bringing up more forces for its defence, Black must undertake something to provide against the threatened onslaught.

The most natural plan is to develop the Q B at K 3, from where it can be exchanged for the Knight should Kt—Q 5 be played. The doubled pawn, which White could force by exchanging the Bishops, is in no way detrimental to Black's game. On the contrary, the opening of the file for the Rook, with the attendant chance of playing P—Q 4 supported by the doubled pawn, gives Black the advantage.

The doubled pawn which Black obtains after 2 Kt—Q 5, B×Kt ; 3 P×B (or 3 B×B), Kt—K 2 ; 4 B×Kt, would also be of no help to White. The apparent weakness created in Black's game at K B 3 and K R 3 by the disappearance of the Kt P does not assist White in this case, because the pieces which could take advantage of such a weakness, the Q B and the Kt at Q 5, have been exchanged. There only remains the K Kt and the Q for an immediate attack, whilst the Black Rook will soon get into effective action on the open Knight's file, e.g. 5 Q—Q 2, K—R 1 ; 6 Q—R 6, K:—Kt 3 ;

7 Kt—R 4, Kt×Kt ; 8 Q×Kt, Q—K 2, followed by the doubling of the Rooks on the Kt file. Considerations of a similar nature would tend to show that 1 B—Kt 5, Kt—K 2 ; 2 B×Kt, P×B is in favour of Black. The White Q B, which is so effective in taking advantage of weaknesses at Black's K B 3 and R 3, has been exchanged. The Queen's Knight is not available for attack on the K B P, as it would be exchanged or else driven off in time by P—B 3. Compared with the position considered above, which occurs after 1...B—K 3, 2 Kt—Q 5, Black has the further advantage of maintaining his Q B, which makes it possible to push the weak K B P on to his fourth, and either exchange it or push it still further to B 5, a useful and secure position.

Matters would be different were Black to allow his King's wing to be broken up without getting rid of White's dangerous pieces by exchanges. Let us consider what happens, if Black takes no measures against Kt—Q 5, but only prevents White's ultimate Q—B 3 by pinning the Knight with B—K Kt 5. White gains a decisive advantage by bringing his Queen into play before Black is able to secure himself against the threatened combined attack of Q and B, or alternately Q and Kt by K—R 1, R—Kt 1—Kt 3. I will give two examples of how the whole game now centres on the attack and defence of the points weakened by the disappearance of the Kt P, and how White pushes home his advantage in the one instance with the help of the B, in the other by the co-operation of the Kt.

I. 1 B—K Kt 5, B—K Kt 5 ; 2 Kt—Q 5, Kt—Q 5 ; 3 Q—Q 2, B×Kt ? ; 4 B×Kt, P×B ; 5 Q—R 6, and there is no reply to the threat of Kt×P ch and Q×P mate, except through the sacrifice of the Q. Forcing the exchange of Knights is of no avail, for after 5...Kt—K 7 ch ; 6 K—R 1, B×P ch ; 7 K×B, Kt—B 5 ch ; 8 Kt×Kt, P×Kt ; 9 K—R 1, White occupies the Kt file first and wins easily : 9...K—R 1 ; 10 R—K Kt 1, R—K Kt 1 ; 11 R×R Q×R ; 12 R—K Kt 1 followed by mate or loss of the Queen.

II. 3 Q—Q 2, P—B 3 ; 4 Kt×Kt ch, P×Kt ; 5 B—R 4 ! B×Kt ; 6 Q—R 6, Kt—K 7 ch ; 7 K—R 1, B×P ch ; 8 K×B, Kt—B 5 ch ; 9 K—R 1, Kt—Kt 3. Now Black has succeeded in interrupting the White Queen's action on the B P. But it has taken many moves, with the sole result that

Black's Queen's Knight is better placed. All the other pieces, however, occupy the positions they took up in the opening. The Black Knight, moreover, is only supported by the R P until Black manages to block the White Bishop's diagonal by P—Q 4. Meanwhile White has gained a big start, and is ready to occupy the open file with his Rooks. The sequel might be : 10 P—Q 4 !, B × P (if P × P ; 11 P—K 5 ! !, Q P × P ; 12 R—K Kt 1, etc.) ; 11 P—B 3, B—Kt 3 ; 12 Q R—Q 1, K—R 1 ; 13 R—K Kt 1, Q—K 2 ; 14 R—Q 3, R—K Kt 1 ; 15 R—R 3, R—Kt 2 (Kt × B ; 16 Q × R P ch ! !) ; 16 R—B 3, followed by B × P (B6).

Taking it all in all, we see from the foregoing that the pinning of the Black Knight can only be injurious to Black if he does not take timely measures to provide against White's Kt—Q 5, which threatens to concentrate more forces for the attack on K B 6 than Black is able to mobilise for its defence.

Beginners, after having experienced frequent trouble through their inadequate defence of this kind of attack, try to avoid their recurrence by making such pinning moves impossible from the first and playing P—R 3 on whichever side the pin is threatened. Apart from the loss of time, on which I remarked at length when discussing the opening, such pawn moves have various other drawbacks.

With every pawn move it should be considered whether the squares protected by the pawn before it has moved may not need the support of that pawn at a later stage. This is particularly the case with regard to squares in front of the castled King. If one of those pawns pushes on, the squares which have lost its protection frequently offer an opening for a direct attack by the enemy's pieces on the King.

A second consideration is the fact that the advancing pawn itself becomes a target for an assault in which the opponent, moving up a pawn on the next file, brings his Rooks into play, or in which he sacrifices a piece for the advanced pawn and the one that protects it, thus robbing the King of the protection he sought to obtain in castling.

The following examples will contribute much to the understanding of this most important subject, the grasp of which will mean a great step forward for the student.

The position in Diagram 93 is from a game v. Scheve-

Teichmann (Berlin, 1907). White played 1 P—R 3 in order to avoid the pinning of his Knight through B—Kt 5. The move is not unjustified, as the Knight is required for the support of the square at Q 4. The pawn move, however, has the drawbacks enumerated above, and White must think of keeping a sufficiency of pieces for the fight on the King's wing, in order to prevent Black from utilising the weakness thus created for a combined assault by superior forces.

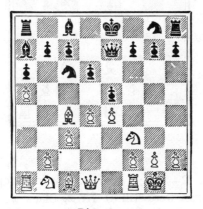

Diag. 93.

In this case White does not take precautionary measures, and succumbs in a surprisingly short time

1...Kt—B 3 ; 2 P×P ? With this move White opens the diagonal for Black's K B for no apparent reason. 2...Q Kt × P ; 3 Kt × Kt ? Instead of providing for the defence of his King's wing, White exchanges one of the King's side pieces, 3...Q × Kt ; 4 Kt—Q 2, B×P ! White has provoked this sacrifice by his last two moves. The K B P is pinned, and the Q enters by way of her Kt 6, the protection of which was given up by pushing on the R P. The rest is easy ; 5 P×B, Q—Kt 6 ch ; 6 K—R 1, Q×P ch ; 7 K—Kt 1, Kt—Kt 5 ; 8 Kt—B 3, Q—Kt 6 ch ; 9 K—R 1, B×P ; 10 resigns.

Diagram 94 shows a position from a game Marshall-Burn (Ostend, 1907). Strong in the knowledge that the Black Queen's side pieces are not developed, and can only with difficulty be of assistance in the defence of the King's side because of their limited mobility, White takes advantage of the weakness created by the advance of the Black K Kt pawn to his third, and initiates an immediate assault on the King's stronghold.

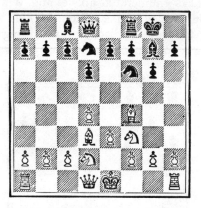

**Diag. 94.**

1 P--K R 4, R—K 1 ; 2 P—R 5. This forces open the Rook's file. If the pawn were still at Kt 2, Black would simply let White push on to R 6 and then reply with P—K Kt 3. 2...Kt × P ; 3 R × Kt, White concludes the game in brilliant style. Black's wrong development has given a welcome opportunity for sacrificial combinations. Now the K B has an open diagonal, the pawn position is broken, and White's Q and R have no difficulty in using the Rook's file for a deadly attack. 3...P × R ; 4 B × P ch, K × B ; 5 Kt—Kt 5 ch, K—Kt 3 (if K—Kt 1, then 6 Q × P, Kt—B 3 ; 7 Q × P ch, K—R 1 ; 8 Castles, etc.) ; 6 Q Kt—B 3, P—K 4 ; 7 Kt—R 4 ch, K—B 3 ; 8 Kt—R 7 ch, K—K 2 ; 9 Kt—B 5 ch, K—K 3 ; 10 Kt × B ch, K—K 2 ; 11 Kt—B 5 ch, K—K 3 ; 12 P—Q 5 ch, K × Kt ; 13 Q × P ch, K—K 5 ; 14 Castles, followed by P—B 3 or R—Q 4 mate.

In cases where both sides have already castled on the same wing, and the opponent has weakened his position by pushing on one of the pawns of that wing, it is seldom advisable to start an attack with the advance of one of the pawns in front of the King, as the latter's position would be weakened. An attack of this kind is only justified if there is a prospect of concentrating with all speed a superior force before the opponent has time for a counter attack.

The Black position in Diagram 95 illustrates one much favoured by " natural " players. Here the advance of the

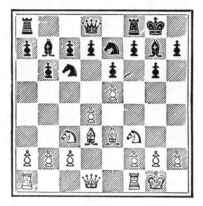

Diag. 95.

K R P would not be a suitable plan of attack for White as his Rook is no longer on the Rook's file, nor could it be brought back in time. In this case White must endeavour to take advantage of the weaknesses at Black's K B 3 and K R 3, produced by his move P—K Kt 3. This will be the *modus operandi :* Q—Q 2 followed by B—R 6, forcing the exchange of Black's valuable K B. After that the Q in conjunction with one of the Knights will attempt to force an entry at K B 6 or K R 6, as for instance in the following, the moves of which are taken from a game I once watched and took note of as being most instructive.

1 Q—Q 2, P—Q 3 ; 2 B—K R 6, P×P ; 3 B×B, K×B ; 4 P×P, Q—Q 2 ; 5 Kt—K 4, Kt—Q 4 ; 6 B—B 4, Q R—Q 1 ; 7 B×Kt, P×B ; 8 Kt—B 6, Q—K 3 ; 9 Q—Kt 5, B—B 1 (to prevent Kt—Kt 4) ; 10 Q R—K 1, Q—B 4 ; 11 Q—R 4, P—K R 3 ; 12 Kt—Q 4, Kt×Kt ; 13 Q×Kt, P—B 4 ; 14 Q—Q 2, P—Q 5 ; 15 P—K B 4, P—B 5 ; 16 P—K Kt 4, Q—K 3 ; 17 P—B 5, Q—B 3 ; 18 R—K 4, B—Kt 2 ;

19 R—B 3 !, Q—B 4 ; 20 Q×P ch, K×Q ; 21 R—R 3 ch, followed by R—R 7 or Kt—R 7 mate.

A somewhat more difficult case is shown in Diagram 96.

Diag. 96.

Here the advance of the White King's side pawns has undeniably produced weaknesses in the pawn skeleton, and these would be fatal had the Black pieces as much mobility as the White ones. But the congestion of Black's pieces on the Queen's side makes his defence unwieldy, and White has no difficulty in accumulating his forces on the King's side for the final assault. The prospects are that White will be able to bring home his attack, before Black has a chance of forcing exchanges and of bringing about the end-game, which through the weakness of the White pawns would probably turn to his advantage. The play (E. Cohn-Ed. Lasker match, Berlin, 1909) is instructive, and shows how the attack should be conducted in such positions. 1 Kt—Kt 3, B—Kt 2 ; 2 K—R 2, P—B 3 ; 3 R—K Kt 1, Kt—Q 2 ; 4 Kt—R 4, K—B 2. The concentration of the White pieces has become alarming, and threatens to be continued by Q—Q 2, R—Kt 2, Q R—K Kt 1, and Kt—B 5. So the Black King decides on flight, but he finds no peace on the Q side either, because there his advanced pawns soon allow White to make a breach in the Black position.

5 Kt—Kt 2, K—K 2 ; 6 Q—K 2, Kt—Kt 3 ; 7 K R—K B 1, B—B 1. It is Black's intention to play P—B 4 as soon as

practicable, and to make an attempt at a counter demonstration on the King's side, 8 P—K B 4, K—Q 1 ?. (Black should have kept to his original intention and played P—B 4); 9 P×P, Q P×P; 10 Q—B 2, Kt—Q 2; 11 P—Q R 4! B—Kt 2; 12 P×P, P×P; 13 R×R, B×R. Now White has achieved what he set out to do, He has opened up avenues of attack on the Queen's side, and is ready to utilise the weakness of Black's Q B P by playing P—Kt 4, on which Black must submit to opening the file for the White K R or the diagonal for the White Q B. In either case White brings vastly superior forces to bear on the Black King's position, and Black should lose. In this game Black escaped only through a mistake on the part of his opponent.

In the foregoing positions it was seen how fatal weaknesses can be, which are produced by the premature advance of the pawns in front of the King, on whom the opposing pieces can force their attack. When the pawns concerned are on the opposite wing to their King, the disadvantages of a premature advance are felt in a different way. The weakness concerns the pawns themselves and not the forces behind them, and is apt to cause the loss of the end-game, particularly of Rook end-games. Let us compare the positions in Diagrams 97

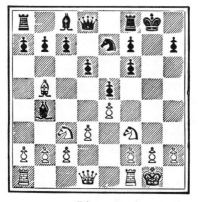

Diag. 97.

and 98. In the one case the chain of Black pawns is broken by the absence of K Kt P, in the other of the Q Kt P. The absence of the K Kt pawn can lead to serious consequences in the middle game, because of the weakness of Black's K B 3 and K R 3 (compare Diagram 90); it can, however, hardly become awkward in the end-game, as the pawns on the B and R files are within the protecting reach of their King.

Diag. 98.

On the other hand, the absence of the Q Kt P is of no consequence for the middle game. There is nothing behind it which could invite an attack. The Q R P and Q B P, however, are very weak for the end-game, as they are quite out of reach of the King (compare Game No. 19). I do not wish to imply that Black should have avoided the exchange at his Q B 3 at all cost; such an exchange has always the compensating advantage of opening a file for the Rooks, which advantage often means a favourable middle game, as will be readily understood. Further, it is often possible to get rid of the weak Q R P by pushing it on, and eventually compelling the exchange of the opposing Kt P, an exchange which can usually be enforced if the Rooks have occupied the open Kt file. The pawn itself is often useful at B 3, in that it can support the advance of P—Q 4 in the centre, should it be desired, or it can, by pushing on, be brought to exercise further pressure on the opposing Kt P.

The break-up of the pawn position on the Q side can become awkward in the end-game and sometimes in the middle-game when the pawns can be attacked, and pieces brought to bear on the Queen's side without leaving the King's side denuded of forces.

This will be illustrated by the position in Diagram 99.

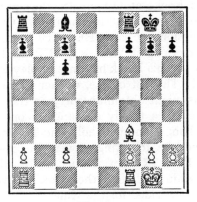

Diag. 99.

*From a game Fr. Lazard-Ed. Lasker (Paris, 1914)*

Here the pawn positions on both sides are broken, and the player that occupies the open files first, gets a decisive advantage. In this case it is Black's move. We can conclude at once that White has played the opening badly. He must have lost two moves, for he has still to capture the B P and then, being White, it should be his move. This disadvantage, small as it may seem, with which White has emerged from the opening, is sufficient to bring him into the greatest difficulties. Black, of course, does not defend the pawn by B—Kt 2 or B—Q 2, as this would practically reduce the B to a P and, moreover, White, by R—Kt 1 or Q 1, would both attack the B and obtain an open file. Instead of that, Black utilises the two moves, which he has, as it were, as a gift in an otherwise equalised position, to bring both Rooks on the Kt file. This policy allows Black to occupy the seventh or eighth rank at will, and to attack the White pawns from the flank or rear, according to circumstances. This menace hampers the radius of action of the White pieces, as they must always be ready for the defence of the threatened pawns, and this gives Black by far the superior game.

The play was continued as follows : 1...R—Kt 1 ; 2 B×P, R—Kt 7 ; 3 B—K 4, B—B 3 ; 4 P—Q R 3, K R—Kt 1. The Knight's file is now definitely in Black's hands. White could occupy the Queen's file, but the Black B at K 3, which prevents the entry of the Rooks at Q 7, makes the operation aimless. Therefore White is condemned to inactivity. On the contrary, Black's line of action is clear. His entry on the seventh can only achieve something if White's Q B P can be deprived of its support. To do this Black has only to play P—Q B 4—B 5 and P—K B 4. This, of course, weakens Black's K B, and the White Rooks might obtain an entry on the K file. Therefore Black will effect a timely exchange of one of his Rooks, after which his King alone will hold the K file. These considerations make the following moves clear : 5 K R—K 1, P—Q B 4 ; 6 P—K R 3, a further awkward necessity in positions of this kind. Before the Rook can venture out, a loophole must be provided for the King.

6...P—B 5 ; 7 R—K 3, R—Kt 8 ch ; 8 R×R, R×R ch ; 9 K—R 2, P—B 4 ; 10 B—B 3, K—B 2 ; 11 B—K 2 (threatening R—Q B 3), R—Kt 2 ; 12 R—Q B 3, K—B 3 (now B×P is not feasible on account of R—Q B 2) ; 13 P—B 4. White wishes to keep the Black King from his Q 5 but cannot do so permanently. Black, however, can occupy the Q file with his Rook, and confine the White King to his wing. 13...R—Q 2 ; 14 K—Kt 3, R—Q 5 ; 15 K—B 3, K—K 2 ; 16 R—K 3, K—Q 3 ; 17 K—Kt 3, R—Q 7 ; 18 P—B 3, B—B 2. R—R 7 would be a mistake on account of R×B ch, but the Q R P cannot escape. 19 P—Q R 4, P—Kt 3 ; 20 B—B 3, R—R 7 ; 21 B—Q 1, B—Q 4 ; 22 R—K 2, R—R 8 ; 23 R—Q 2, R—R 6 ; 24 R—Q B 2, R×R P. Now at last Black has obtained material gain, which was made possible by his command of the open Kt file. To convert it into a win by queening the extra pawn is only a matter of time.

We have now seen how the possession of open files reacts on the mobility of the opposing forces, forever increasing their difficulties until the positional advantage is converted into material gain. We shall meet with cases later on in which the greater mobility of minor pieces achieves the same result and find more and more proofs of the truth of the main general principles which I introduced at the outset.

Let us now recapitulate the chief points touched upon in the course of our deliberations :

1. Generally speaking, attacks should only be directed to objects which cannot be moved away.

2. If in particular cases the attack is aimed at driving off an opposing piece from an especially favourable post, that attack is unwise, if it involves the weakening the pawn position, or if pieces have to take up inferior positions in order to effect their purpose.

3. Pawn moves always create weaknesses, either by leaving other unsupported pawns behind, or by giving opposing pieces access to squares formerly guarded by them, and this more specially so in front of the castled King.

4. Attacks which depend on pawn moves are only justified if overwhelming forces can be accumulated in support, as the advanced pawns might become the object of a counter attack.

5. As pawn moves have very generally some drawbacks, the middle game is the pieces' own hunting ground. As in the opening, the first consideration of sound play in the middle game is to make only such moves as do not reduce the mobility of the pieces.

As illustrative of such manœuvres I shall now give examples from actual master play. In my annotations of these games I have tried to keep before the student's mind constantly the main ideas underlying the different combinations which spring from general strategical principles. I thus avoid burdening his memory with a mass of detail, and bring into prominence the basic principle of each line of play, thereby developing his capacity for conducting a middle game, even after an unusual opening.

I have fixed mainly upon such games as are illustrative of the openings treated in the first part of this book. In most cases the first moves will, therefore, not need any special remarks. The end-games, being typical examples, will only need reference to the chapters in which they have been respectively dealt with.

# PART II

## ILLUSTRATIVE GAMES FROM MASTER TOURNAMENTS

### GAME NO. 1

White : Tartakower.        Black : Burn.
King's Gambit declined (compare p. 30).

| 1. P—K 4 | P—K 4 |
|---|---|
| 2. P—K B 4 | B—B 4 |
| 3. Kt—K B 3 | P—Q 3 |
| 4. P×P | |

On principle this exchange cannot be commended, as the opening of the Queen's file increases the Black Queen's mobility. White derives no benefit from the K B file so long as the Black Bishop makes castling impossible.   White intends to play P—B 3 and P—Q 4, but the manœuvre is doubtful, and the whole opening includes an inordinately large number of pawn moves.   In the present game Black exposes the failings inherent to this system unequivocally.

| 4. ......... | P×P |
|---|---|
| 5. P—B 3 | Kt—Q B 3 |

Black cannot put off White's P—Q 4 by B—K Kt 5, for White can give a check with the Queen and unpin the Knight.

### 6. P—Q Kt 4

The object of this move is not clear, as P—Kt 5 does not win a pawn (Kt--R 4 ;  8 Kt×P ;  9 Q—R 5 ch).   It does not promote development either, and only compromises the Q B P and Q Kt P.

    6. .........               B—Kt 3
    7. B—Kt 5           Kt—B 3

This is aimed at the White King's pawn, which is deprived of its natural support by the Q Kt. In this position Black does well to attack White's K P rather than to defend his own, because an open King's file can only benefit him. Being able to castle, he can occupy the file with his Rook before White has time to bring his King into safety.

    8. Kt × P

It would have been better to protect the pawn by Q—K 2 or P—Q 3.

    8. .........             Castles !

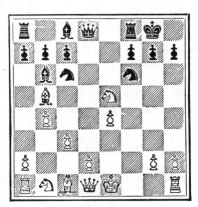

Diag. 100.

The beginning of a brilliant attack. Whether White ex-changes the Bishop or the Knight, he is overwhelmed.

    9. Kt × Kt

After 9 B × Kt, P × B; 10 Kt × P, Q—K 1 wins; 10 P—Q 4 would also lose because Black gains two pawns after Kt × P; 11 O—O, Kt × P. It is interesting to note how speedily the weakness at White's Q B 3 is brought to book.

    9. .........             P × Kt
    10. B × P           Kt × P ! !

Now White can neither take the Kt nor the R. In the first case Q—R 5 ch forces mate very soon, in the second B—B 7 ch, followed by B—Kt 5 ch or B—R 3 ch, wins the Queen.

|     |          |            |
| --- | -------- | ---------- |
| 11. | P—Q 4    | Q—B 3 !    |
| 12. | B × Kt   | Q—R 5 ch   |
| 13. | K—Q 2    | Q × B      |
| 14. | Q—B 3    | Q—R 5 !    |
| 15. | P—Kt 3   |            |

Not Q × R, because of Q—B 7 ch and the loss of the Queen by a discovered check by the Bishop.

|     |          |            |
| --- | -------- | ---------- |
|     |          | Q—Kt 4 ch  |
| 16. | Q—K 3    | Q—Q 4      |
| 17. | R—K 1    | B—Kt 5     |
| 18. | K—B 2    | P—Q R 4    |

Such is the price to pay for premature advances.

|     |          |            |
| --- | -------- | ---------- |
| 19. | P × P    | R × P      |
| 20. | B—R 3    | P—Q B 4    |

Black shatters White's pawn position, and his Bishops and Rooks have full play along open files and diagonals.

|     |          |            |
| --- | -------- | ---------- |
| 21. | P × P    | R × B !    |
| 22. | Kt × R   |            |

or P × B, R × R P ch ; 23 R × R, Q × R ch ; 24 K—B 1, B—B 4.

|     |          |            |
| --- | -------- | ---------- |
| 22. | ......... | B × P      |

The rest speaks for itself.

|     |          |            |
| --- | -------- | ---------- |
| 23. | Q—K 5    | B—B 4 ch   |
| 24. | K—Kt 2   | Q—Kt 2 ch  |
| 25. | K—B 1    | B × Kt ch  |
| 26. | K—Q 2    | R—Q 1 ch   |
| 27. | K—K 3    | R—Q 6 ch   |
| 28. | K—B 2    | Q—B 6 ch   |
| 29. | K—Kt 1   | R—Q 7      |
| 30. | Q—Kt 8 ch | B—K B 1   |
|     | Resigns. |            |

## GAME No. 2

White : Leonhardt.          Black : Marshall.
Falkbeer Counter Gambit (compare p. 35).

| | | |
|---|---|---|
| 1. | P—K 4 | P—K 4 |
| 2. | P—K B 4 | P—Q 4 |
| 3. | P×Q P | P—K 5 |
| 4. | P—Q 3 | P×P |
| 5. | Q×P | Kt—K B 3 |
| 6. | Kt—Q B 3 | |

It would be quite bad to play P—B 4 and try to hold the extra pawn at the expense of development. Black would very soon occupy the King's file with his Rook and there would be no time for White to bring his King into safety, *e.g.* 6 P—B 4, B—Q B 4 ; 7 Kt—K B 3, Castles ; 8 B—K 2, R—K 1, and already now there are threats of Kt—K 5 or Kt—Kt 5 followed by B—B 7 ch or Kt—B 7.

| | | |
|---|---|---|
| 6. | ......... | B—Q B 4 |
| 7. | B—Q 2 | |

White would of course like to continue with B—K 3 in order to make a fight for the possession of the diagonal. He would, however, lose his chance of castling through Black's Q—K 2. This is detrimental in all such cases where the lines in the centre are open or likely to be forced open at any time.

| | | |
|---|---|---|
| 7. | ......... | Castles |
| 8. | Castles | Q Kt—Q 2 |
| 9. | B—K 2 | Kt—Kt 3 |
| 10. | B—B 3 | B—K Kt 5 |
| 11. | B—K 3 ? | |

White has not yet completed his development, and his first care should be to bring out his K Kt. This he could have done without difficulty, thus : 11 B×B, Kt×B ; 12 Kt—R 3. After the move in the text, Black not only occupies the King's file but gains a move in so doing.

| | | |
|---|---|---|
| 11. | ......... | B×B ch |
| 12. | Q×B | R—K 1 |
| 13. | Q—Q 4 | Q—Q 3 |

Black's course is obvious; he must win the Q P. The forces will then be equal in material, but there will remain a

Diag. 101.

flaw in White's position, namely the exposed K B P, and this tells in the ending.

14. P—K R 3

Now the square at K Kt 3 is unprotected, and this is serious in view of a probable Knight's ending, where, moreover, it will sooner or later be necessary to play P—K Kt 3 in order to support the K B P. Both the K Kt P and K B P would be weak, with the King on the other wing, and be under constant threat of being captured. The game does proceed as indicated, and the simple and logical manner in which Marshall brings home his advantage in a very short time shows convincingly how fatal a shattered pawn position can be for the end-game. Instead of the move in the text, White should have played B×B followed by Kt—B 3, which would have completed his development without making another pawn move.

|       |           |            |
|-------|-----------|------------|
| 14.   | ………       | B×B        |
| 15.   | Kt×B      | Q R—Q 1    |
| 16.   | K R—K 1   | R×R        |
| 17.   | R×R       | Q Kt×P     |
| 18.   | Kt×Kt     | Kt×Kt      |
| 19.   | P—K Kt 3  | P—K R 3    |

making a loophole for the King. In this case the move is correct, as the threat of mate ties the Black Rook to his rank.

It is wrong to make a loophole, as weak players are fond of doing, as early as possible "in case," before it is shown that there will be a need for it, or that there will be a Rook ending.

20. P—R 3

White is afraid of playing 20 Q×P on account of Kt—Kt 5, which threatens Kt×B P followed by Q—Q B 3. 21 Q×P would not be a sufficient defence because of Q—B 4 threatening mate, and on the other hand 21 Q—R 4 would conjure up a dangerous attack, beginning with P—Q Kt 4. When the players castle on different wings, there is always the danger of the opponent sacrificing pawns and opening up files for his Rooks and Q against the castled King. The game then assumes a wild character, and as matters are generally settled one way or another in the middle-game, end-game considerations, both with regard to number and position of pawns, can be disregarded. Experience has shown that the player who develops his attack first is likely to win, and that it is of little use to submit tamely to an assault of this kind without attempting a counter attack.

Such games are very difficult for the beginner to understand. There is about them something violent and difficult to estimate, and years of practice are necessary in order to gain the judgment required for weighing up the possibilities of attack and counter attack, where the Kings have castled on opposite wings.

| 20. | ......... | P—R 3 |
| 21. | R—Q 1 | Kt—B 3 |
| 22. | Q×Q | R×Q |
| 23. | R×R | P×R |
| 24. | Kt—Q 4 | Kt—K 5 |
| 25. | Kt—K 2 | K—B 1 |

The Black King now pushes forward irresistibly, and attacks the weakened pawns on the King's wing. The White King cannot get any nearer, as a check by the Black Kt would win a pawn at once. The end is easy.

| 26. | P—B 3 | K—K 2 |
| 27. | K—B 2 | K—K 3 |
| 28. | P—Kt 3 | Kt—B 7 |
| 29. | Kt—Q 4 ch | K—B 3 |
| 30. | P—K R 4 | P—K R 4 |

Now the P at Kt 3 is "backward" and therefore lost.

|  | | |
|---|---|---|
| 31. | P—B 4 | Kt—K 5 |
| 32. | Kt—K 2 | K—B 4 |
| 33. | K—Q 3 | Kt—B 7 ch |
| 34. | K—B 3 | K—Kt 5 |
| 35. | P—Kt 4 | Kt—K 5 ch |
| 36. | K—Q 4 | Kt × P |
|  | Resigns. | |

## GAME No. 3

White : Spielmann.          Black : Prokes.

Vienna Game (compare p. 35).

|  | | |
|---|---|---|
| 1. | P—K 4 | P—K 4 |
| 2. | Kt—Q B 3 | Kt—K B 3 |
| 3. | P—B 4 | P—Q 4 |
| 4. | P × K P | Kt × P |
| 5. | Q—B 3 | |

It is contrary to the principles governing sound play to bring out the Queen early in the game. The opponent frequently has an opportunity of gaining a move by driving off the Queen, developing a minor piece at the same time. In the present case Black might have gained the advantage in the following way : 5...Q Kt—B 3. Now if : 6 Kt × Kt then Kt—Q 5 ! ; 7 Q—Q 3 ?, P × Kt ; 8 Q × P ?, B—K B 4. If, however, 6 B—Kt 5, Black obtains the better game by playing 6...Kt × Kt ; 7 Kt P × Kt, Q—R 5 ch ; 8 P—Kt 3, Q—K 5 ch ; 9 Q × Q, P × Q ; 10 B × Kt ch, P × B, with two Bishops on open diagonals. There is no harm in the doubled pawn, as White cannot attack it. Black's immediate threat is B—R 3 or K B 4, which exerts pressure at Q 6, and White will find it difficult to advance his Q P.

|  | | |
|---|---|---|
| 5. | ......... | P—K B 4 |

This move is open to discussion, as the Kt which it means to support can be driven away by P—Q 3. On the other hand, if White does play his Q P to Q 3, Black can prevent its further advance by P—Q 5, after which the White K P is insecure and the K B somewhat shut in.

|   | 6. P—Q 3 | Kt × Kt |
|---|---|---|
|   | 7. P × Kt | P—Q 5 |
|   | 8. Q—B 2 ! |   |

White offers his Q B P in order to be able to strengthen his
centre by P—Q 4, and to free his pieces. To protect his Q B P
would be inferior, *e.g.* 8 Kt—K 2, Kt—B 3 or 8 B—Kt 2 ?,
P × P ; 9 B × P, B—Kt 5 ! ; 10 B × B, Q × R 5 ch ; 11 Q—B 2,
Q × B ch ; 12 Q—Q 2, Q—Q 5.

|   | 8. ......... | P × P ? |
|---|---|---|

It would have been better, of course, to continue developing
with Kt—B 3, which at the same time maintains the pressure
on Q 5.

|   | 9. P—Q 4 | B—K 3 |
|---|---|---|
|   | 10. Kt—R 3 |   |

Intending Kt—B 4 with a view to exchanging the Bishop.
After that, Black's position on White squares is weak specially
on the diagonal Q R 7, K Kt 1, which was opened by Black's
fifth move, and on which the White Bishop can soon operate.
The game is instructive in showing the development of that
idea.

|   | 10. ......... | B—K 2 |
|---|---|---|
|   | 11. Kt—B 4 | Q—Q 2 |
|   | 12. Kt × B | Q × Kt |
|   | 13. B—Q 3 | P—K Kt 3 |

Black cannot prevent White's threat of Q—K 2 and B—B 4.

|   | 14. Q—K 2 | Q—Q 4 |
|---|---|---|

Diag. 102.

|   | 15. Castles | Q × Q P ch |
|---|---|---|

Black is obliging. The opening of files in the centre is favourable for White, as he can make use of his Rooks in the combined attack. Instead of the move in the text, development with Kt—B 3 and Castles Q R was the last, though slender, chance of saving the game.

16. B—K 3          Q—Q 4

If Q×P, Q—B 2 followed by B—Q 4, B—K 4, K R—K 1 and Q R—Q 1. Black has no sufficient means of defence to oppose this massing of forces.

17. Q R—Q 1          Q—R 4
18. B×B P

The end is swift, and easy to understand.

18. .........          R—B 1
19. Q—Kt 4          P×B
20. Q—R 5 ch          R—B 2
21. P—K 6          Resigns.

## GAME No. 4

White : Tarrasch.          Black : Capablanca.
Giuoco Piano

1. P—K 4          P—K 4
2. Kt—K B 3          Kt—Q B 3
3. B—B 4          B—B 4
4. P—B 3

The beginning of interesting operations in the centre. The steady development with : 4 P—Q 3, P—Q 3 ; 5 Kt—B 3, Kt—B 3 ; 6 B—K Kt 5, B—K 3 or Castles tends to a draw from the very first, and is thought dull.

4. .........          Kt—B 3

Black can avoid the exchange of pawns, which White tries to bring about after P—Q 4, by playing his Queen to K 2. This covers his K P a second time, and White's P—Q 4 can be answered with B—Kt 3. White's Q B P then obstructs the Kt's natural development. In a game von Schewe-Teichmann (Berlin, 1907) the position discussed on p. 117 was reached after the following moves: 5 Castles, P—Q 3; 6 P—Q 4, B—Kt 3; 7 P—Q R 4, P—Q R 3; 8 P—R 5, B—R 2.

| 5. P—Q 4 | P×P |
|----------|-----|
| 6. P×P | B—Kt 5 ch |

Diag. 103.

7. B—Q 2

The pawn sacrifice by 7 Kt—B 3, Kt×K P; 8 Castles! is much more interesting and more in keeping with the spirit of the opening.[1] White obtains a quick development and prevents Black from freeing his game by playing P—Q 4. After 8...B×Kt; 9 P—Q 5 follows (Möller attack), and after

[1] The following two short games will give an idea of the various lines of attack which are to be found in this opening:

*a.* Howell-Michell (cable match, England-America, 1907): 8 ... B × Kt; 9 P—Q 5 (Möller attack), B—B 3; 10 R—K 1, Kt—K 2; 11 R×Kt, P—Q 3; 12 B—Kt 5, B×B; 13 Kt×B, B—B 4 (the only chance of a draw would be this: Castles; 14 Kt×R P, K×Kt; 15 Q R 5 ch, K—Kt 1; 16 R—R 4, P—K B 4!; 17 B—K 2, Kt—Kt 3!; 18 Q—R 7 ch, K—B 2; 19 R—R 6, Kt—B 5; 20 B—R 5 ch, Kt×B; 21 Q—Kt 6 with perpetual check); 14 Q—B 3, Q—Q 2 (B×R; 15 Q×P ch followed by Q—K 6 ch and Q×B); 15 B—Kt 5!, Q×B; 16 Q×B, P—K B 3; 17 Q R—K 1, P×Kt; 18 R×Kt ch and mate in a few moves.

*b.* X *v.* Y, first 10 moves as before: 11 R×Kt, Castles; 12 P—Q 6, P×P 13 B—K Kt 5, Kt—B 4; 14 Q—Q 5!, B×B; 15 Kt×B, Kt—R 3 (Q×Kt; 16 Q×P ch); 16 Q R—K 1, resigns.

9...B—B 3, White wins back his piece by R—K 1 (10 P×Kt
would not be good, as Black could free his game by Kt P×P
and P—Q 4). On the other hand, after 8...Kt×Kt; P×Kt,
White in addition gains a move, as B×P is countered by
Q—Kt 3.

As played here, Black succeeds in playing P—Q 4, and the
game is even. Indeed the isolated Q P is a weakness in the
White position.

| | | |
|---|---|---|
| 7. | ......... | B×B ch |
| 8. | Q Kt×B | P—Q 4 ! |
| 9. | P×P | K Kt×P |
| 10. | Q—Kt 3 | Q Kt—K 2 |
| 11. | Castles K R | Castles |
| 12. | K R—K 1 | P—Q B 3 |

Now the Knight is securely posted in the centre, and Black
can accumulate forces for the attack on the White Q P, possibly by Q—Kt 3, R—Q 1, and Kt—B 4.

13. P—Q R 4

in order to drive the Queen from her Kt 3, but this advance
is " three-edged," as Master Gregory would say, and the pawn
is sure to prove weak in the end-game.

| | | |
|---|---|---|
| 13. | ......... | Q—Kt 3 |
| 14. | Q—R 3 | B—K 3 |
| 15. | P—R 5 | Q—B 2 |
| 16. | Kt—K 4 | |

Kt—K Kt 5 would seem to be stronger here. B—B 4 would
then be answered by 17 B—Q 3. After B×B, 18 Q×B, White
obtains opportunities for a King's side attack, in which the
Rook could co-operate via K 4 and Kt 4 or R 4.

| | | |
|---|---|---|
| 16. | ......... | Q R—Q 1 |
| 17. | Kt—B 5 | B—B 1 |
| 18. | P—K Kt 3 ? | |

This produces weak points at K B 3 and K R 3, and there
being as yet no definite threat in Black's Kt—B 5, should have
been avoided. It is of course difficult to formulate a plan
of attack, for there is no weak place in Black's armour. In

any case White could safely have played Q R—Q 1 and Q 2 in order to double the Rooks on the King's file or Queen's file according to circumstances. But now as soon as a Rook moves to Q 1—and that will have to be done in the end, to support the weak Q P—Black's B—Kt 5 might become awkward.

|  | | |
|---|---|---|
| 18. | ......... | Kt—B 4 |
| 19. | Q R—Q 1 | Kt—Q 3 ! |
| 20. | B × Kt | Kt—Kt 4 |

avoiding an isolated pawn in a subtle manner.

Diag. 104.

|  | | |
|---|---|---|
| 21. | Q—Kt 4 | R × B |
| 22. | Kt—Q 3 | B—Kt 5 |
| 23. | Q Kt—K 5 | P—R 4 |
| 24. | Kt × B | P × Kt |
| 25. | Kt—R 4 | |

Kt—K 5 would be answered by K R—Q 1; 26 Kt × P, Kt × P threatening both Kt—B 6 ch and Kt—B 7. If White stops both threats with Q—B 3, Kt—K 7 ch wins.

|  | | |
|---|---|---|
| 25. | ......... | K R—Q 1 |
| 26. | R—K 7 | Q—Q 3 |

Now Black foregoes his well-earned advantage. He overlooks White's subtle move 28. P—R 6. 26 Q—B 1 was indicated. White's Queen's Pawn could not escape, and there was time to dislodge the White Rook from the seventh by R—Q 2, *e g.*

26...Q—B 1 ; 27 Q—Kt 3 !, Q R—Q 2 ; 28 Q—K 3, R×R ; 29 Q×R, Kt×P.

|     |         |        |
| --- | ------- | ------ |
| 27. | Q×Q     | Kt×Q   |
| 28. | P—R 6 ! | P×P    |
| 29. | R×R P   | Kt—Kt 4 |
| 30. | R×R P   | Kt×P   |
| 31. | K—B 1   | P—Kt 4 |
| 32. | Kt—Kt 2 | Kt—B 6 |
| 33. | R×R     | P×R !  |

The pawn threatens to queen. Taking the Rook's pawn would not be so good, as it would displace the Knight. White would not only regain the pawn easily with Kt—K 3, but would also get his King into play.

|     |        |       |
| --- | ------ | ----- |
| 34. | Kt—K 1 | R—K 1 |

Here R—Q B 1 affords winning possibilities for Black. On account of the threat of R—B 8, the exchange of Knights by White would be forced, and his game would have been badly cramped by the Black K B P, *e.g.* 34...R—Q B 1 ; 35 Kt×Kt, P×Kt ; 36 R—R 1 (K—K 1 ?, R—B 7 ; 37 R—Q 6, R—K 7 ch ; 38 K—B 1, R×P ; 39 K—K 1, R—K 7 ch ; 40 K—B 1, R—K 4), R—Kt 1 ; 37 R—Kt 1, R—Kt 6. After the move in the text the game is drawn.

|     |         |        |
| --- | ------- | ------ |
| 35. | Kt×Kt   | P×Kt   |
| 36. | R—Q 6   | R—Q B 1 |

There is nothing in this move, as the Black passed pawn is now attacked.

|     |        |          |
| --- | ------ | -------- |
| 37. | K—K 1  | R—K 1 ch |
| 38. | K—B 1  | R—Q B 1  |

Drawn.

# GAME No. 5

White : R. C. Griffith.      Black : W. H. Gunston.

Giuoco Piano.

|     |          |          |
| --- | -------- | -------- |
| 1.  | P—K 4    | P—K 4    |
| 2.  | Kt—K B 3 | Kt—Q B 3 |
| 3.  | B—B 4    | B—B 4    |

|   |   |   |
|---|---|---|
| 4. | P—B 3 | Kt—B 3 |
| 5. | P—Q 3 | |

P—Q 4 would seem to be the logical consequence of P—B 3, and therefore preferable. After the text move Black will sooner or later be able to enforce the advance of his own pawn to Q 4, and his pieces will then have the greater mobility.

|   |   |   |
|---|---|---|
| 5. | ......... | P—Q 3 |

Here Black might have played P—Q 4 at once. For if White takes the pawn, he leaves Black in possession of the pawn in the centre. If he does not do so but plays B—Q Kt 5 instead, Black's reply would be Q—K 2 and the exchange of pawns at K 5 would follow. White's P—B 3 is then clearly a lost move.

|   |   |   |
|---|---|---|
| 6. | B—K 3 | B—Kt 3 |
| 7. | Q Kt—Q 2 | Kt—K 2 |
| 8. | Kt—B 1 | P—B 3 |
| 9. | Q—K 2 | Castles |
| 10. | Kt—Kt 3 | P—Q 4 |
| 11. | P×P | P×P |
| 12. | B—Kt 3 | Kt—Kt 3 |

Black has now the superior position on account of his pawn centre.

|   |   |   |
|---|---|---|
| 13. | Castles K R | B—B 2 |
| 14. | B—Kt 5 | P—K R 3 |
| 15. | B×Kt | P×B |

There is nothing in the weakness at Black's K B 3 and K R 3 caused by the disappearance of his K Kt Pawn, as White has lost his K B. On the contrary the open file should be a distinct asset, for, having a strong centre, Black's pieces are more mobile and he is more likely to get an attack.

|   |   |   |
|---|---|---|
| 16. | Q—K 3 | K—R 2 |
| 17. | P—K R 3 | |

in order to play Kt—R 5, which otherwise would be answered by B—Kt 5.

|   |   |   |
|---|---|---|
| 17. | ......... | K R—Kt 1 |
| 18. | K—R 1 | P—B 4 |
| 19. | Kt—R 5 | B—K 3 |

B×P was threatened.

20. R—K Kt 1 P—B 5

Diag. 105.

P—K 5 would seem to be better, as it opens a diagonal for the K B, and a diagonal, too, for the Q B, as White has to exchange the pawns. Indeed Black would soon have obtained a winning advantage, *e.g.* 20...P—K 5; 21 P×P (Kt—R 2, Q—R 5; 22 Q—K 2, Kt—K 4), B P×P; 22 Kt—R 2, Q—R 5; 23 Q—K 2 (P—K Kt 4 or B—Q 1, P—B 4), Kt—K 4, threatening Kt—Kt 5 and Kt—Q 6. As it is, White gains a little time, although Black's position still remains superior.

21. Q—K 2 Q—K 2
22. P—Kt 4 P—B 3

to prevent P—Kt 5.

23. R—Kt 2 Q R—K 1
24. R—K 1 Q—B 2
25. Kt—Q 2

intending to play P—B 3, thus retarding Black's P—K 5, which is still hanging over White like Damocles' sword. The move, however, lets in the Knight.

25. ......... Kt—R 5
26. R—R 2 P—B 4
27. P—B 3 P—K 5

Now this move is no longer feasible, as White's brilliant

sacrifice demonstrates. To make the move possible, long preparations would have been necessary, such as : R—Kt 3, B—Q 2—B 3, etc.

| | | |
|---|---|---|
| 28. | Q P × P | Q P × P |
| 29. | Kt × K P | P × Kt |
| 30. | Q × P ch | R—Kt 3 |
| 31. | R (R 2)—K 2 | |

The scene has changed with startling suddenness. White has open files and diagonals for all his forces, whilst Black's pieces are immobilised. Whatever he plays, Black must lose the piece he has gained.

| | | |
|---|---|---|
| 31. | ......... | B—Q 3 |
| 32. | Q—Q 3 | B × B |
| 33. | R × R | Q—B 5 |

He cannot play B—Q 4 on account of Q—Q 4.

| | | |
|---|---|---|
| 34. | Kt—B 6 ch | K—Kt 2 |
| 35. | Q R—K 7 ch | B × R |
| 36. | R × B ch | K × Kt |
| 37. | Q—Q 6 ch | Resigns. |

## GAME No. 6

White : Mason.          Black : Gunsberg.
Giuoco Piano.

| | | |
|---|---|---|
| 1. | P—K 4 | P—K 4 |
| 2. | Kt—K B 3 | Kt—Q B 3 |
| 3. | B—B 4 | B—B 4 |
| 4. | P—Q 3 | P—Q 3 |
| 5. | B—K 3 | B—Kt 3 |
| 6. | P—B 3 | Kt—B 3 |
| 7. | Q Kt—Q 2 | Q—K 2 |
| 8. | P—Q R 4 | |

A lost move. The logical continuation is Kt—B 1—Kt 3 and Castles.

| | | |
|---|---|---|
| 8. | ......... | B—K 3 |
| 9. | B—Q Kt 5 | B × B |

Generally speaking, exchanges such as this are doubtful. However, in the present case, although it opens the B file for

White, White cannot prevent Black from obtaining the same advantage.

|     |       |        |
|-----|-------|--------|
| 10. | P×B   | P—Q R 3 |

Black gives up the move he has gained. There is no justification for this, as nothing prevents him from proceeding with his development at once with 10...Castles.

|     |           |      |
|-----|-----------|------|
| 11. | B×Kt ch   | P×B  |
| 12. | P—Q Kt 4  |      |

White is anxious lest his Kt P should be made "backward" by P—Q R 4 and P—B 4. This is one of the drawbacks of the premature advance of the Q R P.

|     |          |            |
|-----|----------|------------|
| 12. | ........ | Castles K R |
| 13. | Castles  | Kt—Kt 5    |
| 14. | Q—K 2    | P—K B 4    |
| 15. | P×P      | B×P        |
| 16. | P—K 4    | B—Q 2      |
| 17. | Kt—B 4   | Kt—B 3     |
| 18. | Kt—K 3   | P—Kt 3     |
| 19. | P—B 4    |            |

This creates a weakness at Q 4.

Unimportant as it appears to be, it is the cause of the loss of the game, as the opposing Knight gets in ultimately. The doubling of the Rooks on the K B file would seem to be the best plan.

|     |          |        |
|-----|----------|--------|
| 19. | ........ | Kt—R 4 |
| 20. | P—Kt 3   |        |

White's weaknesses at K B 3 and K R 3 are more damaging than the corresponding ones in the Black camp, as Black still possesses a Bishop of the same colour as the weakened squares. But the move is now compulsory; for were White to allow the Black Knight to his K B 5, and to drive him off then with P—Kt 3, the Knight could play to his R 6 and prevent the doubling of the White Rooks.

|     |          |         |
|-----|----------|---------|
| 20. | ........ | B—R 6   |
| 21. | R—B 2    | Kt—Kt 2 |
| 22. | Q—Kt 2   |         |

White begins to operate in the centre and on the Q wing, as his position on the K side begins to be doubtful. The intention is to play P—Q 4, which, however, Black opposes at once.

22. .........          Kt—K 3

Diag. 106.

If now White plays P—Q 4, he loses a piece by P×P; 24 Kt×P ?, R×R ; 25 K×R, Q—B 3 ch.

23. R—K 1

The Rook has no future here, and R—Q 1, in order to play P—Q 4, is more logical. But as Black obviously threatens to double his Rooks on the K B file, it would be advisable to play for an exchange of Rooks, with : Kt—Kt 2, Q R—B 1 and Kt—K 1.

23. .........          R—B 2
24. Q R—K 2          Q R—K B 1
25. Kt—K 1          Kt—Q 5
26. R—Q 2          Q—Kt 4
27. Kt (K 3)—Kt 2          B×Kt
28. K×B

Kt×B is frustrated by Kt—B 6 ch.

28. .........          Q—K 6

All the Black forces are now in action, and White has no defence, as his pieces can hardly move.

29. K—B 1          Kt—Kt 6 !
          Resigns.

If R—K 2 or B 2, there follows R×R ch; 31 R×R, Kt—Q 7 ch ; 32 Q×Kt, Q×Q.

## GAME NO. 7

White : Marshall.          Black : Tarrasch.
Max Lange Attack.

| | | |
|---|---|---|
| 1. | P—K 4 | P—K 4 |
| 2. | P—Q 4 | P×P |
| 3. | Kt—K B 3 | Kt—Q B 3 |
| 4. | B—Q B 4 | B—B 4 |
| 5. | Castles | Kt—B 3 |

Black can avoid the complications of the Max Lange attack by 5...P—Q 3. In that case White cannot recover the pawn, and in order to develop his Q Kt effectively, would have to play P—B 3, aiming at rapid development in return, after 6...P×P ; 7 Kt×P. But Black can frustrate this plan either by pushing his pawn to Q 6, so that the Q Kt is barred from the square B 3, or by playing B—K Kt 5 with this probable continuation : 7 Q—Kt 3, B×Kt ; 8 B×P ch, K—B 1; 9 P×B, Kt—B 3, and Black has the better game, for White's King's side is broken up and his pieces undeveloped, while Black has prospects of attack on the open K B file.

| | | |
|---|---|---|
| 6. | P—K 5 | P—Q 4 |
| 7. | P×Kt | P×B |
| 8. | R—K 1 ch | B—K 3 |
| 9. | Kt—Kt 5 | Q—Q 4 |

Diag. 107.

This is the typical position in the Max Lange attack. With his ninth move White threatened to win a piece by Kt×B and Q—R 5 ch. Black could not parry the threat by 9...Q—Q 3, on account of P×P followed by Kt—K 4—B 6 ch. The position in the diagram appears to be favourable for Black, as all his minor pieces are in play, whilst White's development is somewhat restricted by Black's strong pawns at Q B 5 and Q 5. For a long time this opening has not been played in tournaments, being considered unsatisfactory for White. With the present game, and his new move of 15 B—R 6, Marshall has reopened the question as to whether White's attack on the K file plus the pawn at K Kt 7 is sufficiently tempting.

| | | |
|---|---|---|
| 10. | Kt—Q B 3 | Q—B 4 |
| 11. | Q Kt—K 4 | Castles Q R |

This is imperative. If Black retires the Bishop from his unsafe position, White permanently prevents Black from castling, which is bound to be fatal in view of the open K file—*e.g.* 11...B—Kt 3 ; 12 P×P, R—K Kt 1 ; 13 P—K Kt 4, Q—Kt 3 ; 14 Kt×B, P×Kt ; 15 B—Kt 5, R×P ; 16 Q—B 3 with a violent attack.

12. Kt×Q B

If White tries to win the exchange in the following way : 12 P—K Kt 4, Q—K 4 ! ; 13 Kt—K B 3, Q—Q 4 ; 14 P×P followed by Kt—B 6, Black can initiate a promising counter attack by 14...B×P ! ! ; 15 P×R=Q, R×Q ; 16 Kt—B 6, Q×Kt ; 17 Q×Q, B×Q. In this case White exposes his King's side by P—K Kt 4 in order to benefit from the unstable position of the Black K B, but unless care is taken, he can easily fall a victim to an attack on the open K Kt file

| | | |
|---|---|---|
| 12. | ......... | P×Kt |
| 13. | P—K Kt 4 | Q—K 4 |

Not Q—Q 4, on account of P×P and Kt—B 6.

| | | |
|---|---|---|
| 14. | P×P | K R—Kt 1 |
| 15. | B—R 6 | |

This is Marshall's innovation. It gets the Bishop out of play, as P—Kt 5 must necessarily follow, yet the pawn at

Kt 7 holds the Black Rook, and there is a permanent threat of Kt—B 6 either winning the exchange or, if the Knight is taken, giving White a pair of formidable passed pawns.

|  |  |  |
|---|---|---|
| 15. | ......... | P—Q 6 |
| 16. | P—B 3 | B—Q 3 |

This is quite to White's liking, since he wishes to advance his centre pawns. Black's only chance of escaping disaster would be : B—K 2, with R—Q 2, Kt—Q 1—B 2. Instead of this, his next few moves do not reveal any concerted plan, and he loses in a surprisingly short time.

|  |  |  |
|---|---|---|
| 17. | P—B 4 | Q—Q 4 |
| 18. | Q—B 3 | B—K 2 |
| 19. | P—Kt 5 | Q—B 4 |
| 20. | Kt—Kt 3 | Q—B 2 |

In manœuvring his Q, Black has achieved nothing either for counter attack or defence. Now White has numerous attacking chances. He first turns his attention to the K P.

|  |  |  |
|---|---|---|
| 21. | Q—Kt 4 | Q R—K 1 |
| 22. | R—K 4 ! | P—Kt 4 |
| 23. | P—Q R 4 | |

and now even the Q R takes part in the assault. Black's game is hopeless.

|  |  |  |
|---|---|---|
| 23. | ......... | P—R 3 |
| 24. | P×P | P×P |
| 25. | K—Kt 2 | |

attacking the K P by avoiding the check.

|  |  |  |
|---|---|---|
| 25. | ......... | Kt—Q 1 |
| 26. | Q—B 3 | Q—Kt 3 |
| 27. | R—Q 4 | P—B 3 |
| 28. | R×Kt ch | K×R |
| 29. | Q×P | Resigns. |

After this, no master has tried to defend a "Max Lange" in an international tournament.

## GAME No. 8

White : Blackburne.          Black : Em. Lasker.

Scotch Game.

|      |           |            |
|------|-----------|------------|
| 1.   | P—K 4     | P—K 4      |
| 2.   | Kt—K B 3  | Kt—Q B 3   |
| 3.   | P—Q 4     | P×P        |
| 4.   | Kt×P      | B—B 4      |
| 5.   | B—K 3     | Q—B 3      |

The threat Kt×Kt and B×B must be met in some way. P—Q 3 is not satisfactory, for Black remains with a trebled pawn after the double exchange. An alternative to the text move is B—Kt 3. Q—B 3, however, has the advantage of developing a piece, and although it is the Queen, White has no early opportunity of driving the same off, such as he often obtains when the Queen comes out so soon in the game.

|      |           |            |
|------|-----------|------------|
| 6.   | P—Q B 3   | K Kt—K 2   |
| 7.   | Kt—B 2    |            |

In order to develop the Q Kt.

|      |           |            |
|------|-----------|------------|
| 7.   | ........  | P—Q Kt 3 ! |

Out of three possible moves, Lasker selects the one which contributes most to development. B—Kt 3 does nothing in that direction, and B×B would bring the White Knight further into play. The text move prepares the development of the B at Kt 2 with the option of Castles Q R. If White exchanges Bishops he gives up the command of his Q 4. Black's P—Q 3 might have had the same result, but then the exchange would have given White a majority of pawns on the K side, whilst White's three Q side pawns would have held the black Q side pawns, one of the latter being doubled.

|      |           |            |
|------|-----------|------------|
| 8.   | Kt—Q 2    | Q—Kt 3     |

The exchange of Bishops allows White to play Kt—K 3, thus avoiding the weakening move P—K Kt 3. 9 B—K B 4 is answered by P—Q 4 !.

|      |           |            |
|------|-----------|------------|
| 9.   | B×B       | P×B        |
| 10.  | Kt—K 3    | R—Q Kt 1   |
| 11.  | P—Q Kt 3  | Castles    |
| 12.  | B—B 4     |            |

To prevent Black's P—B 4.

At first sight it seems as if the Q B P ought to move to B 4, as the advance of the Q Kt P has weakened it. But White dares not allow a Black Knight to settle at Q 5.

| 12. ......... | P—Q 3 |
| 13. P—B 4 ! | |

Diag. 108.

Black threatens to play K—R 1 in order to play P—B 4. White's position would then be very bad, and therefore he rightly decides to anticipate the move, even at the cost of a pawn. In order to gain the Q B P Black must waste a number of moves with the Q, and White gains time for a King's side attack. The pawn sacrifice is very promising indeed.

| 13. ......... | Q—B 3 |
| 14. Castles | Q × Q B P |
| 15. R—B 3 | |

There seem to be many threats here, and the position is a difficult one to fathom. After disentangling his Queen, Black tries very hard to force his P—B 4. As soon as he succeeds in this he has a won game, for the open file is available both for defence and counter-attack.

| 15. ......... | Q—Q 5 |
| 16. K—R 1 | B—K 3 |
| 17. R—Q B 1 | B × B |
| 18. R × B | Q—Kt 7 |

Q—B 3 is impossible apart from the fact that it would block the K B P, *e.g.* 18...Q—B 3; 19 P—K 5, P×P; 20 Kt—K 4, etc.

|  | 19.· R—Q B 2 | Q—B 3 |
|---|---|---|

Now the attack shown in the last note could be answered with Q—R 5.

20. Kt—Kt 4

Here P—K Kt 4 could be answered by Kt—Q 5, *e.g.* 21 P—Kt 5, Q—Kt 3; 22 R—Kt 3, P—B 4.

| 20. ......... | Q—Kt 3 |
|---|---|
| 21. R—Kt 3 | P—B 4 |
| 22. Kt—K 5 | Q—K 3 |
| 23. Kt×Kt | Kt×Kt |
| 24. P—K 5 | Kt—Kt 5 ! |

This prevents the Rook from occupying the Q file which is about to be opened.

| 25. R—B 4 | P×P |
|---|---|
| 26. Q—R 1 | Q—Q 2 ! |

If now Q×P, Black plays R—B 2 with unanswerable threats of R—K 1 or Q 1.

| 27. Kt—B 3 | P×P |
|---|---|
| 28. Kt—K 5 | Q—K 2 |
| 29. R×K B P | Q R—K 1 |
| 30. Kt—B 4 | Q—K 8 ch |
| 31. R—B 1 | Q×Q |
| 32. R×Q | Kt×P |
| 33. P—R 3 | P—B 5 |
| 34. R—Q 3 | Kt—Kt 5 |
| 35. R—Q 7 | P—B 6 ! |
| 36. P×P | R×P |
| 37. R×R P | Kt—Q 6 |

threatens mate in six.

| 38. R—R 1 | Kt—K 8 |
|---|---|

mate is again threatened.

| 39. Kt—Q 2 | R×P ch |
|---|---|
| 40. K—Kt 1 | R—Kt 6 ch |
| 41. K—R 2 | R—Q 6 ! |

| | |
|---|---|
| 42. R × Kt | R × Kt ch |
| 43. R × R | R × R |
| 44. R—Q 7 | R—K 6 |
| 45. R × P | R × P |
| 46. R × P | P—R 3 |
| 47. R—B 6 | |

A few more moves " for fun."

| | |
|---|---|
| 47. ......... | K—R 2 |
| 48. K—Kt 2 | P—R 4 |
| 49. R—R 6 | P—Kt 3 |
| 50. R—R 4 | K—R 3 |
| 51. R—Q B 4 | R—Kt 7 ch |
| 52. K—Kt 3 | K—Kt 4 |
| 53. R—B 3 | P—R 5 ch |
| 54. K—R 3 | K—R 4 |
| 55. R—B 4 | R—Kt 6 ch |
| 56. K—R 2 | P—Kt 4 |
| 57. R—R 4 | R—Kt 7 ch |
| 58. K—R sq | P—R 6 |
| 59. R—Q B 4 | P—Kt 5 |
| 60. K—Kt sq | P—Kt 6 |
| 61. R—B 5 ch | K—Kt 3 |
| 62. R—B sq | K—B 4 |
| 63. R—R sq | R—Q 7 |
| 64. R—K sq | K—B 5 |
| 65. R—R sq | K—K 6 |
| 66. R—R 3 ch | R—Q 6 |
| 67. R—R sq | K—K 7 |
| Resigns. | |

## GAME No. 9

White : Salwe.      Black : Marshall.

### Two Knights' Defence

| | |
|---|---|
| 1. P—K 4 | P—K 4 |
| 2. Kt—K B 3 | Kt—Q B 3 |
| 3. B—B 4 | Kt—B 3 |
| 4. Kt—Kt 5 | |

This attack may be tempting, as the B P cannot be protected, but it is against that elementary principle which says that no attack should be undertaken in the opening until the minor pieces are mobilised, provided of course that Black also has made sound opening moves. There is every likelihood that the attack in the present instance will lead to nothing. It has taken many years to find the correct reply, but now that it is known, the opening has practically disappeared from master practice. Instead of the move in the text, White can play either P—Q 3, leading almost unavoidably to a drawing variation of the Giuoco piano, or Castles which might bring about the Max Lange attack after 4...B—B 4 ; 5 P—Q 4, P×P.

| 4. ......... | P—Q 4 |
| 5. P×P | Kt—Q R 4 ! |

This is a typical position in the Two Knights' defence. The former continuation 5...Kt×Q P has long been abandoned, as the attack that White can initiate by 6 Kt×B P, K×Kt ; 7 Q—B 3 ch, forcing the Black King to K 3, is dangerous though the result is uncertain. The move in the text breaks the attack from the very first, and Black gets the advantage

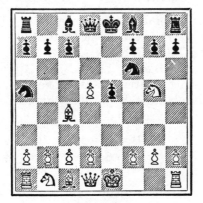

Diag. 109.

as he can gain time by attacking the two minor pieces which it should be noted, are unsupported, and in addition obtain a speedy development, worth more than the pawn given up for it.

6 P—Q 3

B—Kt 5 ch is an alternative. The advantage is Black's
in this case also—*e.g.* P—B 3 ; 7 P×P, P×P ; 8 B—K 2,
P—K R 3 ; 9 Kt—K B 3, P—K 5 ; 10 Kt—K 5, Q—B 2 ;
11 P—Q 4, B—Q 3 (or P×P *e.p.* followed by B—Q 3) ;
12 P—K B 4, P×P *e.p.* ; 13 Kt×P, Kt—Kt 5 or 11 P—B 4,
B—Q 3 ; 12 P—Q 4, P×P *e.p.* ; 13 Kt×P, Castles. Black
has an easy game and open lines.

|       |            |         |
|-------|------------|---------|
| 6.    | ..........  | P—K R 3 |
| 7.    | Kt—K B 3   | P—K 5   |
| 8.    | Q—K 2      | Kt×B    |
| 9.    | P×Kt       | B—Q B 4 |
| 10.   | K Kt—Q 2   |         |

The Knight must move sooner or later.

|       |            |           |
|-------|------------|-----------|
| 10.   | ..........  | Castles   |
| 11.   | Kt—Kt 3    | B—K Kt 5  |
| 12.   | Q—B 1      |           |

A sorry retreat, but the plausible Q—Q 2 would be disas-
trous, *e.g.* P—K 6 ! ; 13 P×P, Kt—K 5 and Q—R 5 ch

|       |            |           |
|-------|------------|-----------|
| 12.   | ..........  | B—Kt 5 ch |

Black's superior development begins to tell in no uncertain
fashion. Now White can neither play 13 B—Q 2 on account of
B×B ch ; 14 Q Kt×B, R—K 1, followed by P—K 6, nor 13 Kt
B 3 on account of B×Kt ; 14 P×B, P—B 3 regaining the pawn
and maintaining positional advantage. White has therefore
no alternative but P—B 3, which weakens his Q 3, where a
Black Knight soon settles down.

|       |            |          |
|-------|------------|----------|
| 13.   | P—B 3      | B—K 2    |
| 14.   | P—K R 3    | B—R 4    |
| 15.   | P—Kt 4     | B—Kt 3   |

At last White can castle. He can, of course, only castle
on the Queen's side, because his King's side pawns are shattered.
Now games in which the Kings castle on different wings are
more or less beyond calculation, as pointed out before. On
the whole, the player who first attacks wins. But experience
has shown that the Queen's side is more difficult to defend
on account of its greater expanse, and this theory is supported by the present game. In addition, White's develop-

ment is not completed yet, whilst all the Black forces are ready to strike.

|     |          |          |
|-----|----------|----------|
| 16. | B—K 3    | Kt—Q 2   |
| 17. | Q Kt—Q 2 | Kt—K 4   |
| 18. | Castles  | P—Kt 4   |

Storming the position with pawns is peculiar to this kind of game. The intention is to break up the opposing pawn position, and to open files for the Rooks. Pawns are cheap in such cases. Open lines for the pieces are the things that matter, and the fewer pawns there are left, the more open lines are available for the attack.

|     |          |          |
|-----|----------|----------|
| 19. | P × P    | Kt—Q 6 ch |
| 20. | K—Kt 1   | Q × P    |
| 21. | K—R 1    |          |

The King was not safe on the diagonal. White wishes to push on his King's side pawns (P—B 4—B 5, and so on). But after P × P *e.p.* there would be a fatal discovered check by the Black Knight.

|     |          |          |
|-----|----------|----------|
| 22. | ........ | Q × P    |

Black's advantage becomes more marked. He has recovered his pawn, and for the ensuing attacks on both sides he is better placed, having already two open files for his Rooks.

|     |          |          |
|-----|----------|----------|
| 22. | P—K B 4  | P—Q R 4  |
| 23. | Q R—Kt 1 | P—K B 4  |
| 24. | Kt—Q 4   | Q—R 5 !  |

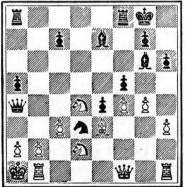

Diag. 110.

The position bristles with chances for daring sacrifices.
After 25 Kt×B P, for instance, Black could play R×Kt !;
26 P×R, Kt—Kt 5 ; 27 P×Kt, P×P ; 28 P—R 3 (Q—B 4 ch ?,
B—B 2), B—B 3 ; 29 K—R 2, Q×P ch ; 30 P×Q, R×P
mate.

|  |  |  |
|---|---|---|
| 25. | P—Kt 3 | Q—Q 2 |
| 26. | P×P | B×P |
| 27. | Q—Kt 2 | P—B 4 |

White's compulsory 25 P—Kt 3 has weakened his Q B 3,
and the move in the text is intended to open the diagonal
K B 3—Q B 6 for the Black Bishop.

|  |  |  |
|---|---|---|
| 28. | Kt×B | Q×Kt |
| 29. | Q×P | B—B 3 |
| 30. | Q—B 4 ch | K—R 1 |
| 31. | Kt—K 4 | Q R—K 1 |

White cannot parry all the threats at once. Though he gets
rid of the threatening B, he lets in the hostile R on the K file
and the end cannot long be delayed.

|  |  |  |
|---|---|---|
| 32. | Kt×B | R×Kt |
| 33. | B—B 1 | K R—K 3 |
| 34. | B—R 3 | R—K 7 |
| 35. | K R—Q 1 | Kt—K 8 |
| 36. | B×P | Kt—B 7 ch |
| 37. | K—Kt 2 | Kt—Kt 5 ch |

and mate at R 7 or B 7.

## GAME No. 10

White : Teichmann.    Black : Amateurs in consultation.
Two Knights' Defence.

|  |  |  |
|---|---|---|
| 1. | P—K 4 | P—K 4 |
| 2. | Kt—K B 3 | Kt—Q B 3 |

| 3. B—B 4 | Kt—B 3 |
| 4. Castles | |

Diag. 111.

The idea underlying this pawn sacrifice is to open the K file for the Rook. It will be seen that, with correct play, Black manages to castle just in time, and White, though winning back his pawn, has no advantage in position. The opening is seldom played by modern masters.

Instead of the move in the text, White can hardly defend the K P with Kt—B 3, as Black simply captures the pawn and recovers his piece by P—Q 4, with a satisfactory position. It is even better for Black if White plays 6 B×P ch in reply to 5...Kt×P. The capture of White's K P is far more important than that of the Black K B P, particularly as the White Bishop, which could be dangerous on the diagonal Q R 2—K Kt 8, is exchanged, e.g. 6...K×B; 7 Kt×Kt, P—Q 4; 8 Kt—Kt 5 ch, K—Kt 1 ! Black continues P—K R 3, K—R 2, R—B 1 and has open lines for Rooks and Bishops.

| 4. ......... | Kt × P |

Black can, of course, develop his B—B 4. Then he must either submit to the Max Lange attack (5 P—Q 4, P×P) or play B×P, giving up the useful B, in which case he loses the pawn gained after 6 Kt×B, Kt×Kt ; 7 P—K B 4, P—Q 3 ; 8 P×P, P×P ; 9 B—K Kt 5, and eventually Q—B 3.

| 5. P—Q 4 | |

R—K 1 at once would lead to nothing.

| | | |
|---|---|---|
| 5. ......... | | P×P |
| 6. R—K 1 | | P—Q 4 |
| 7. B×P! | | Q×B |
| 8. Kt—B 3 | | |

Diag. 112.

This attack has been analysed extensively by Steinitz The only square where the Queen cannot be attacked at once by the minor pieces is at Q 1. After 8...Q—Q 1, Black obtains quite a satisfactory game: 9 R×Kt ch, B—K 2; 10 Kt×P, P—B 4. This is Pillsbury's move, intending to displace the Rook. Black has then open lines for his two Bishops as compensation for his shattered pawn position. 11 R—K B 4, Castles; 12 Kt×Kt, Q×Q ch; 13 Kt×Q, P×Kt. Now it is not easy to find a reasonable plan for White, as Black threatens to cramp White's game with B—Q 3 and P—B 5. It is therefore necessary for White to take measures against that by playing R—B 4 and B—B 4. If Black still plays B—Q 3, B—B 4 follows, with the intention of exchanging and of provoking Black's P—B 4, which leaves the Q P "backward."

| | | |
|---|---|---|
| 8. ......... | | Q—K R 4 |
| 9. Kt×Kt | | B—K 2 |
| 10. B—Kt 5 | | B—K 3 |
| 11. B×B | | Kt×B |
| 12. Kt—Kt 3 | | Q—R 3 |
| 13. Q×P | | Castles K R |
| 14. Q R—Q 1 | | |

Now White is ahead with his development, having both Rooks in play and his Queen better placed. Nor can the latter be attacked by R—Q 1, as White would simply play Q×R. On the Queen being driven away by the Black Knight, he exchanges the latter and plays the Queen back into the same dominating position, eventually producing a dislocation of the Black Queen's side pawns.

|  |  |  |
|---|---|---|
| 14. | ......... | Kt—B 3 |
| 15. | Q—Q R 4 | Q R—Q 1 |
| 16. | Kt—Q 4 ! | Kt×Kt |
| 17. | R×Kt | R×R |
| 18. | Q×R | P—Q Kt 3 |
| 19. | Q—K 5 | P—Q B 4 |

It is instructive to watch how this very slight weakness created by Black's advance of his pawns brings him into trouble. A White Knight settles down at his Q 6, which is no longer guarded by the Black Q B P, and paralyses the whole of Black's game. Another factor in White's superiority of position is the possession of the King's file. The Black Rook cannot move until the King gets a loophole by a pawn move. As we have seen, such a pawn move often affords an entry to the opposing pieces.

|  |  |  |
|---|---|---|
| 20. | P—K B 4 | B—B 1 |

Not B×P, of course, because of P—Q Kt 3 and Q—Kt 2. The Bishop which cannot remain at K 3 is to go to Kt 2, so that the threat of mate after Q—Q B 3 may also hold up a White piece.

|  |  |  |
|---|---|---|
| 21. | P—B 5 | B—Kt 2 |
| 22. | Q—K 7 | Q—Q B 3 |
| 23. | R—K 2 | P—B 3 |

Compulsory, as otherwise P—B 6 forces the Kt P to advance, which is fatal in any case. After P—Kt 3, White would cover his B P and play his Q to K R 6. On the other hand, after P×P there is Kt—R 5—B 6, and Black is in a mating net.

|  |  |  |
|---|---|---|
| 24. | Kt—K 4 | Q—Q 4 |
| 25. | Kt—Q 6 | B—B 3 |

The threat was Q×R ch and R—K 8 mate.

26. P—K R 3

in order to retreat to R 2 in case of Q—Q 8 ch. In a way P—K R 3 creates a certain weakness, as the square at Kt 3 is now defenceless, but Black has no pieces with which to take advantage of it : his Rook cannot move, his Bishop is on the White squares. If Black had a K B instead, the move would be very doubtful, because then Black might break in through White's K Kt 3.

26. ………        P—B 5

White's threat was to repel the Black Queen by P—B 4 and to mate in five moves, beginning with Q—K 6 ch.

27. P—B 3          P—K R 3

Diag. 113.

This disposes of the winning of the Queen by the threatened mate. But it creates a weakness at Black's Kt 3, which White exploits in grand style. He decides to play the King himself to Kt 6, threatening mate at Kt 7. In spite of several raids by the Black Queen, this quaint device is crowned with success. The weakness created by P—K R 3 could not be demonstrated more drastically.

28. K—R 2          P—Q Kt 4
29. K—Kt 3         P—Q R 4
30. K—R 4          P—Kt 3

If White were to play P×P now, Black would mate him one move earlier (Q—Kt 4). Of course he parries the threat first, and Black is helpless.

|  |  |  |
|---|---|---|
| 31. | R—K 3 | Q × Kt P |
| 32. | R—Kt 3 | Q—B 7 |

After P—Kt 4 ch White could not play 33 K—Kt 4 on account of the pretty mate by B—B 6. He would play K—R 5—Kt 6.

|  |  |  |
|---|---|---|
| 33. | P × P | Q—B 5 ch |
| 34. | R—Kt 4 | Q—B 7 ch |
| 35. | K—R 5 | Resigns. |

A most instructive game, showing how the superior position of the pieces can lead indirectly to a win, by reducing the opponent's pieces gradually to impotence and compelling him to move pawns, thereby affording opportunities for a decisive entry.

## GAME No. 11

White : Schlechter.     Black : Janowski.

Ruy Lopez (compare p. 40).

|  |  |  |
|---|---|---|
| 1. | P—K 4 | P—K 4 |
| 2. | Kt—K B 3 | Kt—Q B 3 |
| 3. | B—Kt 5 | Kt—B 3 |
| 4. | Castles | Kt × P |

A continuation, which has lately gained in favour, is : P—Q 3 and B—K 2 (see p. 39).

|  |  |  |
|---|---|---|
| 5. | P—Q 4 | B—K 2 |

It is clearly very dangerous to gratify White's wish for an open file by playing P×P. The move may be playable in the system of defence called the "Riga variation" (see Game No. 17). Here it would be advantageous to be able to close the K B's diagonal. It is better when intending to play the "Riga variation" to have played P—Q R 3 on the third move.

|     |           |          |
| --- | --------- | -------- |
| 6.  | Q—K 2     | Kt—Q 3   |
| 7.  | B×Kt      | Kt P×B   |
| 8.  | P×P       | Kt—Kt 2  |
| 9.  | Kt—B 3    | Castles  |
| 10. | R—K 1     | R—K 1    |

The manœuvre cited on p. 40, namely Kt—B 4—K 3, which makes P—Q 4 possible, is essential for the development of the Q B. Black loses the present game because White is able to keep the Bishop shut in permanently

|     |         |         |
| --- | ------- | ------- |
| 11. | Q—B 4   | Kt—B 4  |

so that the pawn B 3 should not be "hanging" when the Q P moves.

|     |             |         |
| --- | ----------- | ------- |
| 12. | Kt—K Kt 5 ! | B×Kt    |
| 13. | B×B         | Q×B     |
| 14. | Q×Kt        | R—K 3   |

Diag. 114.

After the exchanges the position is clearly in favour of White. Against an undeveloped B, which also hampers a Rook, his Knight is mobile. The Black Queen's side pawns are weak, and give White winning chances even if Black succeeds in playing P—Q 4 and bringing the Bishop into play. The move in the text, which covers the pawn at B 3, again prepares for P—Q 4.

|     |         |         |
| --- | ------- | ------- |
| 15. | Q—Q 4   | B—Kt 2  |

The only chance lay in the pawn sacrifice by P—Q B 4, after

which the Bishop gets to Kt 2 with a threat of mate, and the
Q R is free.

| | | | |
|---|---|---|---|
| 16. | Q—Q Kt 4 | B—B 1 | |
| 17. | Kt—K 4 | | |

Fine play. If Black captures the pawn, White obtains a
combined attack with Q, R, and Kt, to which Black can only
oppose the Q, so that the result cannot be in doubt—*e.g.*
17...Q×K P ; 18 Kt—B 5, Q—Q 3 ; 19 Q—Q B 4, R×R ch ;
20 R×R, P—K R 3 ; 21 R—K 8 ch, K—R 2 ; 22 Q—K 4 ch,
P—Kt 3 (Q—Kt 3 ? ; 23 Q×Q, followed by Kt×P) ; 23
Kt—Q 3 and R—K 7.

| | | |
|---|---|---|
| 17. | ......... | Q—K 2 |
| 18. | Kt—B 5 | R—Kt 3 |
| 19. | R—K 3 | P—Q R 4 |
| 20. | Q—Q 4 | R—Kt 1 |
| 21. | P—Q B 4 | |

preventing R—Kt 4

| | | |
|---|---|---|
| 21. | ......... | P—R 3 |
| 22. | P—Q Kt 3 | K—R 2 |
| 23. | R—Q 1 | Q—Kt 4 |
| 24. | R—Kt 3 | Q—B 4 |
| 25. | R×R | P×R |

Black has built a wall of pawns round his King, but it
does not avail against the superior forces which White can
concentrate.

White's plan is clear. He will advance his pawns, and
break up those that surround the Black King, always taking
care that Black does not free his Queen's side meanwhile.
His pieces will then break in easily, and Black is forced to
look on passively.

| | | |
|---|---|---|
| 26. | P—K R 3 | R—R 1 |
| 27. | P—Q R 4 | |

to prevent the sacrifice of a pawn by P—R 5, which would
bring the Black Rook into play.

| | | |
|---|---|---|
| 27. | ......... | R—Kt 1 |
| 28. | R—Q 3 | Q—Kt 4 |
| 29. | K—R 2 | Q—K 2 |

|     |          |        |
| --- | -------- | ------ |
| 30. | P—B 4    | Q—B 2  |
| 31. | P—K 6!!  |        |

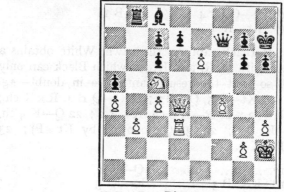

Diag. 115.

A beautiful move which robs Black of his last chance of freeing his Queen's side, which he might have accomplished by the pawn sacrifice of P—Q 3.

|     |           |          |
| --- | --------- | -------- |
| 31. | ........  | P×P      |
| 32. | Q—K 5     | Q—K 2    |
| 33. | P—K Kt 4  | R—Kt 5   |
| 34. | K—Kt 3    | R—Kt 3   |
| 35. | P—R 4     | Q—B 1    |
| 36. | P—R 5     | P×P      |
| 37. | Q×R P     | R—Kt 1   |
| 38. | Q—K 5     | R—Kt 3   |
| 39. | P—Kt 5    | P—R 4    |
| 40. | P—Kt 6 ch |          |

The end is near. Black must take, as Q×R P forces a speedy mate.

|     |            |          |
| --- | ---------- | -------- |
| 40. | ........   | K×P      |
| 41. | Q—Kt 5 ch  | K—R 2    |
| 42. | Q×R P ch   | K—Kt 1   |
| 43. | Q—Kt 5     |          |

threatening R—Q 8

|     |           |          |
| --- | --------- | -------- |
| 43. | ........  | K—B 2    |
| 44. | R—Q 8     | Q—K 2    |
| 45. | Q—R 5 ch  | Resigns. |

Loss of the Queen and mate in a few moves cannot be prevented. Black has played the whole game practically with two pieces less, and the mate was really only a matter of time.

## GAME No. 12

White : Teichmann.          Black : Rubinstein.

Ruy Lopez (see p. 37).

| 1. P—K 4 | P—K 4 |
|---|---|
| 2. Kt—K B 3 | Kt—Q B 3 |
| 3. B—Kt 5 | P—Q R 3 |
| 4. B—R 4 | |

By exchanging the Bishop White could not prove P—Q R 3
to be a lost move, for Black, by retaking with the Q P, obtains
open lines for Q and Q B, and in addition to an easy development, retains two Bishops.  This is a set-off against a certain
weakness in Black's game, which may be found in the fact
that after P—Q 4, P×P, White has four pawns to three on
the King's side, while his three pawns on the Queen's side are
able to hold the four opposing pawns, one of which is
doubled.  But this weakness can only tell in the end-game,
which is too far ahead for practical purposes, and to which
it may not come at all.  An example of the usual line of play will
be found in Game No. 18.

| 4. ........ | Kt—B 3 |
|---|---|
| 5. Castles | B—K 2 |
| 6. R—K 1 | P—Q Kt 4 |
| 7. B—Kt 3 | P—Q 3 |
| 8. P—B 3 | |

Diag. 116.

| 8....... | Castles |

In Capablanca's opinion Black should not castle before White's intentions in the centre have been made clear. It makes a great difference whether White plays his Q P to Q 4 or to Q 3 only.

If after 8...Q Kt—R 4 ; 9 B—B 2, P—B 4 White plays: 10 P—Q 4, his intention is to move his pawn further to Q 5 as soon as Black has castled, and then to attack on the King's wing with Q Kt—Q 2—B 1—K 3, P—K Kt 4 and Kt—B 5. For this reason Black should force White to disclose whether he intends to exchange his Q P or to advance it to Q 5. In the latter case Black can refrain from castling altogether and counter-attack on the King's wing, *e.g.*, 10 P—Q 4, Q—B 2 ; 11 P—K R 3, B—Q 2 ; 12 Q Kt—Q 2, R—QB 1 ; if now : 13 P—Q 5 then P—R 3 followed by P—Kt 4—Kt 5 gives Black many chances. If on the contrary 13 P × P, then Black need no longer fear an attack on the King's side after he has castled, as his Rooks will have a favourable opportunity for operating on the open Queen's file. However, there is still the disadvantage for Black of having advanced Queen's side pawns, which are liable to attack (P—Q R 4).

The game takes a different course when Black exchanges the pawns in the centre. The continuation would then be : 11 ......, Kt—B 3 ; 12 Q Kt—Q 2, B—Q 2 ; 13 Kt—B 1, P × P ; 14 P × P, P × P ; 15 B—Kt 5, Q—Kt 3. It is difficult to decide which side has the advantage. Black has an extra pawn, but White has the initiative.

If in Diag. 116, after 8...Castles White plays 9 P—Q 4 at once, Black has an opportunity for the following interesting attack : 9 P—Q 4, B—Kt 5 ; 10 B—K 3, Kt × K P ; 11 B—Q 5, Q—Q 2 ; 12 B × K Kt, P—Q 4 ; 13 B—B 2, P—K 5 ; 14 P—K R 3, B—R 4 ; 15 Kt—K 5, B × Q ; 16 Kt × Q, B × B ; 17 Kt × R, R × Kt. White cannot take advantage of his Rooks, as there is no open file, whilst Black threatens to initiate a strong attack with P—B 4.

Aljechin has analysed a variation of this line of play, which he thinks leads finally to White's advantage : 12 P × P, Kt—Kt 4 ; 13 B × Kt, B × B ; 14 P—K R 3, B × Kt ; 15 Q × B, Kt × P ; 16 R × Kt, P × R ; 17 B × R, B—B 8 ; 18 Kt—R 3, Q—Q 7. I doubt that White can win this game.

## 9. P—Q 3

In this less aggressive continuation, in which nothing is

immediately attempted against Black's centre, White prepares gradually for a King's side attack, as in this game with Kt—Q 2—B 1—Kt 3. But Black should obtain time for operations in the centre.

|  |  |  |
|---|---|---|
| 9. | :......... | Kt—Q R 4 |
| 10. | B—B 2 | P—B 4 |
| 11. | Q Kt—Q 2 | Kt—B 3 |
| 12. | P—Q R 4 | |

In many variations of the Ruy Lopez, this advance is always good, if Black cannot avoid exchanging the pawn, because the White Queen's Rook, which only gets into play with difficulty, can either be exchanged or hold the Rook's file. In any case the Black Knight's pawn is weak for the end-game. If, as in the present game, Black can play P—Kt 5, P—R 4 is useless and even doubtful, as the Rook's pawn itself may become weak in the end-game.

|  |  |  |
|---|---|---|
| 12. | ......... | B—Kt 2 |

This causes the loss of the game. In the Ruy Lopez the Bishop is nearly always needed on the diagonal Q B 1—K R 6, to prevent a Knight from settling at White's K B 5, which otherwise cannot be repelled except by P—K Kt 3, a most undesirable consummation. The proper continuation would have been P—Kt 5, B—K 3, Q—B 2 and P—Q 4, capturing the Queen's file. Compare note to move 13 in the next game.

|  |  |  |
|---|---|---|
| 13. | Kt—B 1 | Q—B 2 |
| 14. | Kt—Kt 3 | P—Kt 3 |

Diag. 117

Here is the weakness. White first provides against Black's P—Q 4, and then starts a sharp attack on the King's side.

| 15. B—Kt 5 | Q R—Q 1 |

P—Q 4 at once is not feasible, because of B × Kt.

| 16. P×P | P×P |
| 17. Q—B 1 | |

This brings the Q away from her file, which Black could now secure by P—Q 4, followed by P×P.

| 17. ......... | K R—K 1 |

The proper continuation is the one outlined in the note above.

| 18. P—R 3 | |

White has now ample leisure to prepare the advance of his K B P.

| 18. ......... | R—R 1 |
| 19. R×R | R×R |
| 20. Kt—R 2 | B—Q B 1 |
| 21. P—K B 4 | Kt—K 1 |
| 22. P—B 5 | B×B |
| 23. Q×B | Q—K 2 |

Black seeks salvation in exchanges, which White, of course, tries to avoid, having good prospects of driving home his attack. His pieces are concentrated on the King's side, whilst the Black forces are scattered, and unable to get back in time for the defence. Moreover, it is likely that the weakness at Black's K R 3 and K B 3 will prove fatal as the Black K B is exchanged.

| 24. Q—R 6 | Q—B 1 |
| 25. Q—B 1 | Q—Kt 2 |
| 26. R—B 1 | P—Kt 4 |

White was threatening to play Kt—Kt 4 with P×P and Kt—R 6.

| 27. Kt—Kt 4 | Kt—B 3 |
| 28. Kt×Kt ch | Q×Kt |

One of the attacking Knights is eliminated. But there is another, which forces the entry at K B 6 and K Kt 6.

| 29. P—R 4 | |

to gain access for the White Queen at K R 6.    If Black
captures there follows : 30 Kt—R 5, Q—Q 1 ; 31 Q—R 6,
Q—B 1 ; 32 Kt—B 6 ch, an instructive example of the weakness created by P—K Kt 3.

|     |          |       |
|-----|----------|-------|
| 29. | ........ | P—R 3 |
| 30. | Kt—R 5   | Q—Q 1 |
| 31. | P—B 6    |       |

All this is easy to understand.

|     |          |          |
|-----|----------|----------|
| 31. | ........ | K—R 2    |
| 32. | P × P    | B—Kt 5   |
| 33. | Kt—Kt 7  | K—Kt 3   |
| 34. | B—Q 1    | Q—Q 2    |
| 35. | Kt—B 5   | B × Kt   |
| 36. | P × B ch | Resigns. |

The conclusion might be :  K—R 2 ;  37 B—R 5, P × P ;
38 Q × P, R—K Kt 1 ; 39 B—Kt 6 ch, P × B ; 40 Q—R 4
mate.

## GAME No. 13

White : Teichmann.        Black : Schlechter.
Ruy Lopez (see p. 37).

Move 1–8 as in Game No. 12.

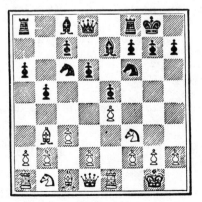

Diag. 118.

|       |          |          |
|-------|----------|----------|
| 9.    | P—Q 3    | Kt—Q R 4 |
| 10.   | B—B 2    | P—B 4    |
| 11.   | Q Kt—Q 2 | Q—B 2    |

Supporting, as it does, the K P, this is not a lost move, although White has not played P—Q 4. It prepares Black's P—Q 4 (after Kt—B 3), the K P being fully protected against White's double attack by P×P.

|       |         |         |
|-------|---------|---------|
| 12.   | Kt—B 1  | Kt—B 3  |
| 13.   | Kt—K 3  | B—Kt 2  |

The logical move would have been B—K 3, to enforce P—Q 4. Black is then very well developed, whilst White labours under a somewhat undeveloped Queen's side. An attempt to exert pressure in the centre with P—Q 4 in order to prevent Black's P—Q 4 would be belated. Black would gain the advantage by : 14...K P×P ; 15 P×P, P×P ; 16 Kt×P, Kt×Kt ; 17 Q×Kt, Kt—Kt 5 ! Nor would B—Kt 5 before Kt—K 3 be more successful ; after B—K 3 ; 14 Kt—K 3, Q R—Q 1 ; 15 P—Q 4, B P×P ; 16 P×P, P×P ; 17 Kt×P, Kt×Kt ; 18 Q×Kt, Q—B 4, Black has the better chances in the end-game. The move in the text is not good because, as we saw before, the Bishop is wanted on the other diagonal to cover the square at K B 4.

|       |         |         |
|-------|---------|---------|
| 14.   | Kt—B 5  | K R—K 1 |
| 15.   | B—Kt 5  | Kt—Q 2  |

Even now it was desirable to aim at P—Q 4, therefore Q R—Q 1 was preferable.

|       |         |
|-------|---------|
| 16.   | B—Kt 3  |

The position of the White pieces points to a dangerous menace to the opposing King's side.

|       |            |        |
|-------|------------|--------|
| 16.   | ......... | Kt—B 1 |
| 17.   | B—Q 5 ! !  |        |

The beginning of a brilliant combination. B × Kt is threatened, and Black must first cover his B at K 2.

17. ..........          Kt—Kt 3
18. B×B                K Kt×B

Q Kt×B is not feasible, because of B×B and Kt×Q P.

19. B×P ch ! !         K×B
20. Kt—Kt 5 ch

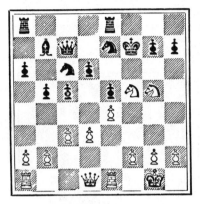

Diag. 119.

Quite a number of charming combinations are hidden in this position. If K—Kt 3 or Kt 1, then 21 Kt×Kt P! If K—B 3 White can capture the R P first with check.

20. ..........          K—Kt 1
21. Q—R 5              Kt×Kt
22. Q×R P ch           K—B 1
23. Q×Kt ch            K—Kt 1
24. Q—Kt 6 ! ! !

The point. This prevents P—Kt 3, which would allow Black to bring up his Q for the defence at Kt 2. Now nothing can be done against the threatening R—K 3—B 3 or R 3.

24. ..........          Q—Q 2
25. R—K 3              Resigns.

A wonderful game in which Teichmann, the great judge of position, proves himself also a master in hand-to-hand fighting, in the wild chaos of sacrificial combinations.

## Game No. 14

White : Spielmann.      Black : Tarrasch.

Ruy Lopez (see p. 41).

| | | |
|---|---|---|
| 1. | P—K 4 | P—K 4 |
| 2. | Kt—K B 3 | Kt—Q B 3 |
| 3. | B—Kt 5 | P—Q R 3 |
| 4. | B—R 4 | Kt—B 3 |
| 5. | Castles | Kt × P |
| 6. | P—Q 4 | |

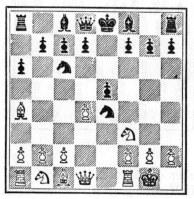

Diag. 120.

In a game between Riga and Berlin P × P was tried for
the first time, a bold venture which anticipates White's desire
to open the King's file. After 7 R—K 1 Black can defend
the Kt by P—Q 4, but after 8 Kt × P White threatens again
to win the Kt by P—K B 3, besides attacking the Q Kt a
second time. However, Black has a surprising answer in
readiness. He initiates a violent counter attack which keeps
White busy until Black, by castling, escapes the dangers
of the double pin. (Compare Game No. 17.)

| | | |
|---|---|---|
| 6. | ......... | P—Q Kt 4 |
| 7. | B—Kt 3 | P—Q 4 |
| 8. | P—Q R 4 | |

This gives Black an opportunity of disposing of his Q Kt
by exchanging it, thereby enabling him to round off his pawn
position by P—Q B 4, at the same time threatening to cut off

the Bishop by P—B 5. 8 P×P followed by P—B 3 is the natural continuation, as shown in the first part of this book, because the Bishop, retreating to B 2, can operate on a useful diagonal.

8. ......... Q Kt×P !

Q R—Kt 1 would not be so good, because White obtains an open file for his Rook. The move in the text is an absolutely valid defence, as was proved by Schlechter in his match against Lasker.

9. Kt×Kt    P×Kt
10. Kt—B 3

P×P and P—B 3 seems a more natural continuation.

10. .........    Kt×Kt

Not P×Kt, on account of B×P.

11. P×Kt    P—Q B 4
12. R P×P    B—K 2

in order to castle in reply to B—R 4.

13. Q—B 3

Here White should have got back his second pawn by P×Q P. If then 13...P—B 5 ; 14 B—R 4, Castles ; 15 P×P, B×P, White plays P—Q B 3, providing a retreat for his R or B. After the move in the text this manœuvre becomes impossible, because the B after P—B 3 can be attacked twice but has lost the support of the Queen.

13. .........    B—K 3
14. R×P    Castles
15. P×P    P—B 5
16. B—R 2

Now the Bishop is hemmed in permanently ; in other words, Black is a piece up and must win easily. Therefore 16 B—R 4 was compulsory in order to get at any rate three pawns for the piece, thus : 16...B—Q 2 ; 17 Q×P, R×R ; 18 P×R, B×B ; 19 Q×P.

16. .........    R×R
17. P×R    Q—R 4
18. B—Kt 1    P—B 6
19. Q—Kt 3

White tries to work up an attack on the King's side while Black is still occupied on the other wing.

| 19. ......... | R—B 1 |
|---|---|
| 20. P—B 4 | B—K B 4 |
| 21. R—K 1 | B—B 3 |
| 22. K—R 1 | |

In order to answer B×Q P by 23 B—K 3 and P—R 7, 22...Q×P is not feasible because of Q×P.

| 22. ......... | P—R 3 |
|---|---|
| 23. P—R 3 | R—Kt 1 |
| 24. B—K 3 | Q×P |
| 25. R—Q 1 | Q—R 8 |
| 26. Q—K 1 | |

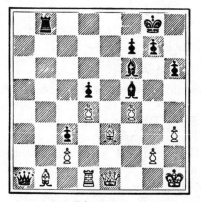

Diag. 121.

The sequel forms an instructive example of how superior development can afford winning chances even when there is no immediate prospect of material gain. The opposing pieces are gradually constricted until the defending lines are weakened by compulsory pawn moves. In the present position Black quietly sets to work to bring his Bishops to bear on the White King.

| 26. ......... | B—K 5 |
|---|---|
| 27. K—R 2 | B—K 2 |
| 28. Q—B 1 | |

to free his game somewhat with P—B 5, which Black prevents at once.

| 28. | ......... | P—B 4 |
| 29. | R—K 1 | B—R 5 |

Being probably short of time, Black makes a few irrelevant moves. If his aim was not the opening of the K Kt file but the subsequent sacrifice of the Queen, he might have played Q—Kt 7 at once, followed by Q—Kt 4.

| 30. | P—Kt 3 | B—K 2 |
| 31. | B—B 2 | B—Q 3 |
| 32. | R—B 1 | K—R 2 |
| 33. | R—K 1 | R—Kt 3 |
| 34. | R—B 1 | B—R 6 |
| 35. | R—K 1 | Q—Kt 7 |
| 36. | Q—K 2 | R—Kt 5 |
| 37. | R—Kt 1 | R—Kt 3 |

Otherwise White might embark upon a counter attack, beginning with P—Kt 4. Now this is impossible on account of R—Kt 3.

| 38. | R—K 1 | Q—Kt 4 |
| 39. | Q—R 5 | |

After the exchange of Queens, Black would win easily by R—Kt 7. 39 B—R 2 also fails on account of Q×Q ; 40 R×Q, R—Kt 7 ; 41 B—Kt 3, B—Q 6 ! ; 42 R—K 5, B×P, and the passed pawn costs a Rook. With the text move, White provokes the sacrifice of the Queen at Kt 8, apparently not seeing the fine continuation at Black's disposal on the forty-first move.

| 39. | ......... | Q×B ! |
| 40. | R×Q | R×R |
| 41. | P—Kt 4 | |

Compulsory. B—Kt 1 would be followed by R—Q B 8, etc.

| 41. | ......... | B—B 8 ! ! |
| | Resigns. | |

There might follow 42 K—Kt 3, P—Kt 3 ; 43 Q—R 4, B×P ch ; 44 K×B, P—Kt 4 ch, and so on. 41...B—Q 3 would have given White a little respite, though his game would still have been hopeless after P×P and R—K 8.

## GAME No. 15

White : Aljechin.            Black : Niemzowitsch.
Ruy Lopez (see p. 41).

| | | |
|---|---|---|
| 1. | P—K 4 | P—K 4 |
| 2. | Kt—K B 3 | Kt—Q B 3 |
| 3. | B—Kt 5 | P—Q R 3 |
| 4. | B—R 4 | Kt—B 3 |
| 5. | Castles | Kt × P |
| 6. | P—Q 4 | P—Q Kt 4 |
| 7. | B—Kt 3 | P—Q 4 |
| 8. | P × P | B—K 3 |
| 9. | P—B 3 | B—K 2 |
| 10. | R—K 1 | |

Diag. 122.

This is one of the most important positions in the Ruy
Lopez. Black has the better development, but his centre is
less secure. Whilst White has a pawn secured in the centre,
Black has a Knight there which will soon be driven away.
White's Q 4, the basis of his centre, is entirely in his hands,
while Black's Q 4 is exposed to a steady pressure by the White
pieces. Finally Black's Q Kt is unfavourably placed, obstructing as it does the Q B P and preventing it from falling
into line with its fellows. In Petrograd, 1909, Lasker tried the

following new defence : Kt—B 4 followed by B—Kt 5, giving up the moves gained before in order to relieve the pressure on the Black Q P and to exchange the same ultimately at Q 5. The various possibilities of the position have been discussed in connection with Diag. **22.** It may be added that after 10...Castles ; Q Kt—Q 2 is surely a better move than the usual Kt—Q 4, as the Queen's side should be developed before undertaking an attack (11...Q—Q 2 ? ; 12 Kt × B, followed by R × Kt). For a long time it was thought that after Kt—Q 4 Black had to exchange Knights, which enables White to make the pawn at Q B 7 " backward " by B—K 3. For Black must first play P—K R 3 to guard his Kt against the threat of P—B 3 and P—K R 4. However, a sensational innovation which refutes the Kt's move was introduced in Breslau in 1912. It is the following sacrifice : 10...Castles ; 11 Kt—Q 4, Kt×K P ! ; 12 P—B 3, B—Q 3 ! ! ; 13 P×Kt, B—Kt 5 ! ! ; 14 Q—Q 2, Q—R 5 with an overpowering attack.

| | |
|---|---|
| 10. ......... | Kt—B 4 |
| 11. B—B 2 | B—Kt 5 |
| 12. Q Kt—Q 2 | Castles |
| 13. Kt—Kt 3 | Kt—K 5 |

Here Lasker played Kt—K 3 against Janowski (Paris, 1912), but it proved to be inferior, because 14 Q—Q 3 disorganises Black's King's side forcibly.

The move in the text is not really a pawn sacrifice. After 14 B × Kt, P × B ; 15 Q × Q, Q R × Q ; 16 K Kt—Q 4, Kt × Kt ; 17 Kt × Kt, R—Q 4, White cannot play 18 R × P, because of P—Q B 4 ; 19 Kt—B 2, B—B 4 or 19 Kt—B 3, R—Q 8 ch ; 20 Kt—K 1, B—B 4 ; 21 R—K 2, B—Q 6 ; 22 R—K 3, B—Kt 4.

| | |
|---|---|
| 14. B—B 4 | P—B 4 |
| 15. P×P *e.p.* | Kt × P (B 3) |
| 16. Q—Q 3 | Kt—K 5 ? |

This loses the Q B P, and weakens the Q P. Black might have tried B × Kt; 17 Q × B, B—Q 3. It would then have been possible to support the Q P by P—B 3 after moving the Kt away. If Black was anxious to preserve his two Bishops he would even have risked P—Kt 3. After 17 B—R 6, R—B 2, the Bishop could have been driven away again by the K Kt from Kt 1 or Kt 5. The open file offered some compensation and chances of counter attack.

|     |        |        |
| --- | ------ | ------ |
| 17. | B × P  | Q—Q 2  |

Not Q × B because of Q × P ch.

|     |        |         |
| --- | ------ | ------- |
| 18. | Kt—K 5 | Kt × Kt |
| 19. | B × Kt | B—R 5   |

R × P is bad because of 20 R × Kt, B—K B 4; 21 Q—Kt 3.

|     |        |       |
| --- | ------ | ----- |
| 20. | B—Kt 3 | B × B |
| 21. | R P × B | B—B 4 |

Now R × P! was feasible with a level game after : 22 R × Kt, B—B 4! 23 K × R, B × R; 24 Q any, Q—B 4 ch, followed by B × B. After missing this chance, Black soon loses the game.

|     |         |            |
| --- | ------- | ---------- |
| 22. | Q—Q 4   | K R—Q 1    |
| 23. | Q R—Q 1 | Q—Q B 2    |
| 24. | Kt—Q 2  | Kt × K B P |

A last and desperate attempt. Black obtains Rook and pawn against two minor pieces, but has no time to initiate an attack with the Rooks. The wisest plan was to give up the P, with a view to effecting the exchange of the minor pieces, because an ending with Queen and Rooks generally produces a draw. Black could not play Kt × Kt P instead of the move in the text because of 25 B—Kt 3 !.

|     |          |          |
| --- | -------- | -------- |
| 25. | B × B    | Kt × R   |
| 26. | R × Kt   | Q × Kt P |
| 27. | B—K 6 ch | K—R 1    |
| 28. | B × P    | Q R—B 1  |
| 29. | Kt—K 4   | Q—R 5    |
| 30. | P—Q Kt 3 | R—B 3    |

White now obtains a passed pawn, and a speedy win.

| | | |
|---|---|---|
| 31. | Q—B 2 | Q—R 4 |
| 32. | Q—B 3 | Q×Q |
| 33. | P×Q | P—Kt 3 |
| 34. | R—Q 2 | R—Kt 3 |
| 35. | P—Q B 4 | P×P |
| 36. | P×P | R—Kt 8 ch |
| 37. | K—B 2 | P—Q R 4 |
| 38. | P—B 5 | R—Q B 8 |
| 39. | P—B 6 | K—Kt 2 |
| 40. | B—B 4 ! | R×B |
| 41. | R×R | R×P |
| 42. | R—Q 7 ch | K—R 3 |
| 43. | K—Kt 3 | R—B 5 |
| 44. | Kt—B 2 | K—Kt 4 |

Mate was threatened by: 45 Kt—Kt 4 ch, K—R 4; 46 R—Q 5 ch, P—Kt 4; 47 R—Q 6 and R—R 6 mate (or if R×Kt ch, P×R mate).

| | | |
|---|---|---|
| 45. | R—Q 5 ch | K—B 3 |
| 46. | R×P | Resigns |


## GAME No. 16

White : Yates.        Black : Gunsberg.

### Ruy Lopez.

| | | |
|---|---|---|
| 1. | P—K 4 | P—K 4 |
| 2. | Kt—K B 3 | Kt—Q B 3 |
| 3. | B—Kt 5 | P—Q R 3 |
| 4. | B—R 4 | Kt—B 3 |
| 5. | Castles | Kt×P |
| 6. | P—Q 4 | P—Q Kt 4 |
| 7. | B—Kt 3 | P—Q 4 |
| 8. | P×P | B—K 3 |
| 9. | P—Q B 3 | B—K 2 |
| 10. | B—K 3 | |

in order to exchange the Black Knight if played to B 4.

| | | |
|---|---|---|
| 10. | ......... | Castles |
| 11. | Q Kt—Q 2 | |

If Q—Q 3, then Kt—R 4 ; 12 Q Kt—Q 2, P—Q B 4.

|  | | |
|---|---|---|
| 11. ......... | Kt × Kt |

This furthers White's development, and should not be played unless there is no other move available. To be considered are P—B 4 and B—K Kt 5. An argument against P—B 4 is that White can deprive Black's weak centre pawn of one protecting piece (12 P×P *e.p.*, Kt×P (B 3) ; 13 Kt— Kt 5), and experience has shown that White obtains the superior game.

| 12. Q × Kt | Kt—R 4 |
|---|---|
| 13. B—B 2 | Kt—B 5 |

A very dangerous manœuvre, as White can evade the exchange of his Bishop and the Black Kt does not get back in time for the defence of the K side, where White's attack becomes virulent. He should have played P—Q B 4 followed by Kt—B 3.

| 14. Q—Q 3 | P—Kt 3 |
|---|---|
| 15. B—R 6 | Kt × Kt P |
| 16. Q—K 2 | R—K 1 |
| 17. Kt—Q 4 | |

Black had probably anticipated that White would be content with regaining his pawn by B×P, but, with fine positional insight, he retains his Bishop for the coming onslaught and speedily concentrates his forces on the K side ; whilst Black, who has won a pawn at the expense of several moves, cannot mobilise an equivalent number of pieces in time for the defence.

| 17. ......... | Kt—B 5 |
|---|---|
| 18. P—B 4 | B—Q 2 |

White was threatening 19 Kt—B 6, 20 Kt × B, 21 B—Kt 5, 22 B—B 6 ; 18...Q—Q 2 is not sufficient, as 19 P—B 5 would follow. Neither can 18...B—Q B 4 be played because of 19 B—Kt 5, Q—B 1 ; 20 B—B 6. Preferable to the text move seems B—K B 1 (19 B—Kt 5, Q—B 1 ; 20 B—B 6, B—Kt 2), as then the Black pieces have more freedom of action.

19. Q R—K 1          P—Q B 4
20. P—K 6

A brilliant sacrifice to which no satisfactory reply can be
found.  For instance, 20…P×Kt ;  21 Q—Kt 4, Kt—K 6 ,
22 R×Kt, P×R ;  23 P—B 5, B×P ;  24 P×B, P×P ,
25 B×P, etc. ; or 24…R—K B 1 ; 25 P×P ch, R×P ; 26 Q—
K 6, Q—K 1 ; 27 B×P, etc. ; or 23…P—Kt 4 ; 24 P×P ch,
K×P ; 25 Q—R 5 ch, K—Kt 1 ; 26 P—B 6, B×P ; 27 B×
P, etc. ; or 21…B—B 4 ; 22 P×P ch, K×P ; 23 B×P ch,
P×B ; 24 P—B 5, etc.  There are many variations, all leading to a speedy end.

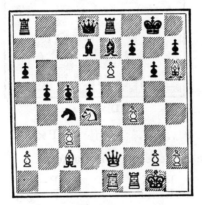

Diag. 123.

20. ………          B—K B 3
21. Q—Kt 4          P×Kt
22. P—B 5          P—Q 6
23. B×P          B×K̃ P

If P×K P then 24 P×Kt P, Kt—K 4 ; 25 R×Kt, B×R ;
26 Q—R 5, Q—B 3 ; 27 R×Q, B×R ; 28 P×P ch, K—R 1 ;
29 Q—B 7, etc. ; or 26…B×P ; 27 B—B 8, etc.

24. P×B          Q—Kt 3 ch
25. K—R 1          Resigns.

## GAME No. 17

White : Berlin.          Black : Riga.
Ruy Lopez.

Move 1–6 as in Game No. 16.

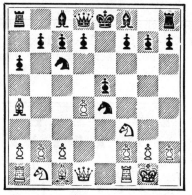

Diag. 124.

6. .........                    P × P

Compare note to move No. 6 in Game 14.

    7. R—K 1                 P—Q 4
    8. Kt × P                 B—Q 3

This is the key to the variation. Black threatens to obtain
a draw by perpetual check through B × P ch, followed by
Q—R 5 ch and Q × P ch. This is not good enough against
a weaker opponent in a tournament, and a strong player
cannot afford to play the Riga defence. But that is not a
point against the variation. To prove it unsound, White has
to find a win.

    9. Kt × Kt                 B × P ch
   10. K—R 1 !

After 10 K—B 1 Black has a tremendous attack, and drives it
home before White can manage to bring his extra piece into
play. A game Maroczy-Berger (Vienna, 1908) is an illustration of this. It continued in this way : 10 K—B 1, Q—R 5 ;

11 B—K 3, Castles ; 12 Kt—Q 4, B—Kt 5 ; 13 Kt—K B 3,
Q—R 4. Now White has no satisfactory continuation.
14 Kt—Q 2 obstructs the Queen, and it is difficult to bring
the Rooks into concerted action. 14 Kt—B 3, Q R—Q 1 ;
15 Q—Q 3, B×Kt ; 16 P×B, Q×P ; 17 Kt×Kt, P×Kt ;
18 Q—B 3, Q—R 6 ch ; 19 K—K 2, Q—Kt 5 ch ; 20 K—B 1,
R—Q 4 ; 21 B—Kt 3, R—K R 4 ; 22 P—B 3, P×P ;
Resigns.

| 10. ......... | Q—R 5 |

It now looks as if White were lost. But a fine sacrifice forces
the exchange of all Black's attacking pieces, and saves the
situation.

| 11. R×Kt ch | P×R |
| 12. Q—Q 8 ch | Q×Q |
| 13. Ǩt×Q ch | K×Ǩt |
| 14. K×B ...... | |

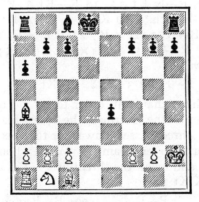

Diag. 125.

After the terrible slaughter, the position is somewhat
clearer. Black has a Rook and two pawns for two minor
pieces, a slight advantage for the end-game, but as yet there
is no thought of an end-game. White, in possession of two
Bishops, with an open Queen's file on which the Black King
stands, has good attacking chances, and most masters would
think the position favourable for White.

| 14. ......... | B—K 3 |

P—K B 4 is a plausible move, but is followed by a pretty mate by 15 B—Kt 5. The move in the text threatens to eliminate the K B by P—Q B 4, P—Q Kt 4.

15. B—K 3          P—K B 4
16. Kt—B 3         K—K 2
17. P—K Kt 4

Tarrasch recommends 17 R—Q 1, threatening Kt—Q 5 ch. If P—B 3, White could play 18 B—Kt 6, thereby permanently preventing Black from contesting the Queen's file, and then try to exchange Black's B by Kt—K 2—Q 4. With two Bishops, White would then have winning chances.

A subtle idea underlies White's move of P—K Kt 4. He wishes to take advantage of the fact that Black has exchanged the K B by playing P—Kt 5, thus holding all the four pawns on the King's side. But Black finds a surprising reply, which seems to refute White's plan.

Capablanca played against Ed. Lasker (New York, 1915), 17 P—K Kt 4, P—K Kt 3 ;  18 K—Kt 3, P—K R 4 ;    19 P × B P, P—R 5 ch ;  20 K—R 2, P × P ;  21 Kt—K 2, P—Kt 4 ; 22 B—Kt 3, B × B ; 23 R P × B, K R—K Kt 1 ; 24 R—Q 1, Q R—Q 1 ;  25 R × R, K × R ;  26 Kt—K 4, winning a pawn.

17. .........    P—K Kt 3     18. P—Kt 5    Q R—K Kt 1 ! ı

Black offers the exchange in order to get rid of White's Q B. If White accepts the sacrifice, he loses his K Kt P, and Black retains three passed pawns for the piece, at least an equivalent for the end-game. White should decline the doubtful gift and meet the threat of P—R 3 and P—K Kt 4 with 19 R— K Kt 1.

19. B—Q 4         P—R 3       20. B—B 6 ch    K—B 2
21. B × R          R × B        22. R—Q 1

in order to play 23 B—Q 7 in answer to P—B 4. This explains White's check at move 20.

22. .........    P × P ch        23. K—Kt 2    K—B 3 !

If now 24 Kt—Q 5 ch, Black would assail the White King with K—K 4 ; 25 Kt × P, B—B 5—K 7—B 6. The Black phalanx of pawns becomes menacing.

24. B—Kt 3      B × B
25. R P × B    K—K 3       26. P—Kt 4    R—R 2

Black need no longer fear to exchange Rooks, for he would then threaten the Queen's side pawns with his King whilst the passed pawns kept the White forces occupied.

|     |            |          |
| --- | ---------- | -------- |
| 27. | Kt—K 2     | R—Q 2    |
| 28. | Kt—Q 4 ch  | K—B 3    |
| 29. | P—Q B 3    | P—B 3    |

The aim of this move is not clear.  Black should adopt a forward policy with P—Kt 5, P—B 5, R—R 2, etc.

|     |          |         |
| --- | -------- | ------- |
| 30. | R—K R 1  | P—Kt 5  |
| 31. | R—R 8    |         |

Now none of the pawns can advance :  P—B 5 would be answered by 32 R—K 8, R—K 2 ; 33 R × R, K × R ; 34 Kt—Kt 3 and one of the pawns is lost.

|     |           |         |
| --- | --------- | ------- |
| 31. | .........  | R—K 2   |
| 32. | Kt—K 2    | R—Q 2   |
| 33. | Kt—Q 4    | R—K 2   |
| 34. | R—B 8 ch  | K—Kt 2  |
| 35. | R—Q 8     | P—B 5   |
| 36. | R—Q 6     | K—B 2   |
| 37. | Kt—B 2    | R—K 3   |
| 38. | R—Q 7 ch  | R—K 2   |
| 39. | R—Q 6     | R—K 3   |
| 40. | R—Q 1     |         |

White tries to win at all costs—and loses.  By a forcible advance on the Queen's side, he creates new chances, but also new weaknesses.

|     |          |         |
| --- | -------- | ------- |
| 40. | .........  | K—B 3   |
| 41. | P—B 4    | R—K 2   |
| 42. | R—Q 4    | K—Kt 4  |
| 43. | R—Q 6    | P—K 6 ! |
| 44. | P—B 3    |         |

P × P fails on account of P—B 6 ch and R—R 2.

|     |          |         |
| --- | -------- | ------- |
| 44. | .........  | P—K 7   |
| 45. | Kt—K 1   | P—Kt 6  |
| 46. | P—Kt 5   |         |

Too late.

|     |          |        |
| --- | -------- | ------ |
| 46. | .........  | R—R 2  |
| 47. | P × B P  | P × P  |

| | | |
|---|---|---|
| 48. | R—K 6 | R—R 7 ch |
| 49. | K—Kt 1 | R—B 7 |
| 50. | Kt—B 2 | R×P |
| 51. | R×K P | R—Q 6 |
| 52. | Kt—K 1 | R—Kt 6 |
| 53. | R—Q 2 | P—B 6 |
| 54. | Kt—Q 3 | P—R 4 |
| | Resigns | |

The R P cannot be prevented from pushing on to R 6, after which a mate is threatened by the Black R on the eighth rank. R—Q 1 would then be compulsory. But that lets the Black Rook in on the seventh (K R—R 7, followed by P—B 7 ch).

## GAME No. 18.

### Emanuel Lasker.  Capablanca.

Ruy Lopez (see p. 37)

| | | |
|---|---|---|
| 1. | P—K 4 | P—K 4 |
| 2. | Kt—K B 3 | Kt—Q B 3 |
| 3. | B—Kt 5 | P—Q R 3 |
| 4. | B×Kt | Q P×B |
| 5. | P—Q 4 | P×P |

Worthy of consideration is : 5...B—K Kt 5 ; 6 P × P, Q × Q ch ; 7 K × Q, Castles ch ; 8 K—K 2, R—K 1 ; 9 P— K R 3, B × Kt ch ; 10 K × B, P—B 3 ; with a good game. In this opening Black is justified in assuming the initiative, as the exchange, which has opened a diagonal for his Q B, has furthered his development. If he does not do so, and confines himself to defending tamely, the chances are that he will lose on account of White's majority of pawns on the King's side.

| | | |
|---|---|---|
| 6. | Q×P | Q×Q |

Compulsory. If B—K 3 instead, 7 B—B 4 attacks Q B 7. B—Q 3 in reply to that would be inferior. By exchanging Bishops White would render the Black Q P " backward," and on the open file its capture would be inevitable.

| | | |
|---|---|---|
| 7. | Kt×Q | B—Q 3 |
| 8. | Kt—Q B 3 | Kt—K 2 |

Black prepares to castle on the King's side. It is more usual, and probably stronger, to castle on the Queen's side, as the King then protects the Q B P, which in the present case would be weak if Black's K B were to be exchanged.

9. Castles          Castles.
10. P—B 4          R—K 1

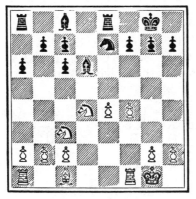

Diag. 126.

Black allows his opponent too much latitude on the King's wing. He should prevent White's P—B 5, which obstructs his Q B, by P—K B 4. After P—K 5 the game would be equalised by B—B 4, B × Kt, and B—K 3.

A draw would then be practically certain, with the Bishops of opposite colours. Black probably thought White would not risk weakening his K P by P—B 5. But with unfailing judgment Lasker foresees that, in consequence of the greater mobility of his pieces, his attack will be successful before a counter attack on the weak K P can be instituted.

11. Kt—Kt 3          P—B 3

Even now P—K B 4 was imperative, though it would keep the Bishop from that square. The continuation could have been 12 P—K 5, B—Kt 5; 13 Kt—K 2 (or R 4), Kt—Q 4, and the Bishop is safe.

12. P—B 5 ! !

This move has a twofold aim. It shuts in the Bishop, and allows B—B 4, exchanging the Black Q B.

12. .......... P—Q Kt 3

The diagonal Q R 1—K R 8 is the only one in which the Bishop has any prospects of action. However, as soon as he relinquishes his present diagonal, a White Knight settles at K 6 and the Black Rooks are very much hampered.

13. B—B 4        B—Kt 2

Black should have exchanged the Bishops. Now he gets a weak pawn at Q 3. Before playing B—Kt 2, P—B 4 should be played to prevent the Knight getting from Kt 3—Q 4—K 6.

| | |
|---|---|
| 14. B×B | P×B |
| 15. Kt—Q 4 | Q R—Q 1 |
| 16. Kt—K 6 | R—Q 2 |
| 17. Q R—Q 1 | Kt—B 1 |
| 18. R—B 2 | P—Q Kt 4 |
| 19. K R—Q 2 | |

This holds Black's Kt at B 1. White's next move prevents the Bishop getting into action by P—B 4. After depriving all the Black pieces of their mobility, White turns his attention to a determined assault on the Black King.

| | |
|---|---|
| 19. .......... | Q R—K 2 |
| 20. P—Q Kt 4 | K—B 2 |
| 21. P—Q R 3 | B—R 1 |
| 22. K—B 2 | R—R 2 |
| 23. P—Kt 4 | P—R 3 |
| 24. R—Q 3 | P—Q R 4 |
| 25. P—K R 4 | P×P |
| 26. P×P | R (R 2)—K 2 |

There are no prospects on the Rook's file, and Black is restricted to keeping his pieces mutually protected. He cannot prevent White from penetrating the King's side.

| | |
|---|---|
| 27. K—B 3 | R—Kt 1 |
| 28. K—B 4 | P—Kt 3 |
| 29. R—Kt 3 | P—Kt 4 ch |
| 30. K—B 3 | |

If Black captures the pawn, he would lose it again forthwith through White's R—R 3, and the pawn at R 3 would also be captured.

| 30. ......... | Kt—Kt 3 |
| 31. P×P | R P×P |
| 32. R—R 3 | R—Q 2 |
| 33. K—Kt 3 | |

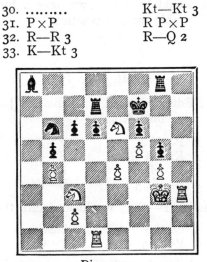

Diag. 127.

The White King leaves the diagonal because Black's P—B 4 would interfere with the combination by which White intends to annihilate Black's game in a few moves.

| 33. ......... | K—K 1 |
| 34. Q R—K R 1 | B—Kt 2 |
| 35. P—K 5 !! | |

A beautiful final stroke.

| 35. ......... | Q P × P |
| 36. Kt—K 4 !! | Kt—Q 4 |
| 37. Kt (K 6)—B 5 | B—B 1 |

Black dares not move the Rook on account of Kt × B and Kt—Q 6 ch.

| 38. Kt × R | B × Kt |
| 39. R—R 7 ch | R—B 1 |
| 40. R—R 1 | K—Q 1 |
| 41. R—R 8 ch | B—B 1 |
| 42. Kt—B 5 | Resigns. |

Mate in two is threatened. Black's only move is Kt—K 2,

after which he is helpless, and White can capture the pawns one by one at his leisure (R—B 7, etc.).   In this game, so beautifully engineered by White, we have a further example of Lasker's remarkable grasp of position.

## GAME No. 19

White : Eduard Lasker.          Black : Janowski.
Four Knights' Game.

|     |           |           |
| --- | --------- | --------- |
| 1.  | P—K 4     | P—K 4     |
| 2.  | Kt—K B 3  | Kt—Q B 3  |
| 3.  | Kt—B 3    | Kt—B 3    |
| 4.  | B—Kt 5    | B—Kt 5    |

B—K 2 ; 5 Castles, P—Q 3 ; would lead into the Ruy Lopez.

|     |         |         |
| --- | ------- | ------- |
| 5.  | Castles | Castles |
| 6.  | P—Q 3   | P—Q 3   |

It is, of course, better to castle before playing P—Q 3, as the opponent could at once play Kt—Q 5 and utilise the pin to initiate an immediate attack, e.g. 5 Castles, P—Q 3 ; 6 Kt—Q 5, B—B 4 ; 7 P—Q 4, P×P ; 8 B—Kt 5.

7. B—Kt 5

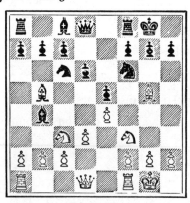

Diag. 128.

The position is not unlike that in Diagram 90, and the same remarks apply to it.   Here B—K 3 is inadvisable,

because P—Q 4, threatening to fork two pieces, forces the exchange of Black's centre pawn. After 7...B—Kt 5; 8 Kt—Q 5,
Kt—Q 5; 9 B—B 4, B—B 4, on the other hand, we get the
position discussed on p. 115, in which White obtains the advantage by Q—Q 2. Instead of 9...B—B 4, Black should
play Q—Q 2 with a similar threat. But he has not the co-
operation of his King's Bishop for the attack, and White just
manages to escape with a draw, *e.g.* 9...Q—Q 2; 10 Kt × Kt ch,
P × Kt; 11 B × P, P—K R 3 (B × Kt; 12 P × B, Q—R 6 fails on
account of K—R 1 and R—K Kt 1); 12 P—B 3, Kt × Kt ch;
13 P × Kt, B—K R 4; 14 K—R 1, K—R 2 (Diagram 129);
15 R—K Kt 1.

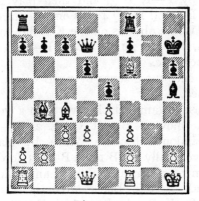

Diag. 129.

This is the saving clause. If now Black had his B at B 4, as
White has in the corresponding attack, White would first have
to protect his B P with 15 Q—K 2, and would be lost after
R—K Kt 1; 16 R—K Kt 1, R—Kt 3; as 17 B—R 4 fails
because of Q—R 6; 18 B—K Kt 3, R—B 3; and on the
other hand, after 17 R × R, P × R Black plays R—K B 1,
attacking the B P a second time.

With the Black Bishop at Kt 5, however, Black does not
succeed. The continuation could be 15...R—K Kt 1; 16
R—Kt 3, R—Kt 3; 17 B—R 4, with a probable draw.

This line of play is most difficult for both sides, and it has
been avoided so far in tournaments.

In Diagram 128 the favourite continuation for many

years was : 7...B×Kt ; 8 P×B, Kt—K 2. The opening of
the K Kt file by 9 B×K Kt is not to be feared, because of the
reasons given when discussing Diagram 90. But White obtains
the advantage with 9 Kt—R 4, preparing the opening of the
K B file by P—B 4 and P×P. 9...Kt—Kt 3, in order to retake
with the B P after 10 Kt×Kt and to open the file for Black's
Rooks, is not a sufficient reply, because after 11 P—B 4 and
P×P White has a clear advantage, having an extra pawn in
effect for the end-game. For the three Black pawns on the
King's side are held by the two adverse pawns, which they
cannot pass.

The attempt to expel the troublesome Bishop after
9...Kt—K 1 by P—K B 3, and then play for a centre by
P—B 3, Kt—B 2 and P—Q 4 fails on account of the withering
attack which White obtains on the K B file, *e.g.* 9...Kt—K 1 ;
10 B—Q B 4, K—R 1 ; 11 P—B 4, P—K B 3 ; 12 Q—R 5,
P×B ; 13 P×P, etc.

In consequence the defence by 7...B×Kt and Kt—K 2 has
been abandoned.

In the present game Black reverts to a very old defence,
comprising the moves : B×Kt, Q—K 2, Kt—Q 1—K 3. It
had been abandoned because White, by playing R—K 1,
P—Q 4, and eventually B—B 1 and B—R 3, forces the exchange
of Black's centre pawn, and obtains an advantage, on well-
known grounds. Here Black strengthens the defence by
interpolating P—K R 3 !, after which White must come to a
decision as to maintaining the pin. If he decides to do so
the White Bishop will no longer be able to threaten the Black
Queen from Q R 3.

|     |           |             |
|-----|-----------|-------------|
| 7.  | .........  | B×Kt        |
| 8.  | P×B       | P—K R 3     |
| 9.  | B—K R 4   |             |

If the B retreats to B 1 or K 3, Black can adopt the defence Kt—K 2—Kt 3. Then Kt—R 4 would be inferior, because
Black can simply play P—K Kt 4. In this case the advance
of the pawns is justified, because Black can bring his Q Kt to
K Kt 3 and have practically one piece more on the King's
side, and good prospects for the attack which he can open with
K—R 2, R—K Kt 1, Kt—Kt 3—B 5.

| 9. ......... | Q—K 2 |

P—K Kt 4 would be premature. White would win at once by 10 Kt × Kt P, P × Kt ; 11 B × P, as he can attack the Knight a second time by P—K B 4 and P × P before Black can either protect it sufficiently or relieve the "pin."

| 10. Q—Q 2 | Kt—Q 1 |
| 11. P—Q 4 | B—Kt 5 |
| 12. Q—K 3 | B × Kt |
| 13. Q × B | Kt—K 3 |

It would be wrong to play for the gain of a pawn with P—K Kt 4 and P × P, e.g. 13...P—K Kt 4 ; 14 B—Kt 3, P × P ; 15 R—K 1 !, P × P ; 16 P—K 5, etc.

14. B × Kt

Black's threat was to develop an attack, similar to that described at move 9, with P—K Kt 4 and Kt—B 5.

| 14. ......... | Q × B |
| 15. Q × Q | P × Q |
| 16. B—B 4 | |

in order to exchange the Knight, which is generally superior to a Bishop in an end-game, as mentioned before.

| 16. ......... | P × P |
| 17. B × Kt | P × B |
| 18. P × P | |

Diag. 130.

In the end-game thus brought about the White Rooks have more freedom, as they can be mobilised easily on the third rank to act on either wing. Black's pawns, however, are stronger, being easily protected by the King, whilst White's weak pawns at Q R 2 and Q B 2 are at too great a distance from the King; therefore White must see to it that Black does not open files for his Rooks on the Queen's side.

|       |              |            |
| ----- | ------------ | ---------- |
| 18.   | .........    | Q R—B 1    |
| 19.   | Q R—Kt 1     | P—Kt 3     |
| 20.   | K R—Q 1      | K R—Q 1    |
| 21.   | R—Kt 3       |            |

White must now allow Black to occupy the Q B or Q file. After 21 P—Q 5 Black would simply play P×P; 22 P×P, P—B 3, with a certain draw.

|       |              |            |
| ----- | ------------ | ---------- |
| 21.   | .........    | P—Q 4      |
| 22.   | R—Kt 3 ch    |            |

P—K B 3 was the correct move here, in view of subsequent threats of mate.

|       |              |            |
| ----- | ------------ | ---------- |
| 22.   | .........    | K—B 2      |
| 23.   | P×P          | R×P        |
| 24.   | R—Q R 3      | P—Q R 4    |
| 25.   | P—K B 4 ?    |            |

A mistake under time pressure, costing a pawn. Q R—Q 3 was the move.

|       |              |            |
| ----- | ------------ | ---------- |
| 25.   | .........    | P—Q B 4    |
| 26.   | R—Q B 3      | Q R—Q 1    |
| 27.   | R—Kt 1       | R×P        |
| 28.   | R×Kt P       | R×P        |
| 29.   | P—K R 3      | R—Q 7      |
| 30.   | R—Kt 5       |            |

Not R×P, on account of R—B 7, and the K Kt P cannot be saved.

|       |              |            |
| ----- | ------------ | ---------- |
| 30.   | .........    | R—(B 5) B 7 |
| 31.   | R—K Kt 3     | P—B 4      |
| 32.   | P—B 4        | P—B 5      |
| 33.   | R—K Kt 4     | P—R 4      |
| 34.   | R—Kt 5       | R×P        |
| 35.   | P—R 4        |            |

Mate was threatened in a few moves through R—Q B 7—B 8 and R (R 7)—R 8.

| 35. ......... | R—(B 7) Kt 7 |

If now R—B 7, White would win the K B P or obtain a perpetual check (36 R—Q Kt 7 ch, followed by R—Q Kt 8— K B 8). After the move in the text, White can still draw, as he wins back his pawn.

| 36. R×R | R×R |
| 37. R×R P? | |

This careless move now loses the game. Of course White should have taken the B P. If then P—R 5, R—R 5 held the pawn from behind, also after 37...K—B 3 ; 38 R×Q R P, P— K 4, a draw would have been the result, as the White B P would soon have become threatening, e.g. 39 R—R 8, K—B 4 ; 40 P—B 5, P—K 5 ; 41 P—B 6, R—Q B 7 ; 42 R—Q B 8, K—Kt 5 ; 43 P—B 7, K×P ; 44 K—R 2, P—K 6 ; 45 R—B 8, R×P ; 46 R×P ch, K—Kt 4 ; 47 R—K 4, R—B 6 ; 48 K—Kt 3, etc. ; or 44 R—K 8, R×P ; 45 R×P, K—Kt 6 ; 46 R—K 1, R—B 7 ; 47 K—R 1, R×P ; 48 R—K 3 ch, and so on.

| 37. ......... | P—R 5 |
| 38. R×P | P—R 6 |
| Resigns. | |

After R—R 5 there follows P—R 7 and R—Kt 8 ch, or (if 40 K—R 2) P—B 6.

### GAME No. 20

White : Eduard Lasker.    Black : Englund.
Four Knights' Game.

| 1. P—K 4 | P—K 4 |
| 2. Kt—K B 3 | Kt—Q B 3 |
| 3. Kt—B 3 | Kt—B 3 |
| 4. B—Kt 5 | Kt—Q 5 |
| 5. Kt×P | |

Black can now get White's K P by playing Q—K 2, and moreover exchange White's valuable Bishop. Instead of the move in the text it is advisable to retire the Bishop to R 4 or B 4, or else to play 5 Kt×Kt, P×Kt ; 6 P—K 5, P×Kt ; 7 P×Kt. Black would then play Q×P and not P×Q P ch, as the latter move allows White to develop quickly, and Black has no time to castle—*e.g.* 8 B×P, Q×P ; 9 Castles, B—K 2 ; 10 B—B 3, followed by R—K 1

|     |          |              |
| --- | -------- | ------------ |
| 5.  | ........ | Q—K 2        |
| 6.  | Kt—B 3   | Kt×P ?       |

Diag. 131.

Here Kt×B was essential, followed by Q×P, freeing the Bishop. After 7 Kt×Kt, Q×P ch ; 8 Q—K 2, Q×Q ch ; 9 K×Q, Kt—Q 4 (10 P—B 4, P—Q R 3), Black completes his development a little later (10 R—K 1, P—K B 3 ; 11 K—B 1 ch, K—B 2), but after the exchange of Queens there is not much to fear from an immediate attack, and the value of the two Bishops soon asserts itself. In a match game Ed. Lasker—Cole (London, 1913) the continuation was 12 P—Q 4, P—Q R 3 ; 13 Kt—B 3, Kt×Kt ; 14 P×Kt, P—Q 4. Here the doubled pawn is a disadvantage, in that the pawn at B 2 is immobile, and constantly liable to be attacked by B—B 4. P—Q 3 was the better move.

|            |              |
| ---------- | ------------ |
| 7. Castles | Kt×Kt        |

Now Kt×B was no longer possible.   After Kt×Q Kt there would be threats of Kt×B P as well as of R—K 1 and P—Q 3. The game is almost lost for Black at this stage, as the King cannot escape the impending attack on the K file by castling.

| | | |
|---|---|---|
| 8. | Q P×Kt | Kt×Kt ch |
| 9. | Q×Kt | Q—B 4 |
| 10. | R—K 1 ch | B—K 2 |
| 11. | B—Q 3 | |

prevents castling, as Q—K 4 would win a piece.

| | | |
|---|---|---|
| 11. | ......... | P—Q 4 |
| 12. | B—K 3 | |

White has the development of the B gratis, as Black must lose time with the Queen.

| | | |
|---|---|---|
| 12. | ......... | Q—Q 3 |
| 13. | B—K B 4 | Q—K B 3 |
| 14. | Q×P ! ! | |

Black being behind with his development is already threatened by sacrificial combinations.   If he takes the Bishop he loses by 15 B—Kt 5 ch, K—B 1 ; 16 Q—Q 8 ch !, B×Q ; 17 R—K 8 mate, or 15...P—B 3 ; 16 B×P ch, and so on.

| | | |
|---|---|---|
| 14. | ......... | P—B 3 |
| 15. | Q—K 4 | B—K 3 |
| 16. | R—K 3 | B—Q B 4 |

Here Black might have castled on the Queen's side, but R—Q 1 would have had much the same sequel as in the actual game.

| | | |
|---|---|---|
| 17. | B—K 5 | Q—R 3 |
| 18. | R—Kt 3 | B—K B 1 |

A sorry retreat.   But after Q—Q 7, which may have been Black's original intention, White plays R—K B 1, threatening B—K B 4.

19. R—Q 1

This move completes White's development, and only seems to give Black a chance of castling.   However, Black has no satisfactory continuation.

19. .........            Castles ?
20. Q×P ch            P×Q
21. B—R 6             Mate

## GAME No. 21

White : Eduard Lasker.        Black : Aljechin.
Three Knights' Defence.

1. P—K 4            P—K 4
2. Kt—K B 3         Kt—Q B 3
3. Kt—B 3           B—Kt 5
4. Kt—Q 5

Developing another piece by B—Kt 5 or B 4 would be more in accordance with principle.

4. .........            B—K 2

There was a threat of Kt×B and Kt×P. If Black plays P—Q 3, the B must retire all the same after 5 B—Kt 5. It seems best to retire the B to K 2 rather than to B 4 or R 4, because there remains the threat of a pin subsequently by B—K Kt 5, which might become serious with the Knight at Q 5.

5. B—B 4            Kt—B 3
6. P—Q 3            P—Q 3
7. Kt×B             Q×Kt
8. P—B 3            P—K R 3

The K Kt is to support the advance of P—Q 4 subsequently, and that is why Black does not want to allow it to be pinned. This is sound strategy, since White has exchanged his Q Kt, which from B 3 prevents P—Q 4 in the ordinary way.

9. B—K 3            Castles
10. Q—Q 2           B—K 3
11. B—Kt 3

The first mistake. B—Q Kt 5 should be played to retard P—Q 4.

| 11. ......... | B×B |
| 12. P×B | P—Q 4 |

Diag. 132.

### 13. P×P

The second mistake. Unimportant as it seems, it leads to the loss of the game. White did not defend the pawn by Q—B 2, because it would have proved 10 Q—Q 2 to have been a lost move. But giving up the centre is a far greater evil. Black now commands his Q 5 and K B 5, and this enables him to start an attack to which there is no defence. The game shows conclusively how important it is to maintain the centre.

| 13. ......... | Kt×P |
| 14. Castles K R | P—B 4 |
| 15. P—Q Kt 4 | P—Q Kt 3 |
| 16. Q—K 2 | |

to prevent P—K 5, which would now be countered by P×P and Q—B 4. However, as P—K 5 cannot be prevented permanently, and the Q must move in any case, Q—B 2 would have been the better move, as there the Queen cannot be molested by a Rook.

| 16. ......... | Q—Q 3 |
| 17. P—Kt 5 | Q Kt—K 2 |
| 18. B—Q 2 | Kt—Kt 3 |
| 19. R—R 4 | Q R—K 1 ! |

Black's game is beautifully developed, whilst White cannot make a combined effort. The Black Rooks are particularly well placed, and threaten to take an effective part in the attack in various ways. All this is the outcome of White losing the centre.

20. P—K Kt 3

Though this prevents Kt (Q 4)—B 5, it weakens K B 3, which is all the more serious as Black threatens to open the file by P—B 5.

20. ......... Q—Q 2

If now White refrains from taking the pawn, Black plays P—Q R 4 !

| | |
|---|---|
| 21. R×P | P—K 5 |
| 22. Kt—Q 4 | P×P |
| 23. Q×P | Kt—K 4 |
| 24. Q—K 2 | P—B 5 |

All the avenues of attack are now open, and White's game collapses quickly.

| | |
|---|---|
| 25. Q—R 5 | Kt—K B 3 |
| 26. Q—B 5 | Kt—B 6 ch |
| 27. K—R 1 | Q×Q |
| 28. Kt×Q | Kt×B |
| 29. R—Q 1 | Kt (B 3)—K5 |
| 30. Kt×P | Kt×B P ch |
| 31. K—Kt 2 | P—B 6 ch |
| Resigns. | |

GAME NO. 22

White : Forgacz.        Black : Tartakower.
French Defence (see p. 48).

| | |
|---|---|
| 1. P—K 4 | P—K 3 |
| 2. P—Q 4 | P—Q 4 |
| 3. Kt—Q B 3 | Kt—K B 3 |
| 4. B—Kt 5 | B—K 2 |
| 5. P—K 5 | Kt—K 5 |

K Kt—Q 2 is better, because it would support the advance of P—Q B 4 and also be of use eventually in an attack on White's centre by P—K B 3. The text move allows the exchange of two minor pieces, which can only be to White's advantage, as Black cannot get his Q B into play, and is for a long time practically a piece down.

6. Kt × Kt          B × B

After P × Kt the pawn would be very weak, and could hardly be held for long.

7. Kt × B          Q × Kt
8. P—K Kt 3

To be able to play P—K B 4 before developing the Kt (see p. 49).

| 8. ......... | P—Q B 4 |
|---|---|
| 9. P—Q B 3 | Kt—B 3 |
| 10. P—K B 4 | Q—K 2 |
| 11. Q—Q 2 | B—Q 2 |
| 12. Kt—B 3 | Castles K R |
| 13. B—Q 3 | P—B 5 |
| 14. B—B 2 | P—Q Kt 4 |
| 15. Castles K R | P—Kt 5 |
| 16. Q R—K 1 | P—Q R 4 |

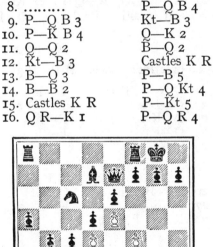

Diag. 133.

So far the game is easy to understand in the light of the remarks made on page 44, when treating of the openings. The continuation shows in an instructive fashion that White's attack is the more effective, being directed against the King's side.

17. P—B 5 !   K P×P

This sacrifice of a pawn in conjunction with a second sacrifice on the next move, produces a combination of rare beauty.

18. P—Kt 4 ! !   P×P

If Black did not capture White would. In either case the storming of the position by pawns achieves its object and the lines of attack are free for the pieces.

19. Kt—Kt 5   P—Kt 3

Now that White has made an opening for himself at K B 6, the rest is easy. 19...P—R 3 is of no avail. The sequel might have been : 20 Kt—R 7, K R—Q 1 ; 21 Kt—B 6 ch, after which White wins after either P×Kt ; 22 Q×P, or K—R 1 Kt×P.

20. R—B 6   K—Kt 2

Black gets no breathing space. If P—R 3, then 21 B×P.

| | |
|---|---|
| 21. Q R—K B 1 | B—K 1 |
| 22. Q—B 4 | Kt—Q 1 |
| 23. P—K 6 | R—R 3 |
| 24. Q—K 5 | K—R 3 |
| 25. Q R—B 5 | |

Help !

| | |
|---|---|
| 25. ......... | B P×P |
| 26. Kt—B 7 ch | Q×Kt |
| 27 R—R 5 ch | K—Kt 2 |
| 28. R×Kt P mate | |

GAME No. 23

White : Yates.   Black : Esser.
French Defence.

| | |
|---|---|
| 1. P—K 4 | P—K 3 |
| 2. P—Q 4 | P—Q 4 |
| 3. Kt—Q B 3 | Kt—K B 3 |
| 4. B—Kt 5 | P×P |
| 5. B×Kt | P×B |

If the Queen recaptures, White obtains too great an advantage in development, and therefore Black submits to the doubling of his pawns. It is doubtful if this means a handicap, although the King's side gets broken up. For Black keeps his two Bishops, a powerful weapon, unless White succeeds in developing swiftly an attack on the King's side. The present game is instructive and shows the chances afforded to both sides by the position brought about by the exchange at K B 6.

6. Kt×P        P—K B 4

As the K B obtains a long diagonal at Kt 2, this advance is justified. Otherwise there would be strong objections to it, as the pawn is likely to be subjected to attack, and apart from that, it gives up command of Black's K 4.

7. Kt—Q B 3

Kt—Kt 3 would seem more natural, firstly, because Black has weaknesses on the K side, and White will need his pieces for attack in that quarter, and secondly, because the Q P ought to be supported by P—B 3, as Black will attack it by B—Kt 2.

7. ..........        B—Kt 2
8. Kt—B 3        Castles
9. B—B 4

If now the Knight were at Kt 3, White could play P—B 3 and B Q 3. This is the proper place for the B, which might obtain an open diagonal after P—K Kt 4.

9. ..........        Kt—B 3
10. Kt—K 2        Kt—R 4
11. B—Q 3        P—B 4
12. P—B 3        P—Q B 5

P—Kt 3 seems preferable, as the text move releases the hold on White's Q 4. The isolated pawn resulting after 13 P×P is not to be feared, as the B at Kt 2 would have greater efficiency (Q R—Kt 1), and White would not be so firmly established in the centre.

13. B—B 2        P—Kt 4
14. Q—Q 2

There now ensues an interesting struggle. White builds up an attack with Q and both Knights and eventually the B (P—K Kt 4). If Black can manage to play his King into safety at R 1 in time, and then occupies the Kt file with his Rooks, he would have the better of it, his pieces having by far the greater range of action.

|      |            |        |
|------|------------|--------|
| 14.  | .........  | B—Kt 2 |
| 15.  | Q—B 4      | Q—B 3  |

K—R 1 and K R—Kt 1 might be considered.

|      |            |        |
|------|------------|--------|
| 16.  | Kt—Kt 3    | B—K R 3 |
| 17.  | Q—B 7      | Q—Q 1   |
| 18.  | Q—K 5      |         |

White gains a move by attacking the Knight's Pawn. It may seem far fetched if I now point out that this could not have happened if from the first Black had given preference to the pawn formation at Q Kt 3 and B 4 instead of Kt 4 and B 5, though the whole game would almost certainly have taken a different course. Still, when advancing a pawn into an unprotected position there always is the risk of its becoming the object of an attack at an opportune moment, and whenever the plan of development does not necessitate such moves they are best avoided.

|      |              |          |
|------|--------------|----------|
| 18.  | .........    | B—Q 4    |
| 19.  | Kt—R 5       | Kt—B 3 ? |
| 20.  | Q—Kt 3 ch ? ? |         |

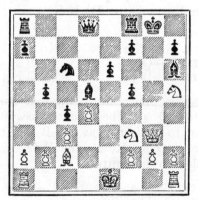

Diag. 134.

The last moves have decided the game.  Both players have overlooked that 20 Q—B 6 would have won a pawn at least (Q×Q, 21 Kt×Q ch with Kt×B and B×P).  20...B×Kt leads to an immediate loss by 21 Q×B, B×Kt ; 22 Q×B followed by P—K Kt 4 ! with an overwhelming attack.

Instead of 19...Kt—B 3, Black should have played P—B 3, followed by K—R 1 and the occupation of the Kt file by the Rooks.  White's last move allows him to do this with even greater effect.

|      |           |            |
|------|-----------|------------|
| 20.  | ......... | K—R 1      |
| 21.  | Q—R 3     | R—K Kt 1   |

Black has now a preponderance of material on the field of battle, and it can be concluded off-hand that White, not being able to bring his Rooks into play, must lose.

|      |           |        |
|------|-----------|--------|
| 22.  | Kt—Kt 3   | Q—B 3  |
| 23.  | K—B 1     |        |

K—K 2 is a shade better.  But there is no longer any adequate defence.

|      |           |              |
|------|-----------|--------------|
| 23.  | ......... | R—Kt 5       |
| 24.  | R—K 1     | Q R—K Kt 1   |
| 25.  | Kt—K 5    |              |

Black was threatening B×Kt, followed by R—R 5 and P—B 5

|      |           |          |
|------|-----------|----------|
| 25.  | ......... | Kt×Kt    |
| 26.  | P×Kt      | Q—Kt 4   |
| 27.  | Q—R 5     | B×P ch   |
| 28.  | K—Kt 1    | R×Kt ?   |

Q×Q and B—K 5 ch was simple and effective.

|      |           |        |
|------|-----------|--------|
| 29.  | R P×R     | B×R    |
| 30.  | Q×Q       | B×Q    |
| 31.  | K×B       | R—Q 1  |
| 32.  | P—B 4     |        |

R—Q 1 is much more promising, although it means the loss of a pawn (R×R and B—B 8, etc.).  With Bishops of different colour the game is not easy to win even now.

| 32. ........ | R—Q 7 |
| 33. P×B | R×B |
| 34. R—Q 1 | R×Kt P |
| 35. R—Q 7 | K—Kt 2 |
| 36. R×R P | R—Q B 7 |

He could have played P—Kt 5 at once.

| 37. R—R 5 | R—Q Kt 7 |
| 38. P—R 4 | |

R—R 3 would only have drawn out the agony a little longer.

| 38. ......... | P—Kt 5 |
| Resigns. | |

## GAME No. 24

White : Atkins.          Black : Barry.

### French Defence.

| 1. P—K 4 | P—K 3 |
| 2. P—Q 4 | P—Q 4 |
| 3. Kt—Q B 3 | Kt—K B 3 |
| 4. B—Kt 5 | B—K 2 |
| 5. P—K 5 | K Kt—Q 2 |
| 6. B×B | Q×B |

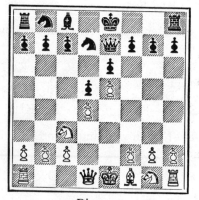

Diag. 135.

7. Kt—Kt 5

The intention is to strengthen the centre by P—Q B 3.
Though it takes a number of moves to bring the Knight into

play again, yet most of the tournament games in this variation have been won by White, mostly through a King's side
attack on the lines set out in the notes to Game No. 22.
Investigations by Alapin tend to show that this is due to the
fact that Black in all cases devoted his attention to Queen's
side operations (just as in Game No. 22 ) when he could have
utilised White's backward development, by himself starting a
counter attack on the King's side.  He can then either aim at
the White centre at once with P—K B 3, or else play P—K B 4
and prepare the advance of the K Kt P by Kt—B 3—Q 1—B 2.
These various lines of play are still under discussion.  Simple
development is probably preferable to the move in the text,
*e.g.* 7 B—Q 3, Castles ; 8 P—B 4, P—Q B 4 ; 9 Kt—B 3.

7. ......... K—Q 1

There can be no advantage in forfeiting the option of
castling unless there be no other way of getting the King into
safety and of bringing the Rooks into concerted action.  It
is obvious that otherwise the free development of pieces is
hindered, and the King is in appreciable danger, for it is easier
to open files in the centre than on the wings where the pawns
have not advanced yet.  Therefore Kt—Kt 3 is the only move
worth considering.

8. P—Q B 3 P—K B 3
9. P×P

With the Black King remaining in the centre, White has no
further interest in the maintenance of his pawn at K 5.  On
the contrary he will try to clear the centre.

9. ......... P×P
10. Q—Q 2 P—B 3
11. Ǩt—Q R 3 Kt—B 1

At this early stage it is clear that Black will have to
contend with difficulties in trying to complete his development.  The usual way (P—Q B 4) is barred on account
of the dangers to Black's King with which a clearance in the
centre is fraught.

12. Kt—B 3 B—Q 2
13. P—K Kt 3 !

As Black can force this advance at any time by playing R—K Kt 1, White decides to develop his K B at Kt 2, thereby covering his K B 3 and K R 3. The weakness of the latter squares would not be of any great moment if White were to castle on the Queen's wing. But as P—Q B 4 is necessary in order to break up the centre, castling K R is the right course.

| 13. ......... | B—K 1 |
| 14. B—Kt 2 | Q Kt—Q 2 |
| 15. P—B 4 | P×P |
| 16. Kt×P | Kt—Q Kt 3 |
| 17. Kt×Kt | P×Kt |
| 18. Castles K R | Kt—Kt 3 |
| 19. K R—K 1 | B—Q 2 |
| 20. Q—B 3 | R—K 1 |
| 21. Kt—Q 2 | Q—B 1 |
| 22. P—Q R 4 ! | |

White wishes to get rid of the pawn at Black's Kt 3, in order to break in with his Knight at B 5. Black has no means of preventing this, and soon succumbs to the overwhelming array of White forces.

| 22. ......... | Kt—K 2 |
| 23. P—R 5 | P—Q Kt 4 |
| 24. Kt—Kt 3 | Kt—Q 4 |
| 25. B×Kt | K P×B |
| 26. R×R ch | B×R |
| 27. Kt—B 5 | Q—B 2 |
| 28. R—K 1 | K—B 2 |
| 29. Q—K 3 | B—Q 2 |
| 30. Q—B 4 ch | Resigns. |

If K—Q 1, 31 Kt×P ch followed by Kt—Q 6 ch. If K—B 1 White wins by 31 Q—Q 6 and R—K 7.

## GAME No. 25

White : Emanuel Lasker.     Black : Tarrasch.
French Defence.

| 1. P—K 4 | P—K 3 |
| 2. P—Q 4 | P—Q 4 |

3. Kt—Q B 3          Kt—K B 3
4. B—Kt 5            B—Kt 5

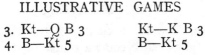

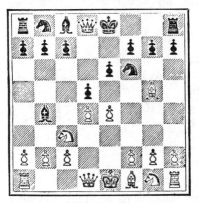

Diag. 136.

This line of defence, called the McCutcheon variation, was recommended for many years by Tarrasch as being the strongest. The most obvious continuation 5 P—K 5 leads to complications, and the final verdict has not yet been reached. After 5...P—K R 3, the best continuation is thought to be: 6 P×Kt, P×B; 7 P×P, R—Kt 1; 8 P—K R 4, P×P; 9 Q—R 5, Q—B 3; 10 Q×R P, Q×P.

White has an easy development, whilst Black, as in most variations in the French defence, finds it difficult to bring his Q B into play. After P—K R 3, it is not advisable to retire the Bishop; 6 B—R 4, P—K Kt 4; 7 B—Kt 3, for here the Bishop is out of play, and Black's King's Knight being free can play to K 5 for concerted action with Black's K B. Lasker's continuation in the present instance is at once simple and effective. It leads to an entirely different system of development.

5. P×P                Q×P

If Black recaptures with the pawn, he must lose a move with the Bishop in order to avoid getting an isolated doubled pawn after 6 Q—B 3. The doubled pawn which Black may get after the move in the text would not be isolated, and therefore not necessarily weak. It could become a weakness if Black were to castle on the King's side. But otherwise it might even become a source of strength, supporting, as it would, an advance of Black's K P against the White centre.

|  | 6. Kt—B 3 | P—B 4 ? |
|---|---|---|

Black should retain the option of castling Q R, in case White exchanges at his K B 6 ; P—Q Kt 3 and B—Kt 2 would have been better.

| 7. | B × Kt | P × B |
|----|--------|-------|
| 8. | Q—Q 2 | B × Kt |
| 9. | Q × B | Kt—Q 2 |
| 10. | R—Q 1 | R—K Kt 1 |
| 11. | P × P | Q × P |
| 12. | Q—Q 2 | Q—Kt 3 |

guarding against the mate at Q 1 before moving the Kt. But this would have been better effected by Q—K 2. After Q—Kt 3 the Knight cannot move yet because of B—Kt 5 ch.

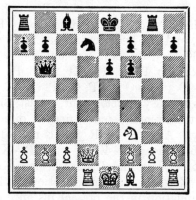

Diag. 137.

| 13. | P—B 3 | P—Q R 3 |
|-----|-------|---------|
| 14. | Q—B 2 | P—B 4 |
| 15. | P—K Kt 3 | Kt—B 4 |
| 16. | B —Kt 2 | Q—B 2 |

Black wishes to push on the K P. White, however, prevents this at once.

| 17. | Q—K 2 | P—Kt 4 |
|-----|-------|--------|
| 18. | Castles | B—Kt 2 |

The Black position has any number of weaknesses. The King cannot castle into safety ; the pawn position is full of holes, and open to attack. White takes full advantage of this and wins in masterly fashion with a few strokes.

|  | | |
|---|---|---|
| 19. | P—B 4 | P—Kt 5 |
| 20. | Q—Q 2 | R—Kt 1 |

Now White cannot capture the Kt P because of B × Kt. But he does not want the pawn, he wants the King.

|  | | |
|---|---|---|
| 21. | Q—R 6 | B × Kt |
| 22. | B × B | Q—K 4 |
| 23. | K R—K 1 | Q × P |
| 24. | Q—B 4 | Q R—B 1 |
| 25. | Q—Q 6 | P—B 3 |

Mate in two was threatened (B—B 6 ch, etc.).

|  | | |
|---|---|---|
| 26. | B—R 5 ch | R—Kt 3 |
| 27. | B × R ch | P × B |
| 28. | R × P ch | Resigns. |

## GAME No. 26

White : Capablanca.          Black : Blanco.
French Defence.

|  | | |
|---|---|---|
| 1. | P—K 4 | P—K 3 |
| 2. | P—Q 4 | P—Q 4 |
| 3. | Kt—Q B 3 | P × P |
| 4. | Kt × P | Kt—Q 2 |
| 5. | Kt—K B 3 | K Kt—B 3 |
| 6. | Kt × Kt ch | Kt × Kt |
| 7. | Kt—K 5 | |

This crosses Black's plan of developing the Q B at Kt 2.

|  | | |
|---|---|---|
| 7. | ......... | B—Q 3 |
| 8. | Q—B 3 | P—B 3 |

9 B—Kt 5 ch, P—B 3 ; 10 Kt × P was threatened.

|  | | |
|---|---|---|
| 9. | P—B 3 | Castles |
| 10. | B—K Kt 5 | B—K 2 |
| 11. | B—Q 3 | |

Whatever Black plays now, he must create some weakness in order to provide against White's Q—R 3, B×Kt, Q×R P, and White's attack must succeed. The whole of Black's plan is thus frustrated, as the only reason for abandoning the centre by P×P was the occupation of the long diagonal by the Q B. Now the Queen's side pieces cannot get into play without much difficulty, and by the time they have succeeded it is too late.

Diag. 138.

| 11. ......... | Kt—K 1 |

Intending to intercept the diagonal of the White K B by P—K B 4. If Black plays P—K Kt 3 with the same intention, White plays P—K R 4–5 and P×P, and brings the Rook into play.

| 12. Q—R 3 | P—K B 4 |

P—K R 3 would lead to an immediate disaster : 13 B×P, P×B ; 14 Q×R P, P—K B 4 ; 15 P—K Kt 4. The move in the text avoids the immediate attack on the King, but the King's Pawn is now " backward," and White immediately fastens on this weakness.

| 13. B×B | Q×B |
| 14. Castles K R | R—B 3 |
| 15. K R—K 1 | Kt—Q 3 |
| 16. R—K 2 | B—Q 2 |
| 17. Q R—K 1 | R—K 1 |
| 18. P—Q B 4 | Kt—B 2 |

|       |          |          |
|-------|----------|----------|
| 19.   | P—Q 5    | Kt × Kt  |
| 20.   | R × Kt   | P—K Kt 3 |

21 B × P was threatened.

|       |          |          |
|-------|----------|----------|
| 21.   | Q—R 4    | K—Kt 2   |
| 22.   | Q—Q 4    | P—B 4    |
| 23.   | Q—B 3    | P—Kt 3   |
| 24.   | P × P    | B—B 1    |
| 25.   | B—K 2    |          |

The Bishop now settles at Q 5, and whether Black takes the pawn or not, he is paralysed either by the pawn itself, or the pin of the Bishop if the pawn is taken.

|       |          |          |
|-------|----------|----------|
| 25.   | .........| B × P    |
| 26.   | B—B 3    | K—B 2    |
| 27.   | B—Q 5    | Q—Q 3    |
| 28.   | Q—K 3    | R—K 2    |
| 29.   | Q—R 6    | K—Kt 1   |
| 30.   | P—K R 4  |          |

The deciding manœuvre, tearing up the chain of pawns in front of the K.

|       |          |          |
|-------|----------|----------|
| 30.   | .........| P—Q R 3  |
| 31.   | P—R 5    | P—B 5    |
| 32.   | P × P    | P × P    |
| 33.   | R × B    | Resigns. |

After R × R, 34 R × R, R × R ; 35 Q × P ch wins a piece. A beautifully concise game.

## GAME No. 27

White : Niemzowitsch.          Black : Tarrasch.
French Defence.

|       |          |          |
|-------|----------|----------|
| 1.    | P—K 4    | P—Q B 4  |

This opening is called the Sicilian Defence. White, however, adopts a continuation which leads into a variation of the French Defence.

|       |          |          |
|-------|----------|----------|
| 2.    | P—Q B 3  | P—K 3    |
| 3.    | P—Q 4    | P—Q 4    |
| 4.    | P—K 5    | Kt—Q B 3 |
| 5.    | Kt—B 3   | Q—Kt 3   |
| 6.    | B—Q 3    | P × P    |

Black seeks to demonstrate that White's Q P is weak. The present game, however, seems to prove that White is able to guard it adequately, thus permanently supporting the K P too. It would therefore appear to be better to attack the K P itself, and to play P—B 3 on the fifth move. Now B—Q 2 would be better than the text move. As White cannot give further support to his Q 4, he would have to play P × P, and the protection of the K 5 would have to be undertaken by pieces, which is not desirable.

7. P × P           B—Q 2

Not Kt × P, 8 Kt × Kt, Q × Kt, because of B—Kt 5 ch.

8. B—K 2

The B cannot go to B 2 on account of Kt—Kt 5 and B—Kt 4.

8. .........           K Kt—K 2
9. P—Q Kt 3       Kt—B 4
10. B—Kt 2

Now White's centre is safe from further attacks. True, White has forfeited castling, but as he dominates the King's side, where Black cannot undertake anything, there is no harm in P—Kt 3, preparatory to " artificial castling."

10. .........           B—Kt 5 ch
11. K—B 1           B—K 2

Directed against 12 P—Kt 4, driving off the Kt. Now Kt—R 5 would follow.

12. P—Kt 3           P—Q R 4

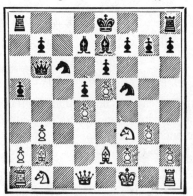

Diag. 139.

This manœuvre is unwise ; White counters with 13 P—Q R 4, a move which was necessary in any case, in order to develop the Q Kt via R 3, this being the Knight's only chance of getting into play, because.as long as the Q P is attacked three times the lines of B and Q must not be interrupted. That is a weakness in White's game, and it was necessary for Black to prevent his Kt being driven off by P—K Kt 4. P—K R 4 was the correct move. Then White also had to play P—K R 4 to prevent P—K Kt 4–5, in which case Black could have played 13...P—K Kt 3, and have brought his Rooks into concerted action. P—K Kt 3 would have been necessary before castling, because White's B—Q 3 would have attacked the K Kt. The latter could not then capture the Queen's Pawn on account of a discovered check, e.g. 12...Castles ; 13 B—Q 3, Kt × P ? ; 14 Kt × Kt, Kt × Kt ; 15 B × Kt, Q × B ? ; 16 B—R 7 ch, and Q × Q.

In Diagram 139 Black's P—Q R 4 is not only a lost move, but moreover allows a White piece to settle permanently at Q Kt 5. It also prevents the Knight from playing to Q R 4, from where White's P—Q R 4 could be answered by Kt—Kt 6 eventually.

|  |  |  |
|---|---|---|
| 13. | P—Q R 4 | R—Q B 1 |
| 14. | B—Kt 5 | Kt—Kt 5 |

All these skirmishes only result in the exchange of pieces, and as long as Black's K R is out of play this can only be of advantage to White.

|  |  |  |
|---|---|---|
| 15. | Kt—B 3 | Kt—Q R 3 |

This is in order to drive off the B. Black should have exchanged his own inactive Q B, as the White B might become effective on the Diagonal Q Kt 1—K R 7, whilst Black's Q B has no future.

|  |  |  |
|---|---|---|
| 16. | K—Kt 2 | Kt—B 2 |
| 17. | B—K 2 | B—Kt 5 |

Black cannot yet castle, because of 18 B—Q 3 Kt—K R 3, 19 B—Q B 1).

| 18. Kt—R 2 | Kt—Q R 3 |
| 19. B—Q 3 | Kt—K 2 |
| 20. R—Q B 1 | Kt—B 3 |
| 21. Kt×B | Q Kt×Kt |
| 22. B—Kt 1 | |

White's last eight moves completed his development, and his Bishops lie in wait for the attack on the Black King. Meanwhile Black has effected nothing. On the contrary, he

Diag. 140.

has exchanged his valuable K B, and also allowed his K Kt to be driven off. His King's side is bare, and castling would be fraught with danger. If Black castles now, White plays Kt—Kt 5, and Black must weaken his position by P—R 3 or P—Kt 3, and White would advance his Kt P or R P and force an exchange, opening a file for his Rook. In consequence Black decides to forfeit castling and to bring his K R to bear on the K B file. For this also Black must first play P—R 3, and White obtains an open file by P—Kt 4—Kt 5. The sequel is shown here.

| 22. ......... | P—R 3 |
| 23. P—Kt 4 | Kt—K 2 |
| 24. R×R ch | B×R |
| 25. Kt—K 1 | |

White waits first, to see whether Black is going to castle, and meanwhile tries to exchange Black's Q Kt, which commands his Q B 2 and Q 3.

| 25. ......... | R—B 1 |
|---|---|
| 26. Kt—Q 3 | P—B 3 |
| 27. Kt × Kt | Q × Kt |
| 28. P × P | R × P |
| 29. B—B 1 | Kt—B 3 |
| 30. P—Kt 5 | P × P |
| 31. B × P | R—B 1 |
| 32. B—K 3 | Q—K 2 |
| 33. Q—Kt 4 | |

This provides against Black attempting to free his Bishop by P—K 4. Black's B—Q 2 is countered by B—Kt 6 ch. White now wins surprisingly quickly, through the greater mobility of his pieces.

| 33. ......... | Q—B 3 |
|---|---|
| 34. R—Kt 1 | R—R 1 |
| 35. K—R 1 | R—R 5 |

Here Black could have held out a little longer by defending his Kt P : 35...K—B 1 ; 36 R—Kt 3, R—R 5 ; 37 Q—Q 1, K—Kt 1 ; 38 B—Kt 5, Q × P (R × P, 39 Q—R 5); 39 R—Q 3, Q × P ; 40 B × R, Q × B.

| 36. Q—Kt 3 | R × P |
|---|---|

Compulsory. B—Kt 5 was threatened, and after R—R 1, Q × P, Q × Q, R × Q, the R P wins easily.

| 37. B × R | Kt × B |
|---|---|
| 38. Q × P | Q—B 6 ch |
| 39. Q—Kt 2 | Q × Q ch |
| 40. R × Q | Kt × P |
| 41. P—R 4 | Resigns. |

## GAME No. 28

White : Alapin.        Black : Rubinstein.
Sicilian Defence.

| 1. P—K 4 | P—Q B 4 |
|---|---|

At first glance this move would seem to lose time, as it does nothing towards the main object of opening strategy, namely, the development of pieces. But we shall find that it does contribute to that aim, although indirectly. For one thing it could, by a transposition of moves, lead into an opening in which P—Q B 4 is played in any case ; in other openings it is of use, in that it acts from the first against the formation of a strong white centre. Concurrently it prepares the opening of a file for the Rooks.

2. Kt—K B 3       Kt—K B 3 ?

Black should not play Kt—K B 3 as long as White's P—K 5 means the clear gain of a move. There are plenty of developing moves to choose from.

Two systems of development can be followed by Black according to whether the K B is to develop at K 2 or Kt 2. In the first case (compare Game No. 29) P—K 3 is played. In the second case, the opening might take this course : 2...Kt—Q B 3 ; 3 P—Q 4, P×P ; 4 Kt×P, Kt—B 3 ; 5 Kt—Q B 3, P—Q 3 (not P—K Kt 3 at once, because White would exchange Knights and drive off the K Kt by P—K 5) ; 6 B—K 3, P—K Kt 3, and B—Kt 2. White's position is superior, as he has a pawn in the centre in conjunction with greater mobility. Black will find it difficult to bring his Q B into play. Nevertheless his position is compact and difficult to get at.

3. P—K 5

Undoubtedly Rubinstein had taken this move into account when playing 2...Kt—K B 3. His idea was to provoke the advance of the K P. The pawn at K 5 is weaker than at K 4, particularly as Black's Q B P prevents its natural support by P—Q 4. Moreover Black's Q 4 is free from interference by White. White refutes this ultra subtilty by simple and straightforward play, and he gets such an advantage in development that his attack succeeds before Black is able to demonstrate any weakness in White's game.

3. .........       Kt—Q 4
4. Kt—B 3       Kt × Kt
5. Q P × Kt       Kt—B 3
6. B—Q B 4       P—Q 3

After 6...P—K 3, 7 B—B 4 would restrain the Q P.

7. B—B 4       P × P

At this early stage Black has no satisfactory means of development. The Q P is attacked three times, and therefore the K P cannot move, nor can the K B be developed at Kt 2. B—Kt 5, in order to play B×Kt and P×P, is refuted by B×P ch. The move in the text which brings about the exchange of Queens, but develops another White piece at the same time, is more or less forced. It is instructive to watch how White's advantage in development soon materialises.

|      |        |          |
|------|--------|----------|
| 8.   | Kt×P   | Q×Q ch   |
| 9.   | R×Q    | Kt×Kt    |
| 10.  | B×Kt   | P—Q R 3  |

White's threat of B—Kt 5 ch could not be parried by B—Q 2 because of 11 B×P ch.

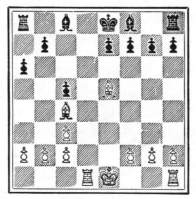

Diag. 141.

|      |         |         |
|------|---------|---------|
| 11.  | B—B 7   | B—Kt 5  |
| 12.  | P—B 3   | Q R—B 1 |
| 13.  | B—Kt 6  | B—B 4   |
| 14.  | B—Kt 3  | P—K 4   |
| 15.  | B—R 4 ch| K—K 2   |
| 16.  | P—Q B 4 |         |

Here White could have won a pawn at once by R—Q 5. If then K—K 3, 17 P—Q B 4.

|      |         |         |
|------|---------|---------|
| 16.  | ......... | P—B 3  |
| 17.  | K—B 2   | K—B 2   |
| 18.  | B—Q 7 ! | B×B     |
| 19.  | R×B ch  | B—K 2   |
| 20.  | K R—Q 1 ! |       |

The pawns can wait. 20 R×P would not have been profitable because of R—Q Kt 1.

| | |
|---|---|
| 20. ......... | K—K 3 |
| 21. R×P | B—Q 3 |

Black might have resigned here. It is only a question of time.

| | |
|---|---|
| 22. B—R 7 | R—B 3 |

Otherwise there follows R—Kt 6.

| | |
|---|---|
| 23. R×P | P—Q R 4 |
| 24. R—Kt 7 | R—R 1 |
| 25. R—Q 5 | P—R 4 |
| 26. P—Q R 4 | P—R 5 |
| 27. P—Q Kt 3 | R (R 1)—Q B 1 |
| 28. R—Kt 5 | Resigns. |

## GAME No. 29

White : Teichmann.     Black : Spielmann.

### Sicilian Defence (see p. 215).

| | |
|---|---|
| 1. P—K 4 | P—Q B 4 |
| 2. Kt—Q B 3 | P—K 3 |
| 3. K Kt—K 2 | |

This comes to the same as Kt—B 3, as after P—Q 4, P×P the Knight recaptures. If, however, Black plays P—Q 4 there is a certain advantage for White to have the Kt at K 2, e.g. 3...P—Q 4; 4 P×P, P×P; 5 P—Q 4. If now Black does not exchange pawns, White is able to bring his K B to bear on the centre after P—K Kt 3 and B—Kt 2.

| | |
|---|---|
| 3. ......... | Kt—Q B 3 |

White can exchange this Knight later on, and thus make P—K 5 possible as soon as he should deem it advisable to drive the Black Knight from his K B 3, where the same is bound to develop sooner or later. It is perhaps wise to prevent P—K 5 by Q—B 2 instead of the move in the text. This is an old defence, introduced by Paulsen. Though it retards the development of Black's minor pieces, it produces a strong defensive position, and the opening of the Q B file gives attacking chances on the Queen's side. The defence might run like this : 3...P—Q R 3 ; 4 P—Q 4, P×P ; 5 Kt×P, Q—B 2 ; 6 B—K 3, Kt—K B 3 ; 7 B—K 2, B—K 2 ; 8 Castles, P—Q Kt 4 followed by B—Kt 2, P—Q 3, Q Kt—Q 2, etc.

| 4. P—Q 4 | P×P |
|---|---|
| 5. Kt×P | P—Q R 3 |
| 6. Kt×Kt | Kt P×Kt |
| 7. B—Q 3 | P—Q 4 |
| 8. Castles | Kt—B 3 |
| 9. B—K B 4 | B—Kt 5 |

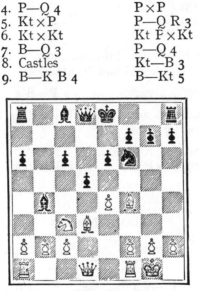

Diag. 142.

As White can force Black to play P—Kt 3, a weakening move, by P—K 5 and Q—Kt 4, Black should have played P—Kt 3 at once, so as to have Kt—R 4 in answer to P—K 5, thus keeping one piece for the defence of the King's side. The latter is in jeopardy after the move in the text, and White's attack succeeds.

| 10. P—K 5 | Kt—Q 2 |
|---|---|
| 11. Q—Kt 4 | P—Kt 3 |
| 12. K R—K 1 | P—Q B 4 |

Of course Black must not accept the sacrifice of the exchange by playing P—Q 5. After 13 Kt—K 4, B×R ; 14 Kt—Q 6 ch, K—B 1 ; 15 R×B, Black is in a mating net, from which there is no escape, as he has no time to collect sufficient forces for the defence. The move in the text does not stem the tide either, and White quickly forces the win by a beautiful combination.

|      |              |        |
|------|--------------|--------|
| 13.  | P—Q R 3      | B—R 4  |
| 14.  | B—K Kt 5     | Q—Kt 3 |

Q—B 2 leads to the same conclusion.

|      |              |        |
|------|--------------|--------|
| 15.  | P—Kt 4 !     | P×P    |
| 16.  | Kt×P         | P×Kt   |
| 17.  | P—K 6        |        |

The object of White's fifteenth move is revealed. Without it the R at K 1 would now be attacked.

|      |       |       |
|------|-------|-------|
| 17.  | ........ | P—B 4 |

Kt—B 4 fails on account of 18 P×P ch, K×P ; 19 R—K 7 ch, followed by Q—K B 4.

|      |                    |          |
|------|--------------------|----------|
| 18.  | P×Kt double ch     | K×P      |
| 19.  | B×P ch             | Resigns. |

## GAME No. 30

White : Tarrasch.        Black : Spielmann.
### Sicilian Defence.

|      |             |          |
|------|-------------|----------|
| 1.   | P—K 4       | P—Q B 4  |
| 2.   | Kt—Q B 3    | Kt—Q B 3 |
| 3.   | P—K Kt 3    |          |

Speedy development by Kt—B 3 and P—Q 4 is more desirable, as otherwise Black may have time to get a firm footing at his Q 5.

|      |          |         |
|------|----------|---------|
| 3.   | ........ | P—K Kt 3 |
| 4.   | B—Kt 2   | B—Kt 2  |

The Black Bishop is the more effective, as the line of the White Bishop is masked by the K P. Small as this advantage would seem, it becomes serious later on. It is another confirmation of the doctrine that the value of each manœuvre in the opening depends on the measure of mobility it affords for the pieces.

|      |             |        |
|------|-------------|--------|
| 5.   | K Kt—K 2    | Kt—B 3 |
| 6.   | P—Q 3       |        |

Here White could still obtain a freer game with P—Q 4. Perhaps he was afraid of losing a pawn after 6...P×P; 7 Kt×P, Kt×P. But there is nothing in it, *e.g.* 8 K Kt×Kt, Kt×Kt; 9 Kt×Q, Kt×Q; 10 Kt×B P! (Kt×Kt P? B×Kt; 11 B×B, R—Q Kt 1), K×Kt (Kt×B P?; 11 Kt×R, Kt×R; 12 Kt×P, Kt×P; 13 Kt×P), K×Kt. There was nothing else to be feared after P—Q 4.

| 6. ......... | P—Q 3 |
| 7. Castles | B—Q 2 |

in order to play Q—B 1 and B—R 6 and to exchange Bishops, after which there would be weak points at White's K R 3 and K B 3.

| 8. P—K R 3 | Castles |
| 9. B—K 3 | P—-K R 3 |

Black also prevents an exchange of Bishops.

| 10. Q—Q 2 | K—R 2 |
| 11. P—B 4 | Kt—K 1 |

The position has now become exceedingly difficult. In order to make the most of the favourable development of his K B, Black must advance on the Queen's side. But in moving his King's side pieces over to the Queen's side, Black must proceed warily, as White might get chances of an attack with overwhelming forces on the King's side.

| 12. P—K Kt 4 | Kt—B 2 |
| 13. Kt—Kt 3 | |

Here it was necessary to play R—B 2 in order to play the Q R to K B 1 before Black could manage to drive the Kt to Q 1 by P—Q Kt 4-5.

| 13. ......... | P—Q Kt 4 |
| 14. Kt—Q 1 ? | |

It would still have been better to play Q R—K 1 and to leave the Queen's side to itself as long as possible after P—Kt 5, 15 Kt—Q 1, in order to start an assault on the King's side with P—B 5, P—K R 4, and P—Kt 5. After the text move the Queen's Rook remains shut in.

| 14. ......... | Q R—Kt 1 |
| 15. Kt—K 2 | |

in order to play P—B 3 and P—Q 4.  The whole plan, however, is inconsequent, as he has started an attack on the
King's side.  Now he suddenly opens up files on the Queen's
side where Black has assembled superior forces.  The result
is that White gets into trouble on both wings, for as soon as he
gives up his King's side attack, the advanced pawns there,
as one knows, are only a source of weakness.

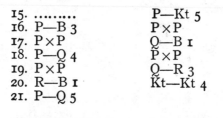

| 15. | ......... | P—Kt 5 |
| 16. | P—B 3 | P×P |
| 17. | P×P | Q—B 1 |
| 18. | P—Q 4 | P×P |
| 19. | P×P | Q—R 3 |
| 20. | R—B 1 | Kt—Kt 4 |
| 21. | P—Q 5 | |

Diag. 143.

This shuts in the White K B altogether, and at the same
time opens the diagonal of Black's K B.  Therefore, on
principle alone the move is questionable.  In effect it gives
Black an opportunity for a beautiful winning combination.
Only P—K 5 was worth considering, as then the opposing
Bishop would have been shut in and White's own diagonal
opened.

| 21. | ......... | Kt—Kt 5 ! ! |
| 22. | Q×Kt | Kt—Q 5 |
| 23. | Q×Kt | B×Q |
| 24. | Kt×B | |

Although three minor pieces are generally an equivalent for the Queen, in this case the White game collapses quickly. The advanced pawns have produced too many weak points which afford an entry for the Black forces.

| | |
|---|---|
| 24. ......... | K R—B 1 |
| 25. R×R | R×R |
| 26. R—B 2 | Q—R 6 |
| 27. R—K 2 | |

B—R 5 was threatened. But the text move is of no avail either. Black winds up the game with another fine combination.

| | |
|---|---|
| 27. ......... | R—B 8 ! |
| 28. B×R | Q×B |

If R—K 1, Q—B 4.

| | |
|---|---|
| 29. Kt—B 3 | Q×Kt ch |
| 30. K—B 2 | B—Kt 4 |
| Resigns. | |

## GAME No. 31

White : John.          Black : Janowski
### Sicilian Defence.

| | |
|---|---|
| 1. P—K 4 | P—Q B 4 |
| 2. Kt—K B 3 | Kt—Q B 3 |
| 3. P—Q 4 | P×P |
| 4. Kt×P | Kt—B 3 |

The aim of this move is to provoke Kt—B 3, and incidentally to prevent P—Q B 4. The latter move would give White command of his Q 5 and not only prevent Black's P—Q 4 but also immobilise Black's K P unless his Q P is to remain " backward."

| | |
|---|---|
| 5. Q Kt—B 3 | P—K Kt 3 |

As shown on p. 216, P—Q 3 must be played first. In any case Black must be wary of playing P—K Kt 3. If, for instance, after P—Q 3 White plays 6 B—Q B 4, and Black replies with P—K Kt 3, there follows 7 Kt×Kt, P×Kt ; 8 P—K 5 !,

Kt—Kt 5 (P×P ?, 9 B×P ch) ; 9 P—K 6, P—K B 4, with advantage to White (see game in the match Schlechter-Lasker).

| | | |
|---|---|---|
| 6. | Kt×Kt | Kt P×Kt |
| 7. | P—K 5 | Kt—Kt 1 |
| 8. | B—Q B 4 | P—Q 4 |
| 9. | P×P, *e.p.* | P×P |
| 10. | Q—B 3 | |

Diag. 144.

White has now three pieces in action and Black none. Black's game is hopeless already ; his B 2 cannot be covered by Q—Q 2 because of : 11 B×P ch, Q×B ; 12 Q×P ch, and after Q—K 2 ch there follows : 11 B—K 3, B—Kt 2 ; 12 Castles Q R, and 13 K R—K1, with an overwhelming attack.

| | | |
|---|---|---|
| 10. | ......... | Q—Q 2 |
| 11. | Kt—Q 5 ı | |

In view of the fact that his game is so much more developed, and that the opposing King will hardly be able to escape from the centre of the board, White decides to sacrifice a Knight in order to open the files in the centre for his Rooks, instead of following the simple line indicated in the previous note.

| | | |
|---|---|---|
| 11. | ......... | P×Kt |
| 12. | B×P | Q—K 2 ch |
| 13. | B—K 3 | R—Kt 1 |
| 14. | Castles K R | |

Castles Q R is stronger still, as the Q R gets into action at once.

| 14. ......... | B—K Kt 2 |
| 15. B—K B 4 | R—Kt 3 |
| 16. B—3 6 ch | R × B |

If B—Q 2, the continuation might have been : 17 B × B, Q × B ; 18 Q R—Q 1, Q—Kt 2 ; 19 K R—K 1 ch, Kt—K 2 ; 20 R × Kt ch, K × R ; 21 B × P ch, etc. ; or 18...Q—B 1 ; 19 B × P, etc.

After 17 R—K 1 Black could have held out a little longer with B—B 3. After the text move, however, Black's game collapses quickly before the concentrated onslaught of the White forces.

| 17. Q × R ch | Q—Q 2 |
| 18. Q R—K 1 ch | Kt—K 2 |
| 19. R × Kt ch ! | K × R |
| 20. R—K 1 ch | K—B 1 |
| 21. B × P ch | K—Kt 1 |
| 22. R—K 8 ch | B—B 1 |
| 23. R × B ch | K—Kt 2 |
| 24. Q—B 3 ch | Resigns. |

## GAME No. 32

White : Ed. Lasker.          Black : Mieses.
Centre Counter Defence.

| 1. P—K 4 | P—Q 4 |
| 2. P × P | Kt—K B 3 |

This is to tempt White to play P—Q B 4, a weak move (see p. 35). By playing P—Q B 3 Black would obtain by far the better game in exchange for the pawn.

| 3. P—Q 4 | Q × P |

Kt × P can also be played. In either case White wins a move by driving off the Black piece by Kt—Q B 3 or P—Q B 4. Furthermore, White has a pawn in the centre. Black's plan in retaking with the Queen might be to castle early on the

Queen's side and attack White's centre pawn by P—K 4, and White must be on the alert against this plan, though it will not be easy for Black to put the same into execution, because of the exposed position of his Queen. After 4 Kt—Q B 3, Q—Q R 4 is the only move which brings the Queen into momentary security, and even then Black must provide for a retreat, as after White's B—Q 2 there would be a threat of an advantageous " discovery " by the Kt. P—Q B 3 provides such a retreat, but it bars the Q Kt from its natural development at B 3, where the Kt could exert further pressure on White's Q 4. The Q B, too, is difficult to get into play and easily becomes an object of attack, as in the present game.

| 4 Kt—Q B 3 | Q—Q R 4 |
| 5. Kt—B 3 | B—B 4 |

B—Kt 5 would only help White's intentions to attack on the King's side in the absence of Black's Queen, *e.g.* 6 P—K R 3, B—R 4 ; 7 P—K Kt 4, B—Kt 3 ; 8 Kt—K 5 (threatening Kt—B 4), P—B 3 ; 9 P—K R 4, Q Kt—Q 2 ; 10 Kt—B 4, Q—B 2 ; 11 P—R 5, B—K 5 ; 12 Kt × B, Kt × Kt ; 13 Q—B 3 and B—B 4 with the superior game.

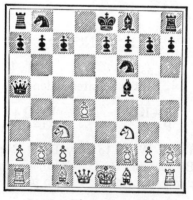

Diag. 145.

6. Kt—K 5 !          Kt—K 5

P—B 3 was urgent here, to provide against Kt—B 4 and Q—B 3. Now the game is as good as lost. White obtains a violent attack with superior forces, and brings it home before Black has time to complete his development.

|  | 7. Q—B 3 | Kt—Q 3 |
|---|---|---|

If Kt × Kt, B—Q 2.

|  | 8. B—Q 2 | P—K 3 |
|---|---|---|
|  | 9. P—K Kt 4 | B—Kt 3 |

Black had to guard his K B 2 because of Kt—Kt 5, Kt × Kt, Q × P ch.

|  | 10. P—K R 4 | Q—Kt 3 |
|---|---|---|
|  | 11. Castles | P—K B 3 |

Compulsory. Kt—B 3 is refuted by 12 Kt × Kt, Q × Kt; 13 Q × Q, P × Q; 14 B—Kt 2 and P—R 5. On the other hand, the answer to 11...Q × P would be 12 B—K B 4, Q—B 4; 13 P—R 5, P—B 3; 14 P × B, P × Kt; 15 B—K Kt 5 followed by R × Kt and R—Q 8 or Q—B 7 mate.

|  | 12. Kt × B | P × Kt |
|---|---|---|
|  | 13. B—Q 3 | Q × P |

K—B 2 or P—K B 4 were also unavailing in consequence of Black's poor development.

|  | 14. B × P ch | K—Q 2 |
|---|---|---|
|  | 15. B—K 3 | Q—Kt 5 |
|  | 16. P—R 3 | Q—B 5 |
|  | 17. Q × Kt P | Q—B 3 |
|  | 18. B—K 4 | Resigns. |

## GAME No. 33

White : Barasz.        Black : Mieses.
Centre Counter Defence.

|  | 1. P—K 4 | P—Q 4 |
|---|---|---|
|  | 2. P × P | Q × P |
|  | 3. Kt—Q B 3 | Q—Q R 4 |
|  | 4. Kt—B 3 |  |

It is better to advance the Q P at once and so threaten B—Q 2, after which Black is almost under compulsion to provide a retreat for his Q by P—Q B 3, thus blocking his Q Kt.

| 4. ......... | Kt—Q B 3 |
| 5. B—K 2 | B—B 4 |
| 6. P—Q 3 | |

Already now the mistake of having allowed Black to develop his Queen's side unmolested is apparent. P—Q 4 is now impossible, for Black would castle on the Queen's side and keep the initiative by exerting a permanent pressure on White's Q P by P—K 4. White must yield up the centre to Black.

| 6. ......... | P—K 4 |
| 7. B—Q 2 | Castles |
| 8. P—Q R 3 | Q—B 4 |

The Queen must escape from White's threat of P—Q Kt 4.

| 9. Castles | Kt—B 3 |
| 10. P—Q Kt 4 | Q—K 2 |
| 11. P—Kt 5 | |

This advance is somewhat purposeless, as the White pieces are not ready for an attack on Black's King. It is difficult, though, to find a sensible plan, as the White pieces have so little mobility. It would perhaps be best to play R—K 1, B—B 1, and Kt—K 4.

| 11. ......... | Kt—Q 5 |
| 12. R—K 1 | Q—B 4 |
| 13. B—K B 1 | B—Q 3 |
| 14. Q—Kt 1 ? | |

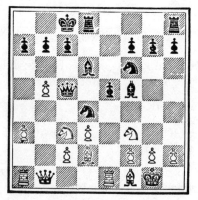

Diag. 146.

The purpose of this move is not clear. The advance of the Kt P could only be condoned by a desire to obtain an open file, and it seems illogical to protect it now. If White wanted to escape the pinning of his K Kt he need not have moved the Queen. Kt × Kt would have effected this and prevented the King's side from being laid bare.

White's game would still have been bad, particularly as the exchange at Q 4 opens the diagonal for the Black K B, but the move in the text has even a worse effect. Mieses concludes the game with an elegant sacrifice.

| | |
|---|---|
| 14. ......... | Kt × Kt ch |
| 15. P × Kt | P—K 5 ! |
| 16. Q P × P | B × P ch |
| 17. K × B | Q × P ch |
| 18. B—Kt 2 | R × B |
| 19. R—K 2 | R × R |
| 20. Kt × R | Q × Kt |
| 21. P × B | Q—K 4 ch |
| 22. K—R 1 | R—K 1 |

Black has wrought fearful havoc in the White ranks, and the defenceless King cannot withstand the onslaught of the three White pieces for long.

| | |
|---|---|
| 23. P—Q B 4 | Kt—R 4 |
| 24. K—Kt 1 | Q—Q 5 ch |
| 25. K—R 2 | R—K 7 |

threatening Q—R 5 ch, Q—B 7 ch, and mate at Kt 7 or R 7.

| | |
|---|---|
| 26. Q—R 1 | Q—K 4 ch |
| 27. P—B 4 | Q × P ch |
| 28. K—Kt 1 | Q—Q 5 ch |
| Resigns. | |

## GAME No. 34

White : Em. Lasker.     Black : Niemzowitsch.
Caro-Kann Defence (compare p. 50).

| | |
|---|---|
| 1. P—K 4 | P—Q B 3 |
| 2. P—Q 4 | P—Q 4 |

|       |              |            |
| ----- | ------------ | ---------- |
| 3.    | Kt—Q B 3     | P × P      |
| 4.    | Kt × P       | Kt—B 3     |
| 5.    | Kt × Kt      | Kt P × Kt  |
| 6.    | B—K 2        | B—B 4      |
| 7.    | B—B 3        | Q—R 4 ch   |
| 8.    | P—B 3        | P—K R 4 !  |

A deep conception. If White accepts the proffered sacrifice of a pawn, he loses time, as he must retire his B before
bringing out his Kt, and, moreover, the K R file being open, he
can only castle on the Q side. But there the Black Queen
is ready for the attack. If he refuses the sacrifice, the text
move is still of value, as even then it is hardly advisable for
White to castle on the K side, whilst Black can play B—R 3
as soon as it might be desirable to exchange White's Q B.

|       |              |             |
| ----- | ------------ | ----------- |
| 9.    | B × P        | Kt—Q 2      |
| 10.   | B—Kt 4       | B × B       |
| 11.   | Q × B        | Castles     |
| 12.   | Kt—K 2       | P—K 3       |
| 13.   | B—B 4        | Q—Q Kt 4 !  |

Black is the first to complete his development, and he
assumes the offensive.

14. Castles Q R !

This is much stronger than the alternative P—Q Kt 3,
which would fatally disturb the pawn skeleton, particularly
as castling is only possible on the Q side. Although Black
can now gain two pawns, White obtains an attack and Black
only just manages to escape with a draw.

|       |              |             |
| ----- | ------------ | ----------- |
| 14.   | .........    | Kt—Kt 3     |
| 15.   | Kt—Kt 3      |             |

intending Q—K 2 in answer to Kt—B 5. Again P—Q Kt 3
is not to be thought of, and R—Q 2 also fails because of
Kt—B 5; 16 R—B 2, Kt × P.

|       |              |             |
| ----- | ------------ | ----------- |
| 15.   | .........    | Q—Q 4       |
| 16.   | K—Kt 1       | Q × Kt P    |
| 17.   | Q R—Kt 1     | Q × B P     |

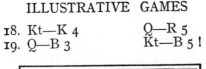

18. Kt—K 4          Q—R 5
19. Q—B 3          Kt—B 5 !

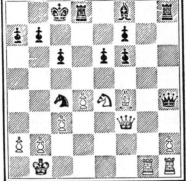

Diag. 147.

Whilst Black was busy capturing two pawns by moving the Queen four times, White was concentrating the whole of his forces, and now threatens to win back the pawn with R—Kt 4. The move in the text anticipates the threat, for now the answer to 20 R—Kt 4 would be Q—R 4 ; 21 Kt×P ?, Q—B 4 ch ; 22 Kt—K 4 ? ? Kt—Q 7 ch, winning the Q.

20. K—R 1          P—K B 4
21. Kt—Kt 5        B—Q 3
22. B—B 1          R—Q 2
23. R—Kt 2         B—B 2

intending to get rid of the awkward White Knight by Kt—Q 3—K 5.

24. K R—Kt 1       Kt—Q 3
25. Q—K 2          Kt—K 5
26. Kt—B 3         Q—R 6
27. P—R 3

White appears to be in " time " difficulties, or else he remains passive, in order to give Black an opportunity for making the risky attempt to hold the extra pawn by P—B 3 and P—K 4.

27. ..........      P—R 3
28. B—K 3          K R—Q 1
29. K—R 2          R—R 1

If Black wants to play for a win, he must play P—B 3. In view of the favourable position of the White pieces, he prefers to risk nothing and to avoid the weakening of position which follows upon practically every pawn move.

| | | |
|---|---|---|
| 30. | K—R 1 | K R—Q 1 |
| 31. | K—R 2 | R—K 1 |
| 32. | R—Kt 8 | R × R |
| 33. | R × R ch | R—Q 1 |
| 34. | R—Kt 7 | R—Q 2 |
| 35. | R—Kt 8 ch | |

As long as Black plays steadily, White cannot hope for more than a draw.

| | | |
|---|---|---|
| 35. | ......... | R—Q 1 |
| 36. | R—Kt 7 | R—B 1 |
| 37. | P—B 4 | Kt—B 3 |

In order to drive off the Rook; White now enforces the draw by a fine combination.

| | | |
|---|---|---|
| 38. | B—Kt 5 ! | Kt—R 4 |
| 39. | R × P ! | R × R |
| 40. | Q × P ch | R—Q 2 |

Not K—Kt 1 on account of 41 Q—K 8 ch, K—R 2; 42 Q × R, Q × Kt ; 43 Q × B, threatening B—K 7.

| | | |
|---|---|---|
| 41. | Kt—K 5 ! | Draw. |

For after B × Kt there follows 42 Q—K 8 ch, K—B 2; 43 Q × B ch, with perpetual check.

Both players have shown a deep positional insight, and the game shows in an interesting manner how a preponderance of material can be counterbalanced by the greater mobility of the pieces.

## GAME No. 35

White : Reti.      Black : Tartakower.
Caro-Kann Defence.

| | | |
|---|---|---|
| 1. | P—K 4 | P—Q B 3 |
| 2. | P—Q 4 | P—Q 4 |

| | |
|---|---|
| 3. Kt—Q B 3 | P×P |
| 4. Kt×P | Kt—K B 3 |
| 5. Q—Q 3 | |

White wishes to castle as soon as possible on the Queen's side, in order to operate on the Queen's file with the help of the Rook.

| | |
|---|---|
| 5. ......... | P—K 4 |

Here Black loses two moves in bringing White's centre pawn away. The manœuvre therefore is not sound. Q Kt—Q 2, Kt×Kt, and Kt—B 3, or any other developing moves would be preferable.

| | |
|---|---|
| 6. P×P | Q—R 4 ch |
| 7. B—Q 2 | Q×P |
| 8. Castles ! | |

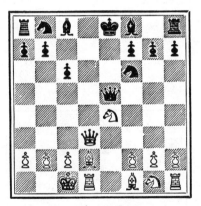

Diag. 148.

White prepares a magnificent mating combination, which can only be made possible at such an early stage, when the opponent has utterly neglected his development.

| | |
|---|---|
| 8. ......... | Kt×Kt |
| 9. Q—Q 8 ch ! ! | K×Q |
| 10. B—Kt 5 double ch | K—B 2 |
| 11. B—Q 8 mate | |

A beautiful mate. If 11...K—K 1, 11 R—Q 8 mate.

## · GAME No. 36

White : Forgacz.　　　　　　Black : E. Cohn.
Queen's Gambit.

|     |          |          |
|-----|----------|----------|
| 1.  | P—Q 4    | P—Q 4    |
| 2.  | Kt—K B 3 | P—K 3    |
| 3.  | P—B 4    | P × P    |
| 4.  | Kt—B 3   | Kt—K B 3 |
| 5.  | B—Kt 5   | B—K 2    |
| 6.  | P—K 4    | P—K R 3  |

Through 3...P × P Black's development is one move behind, and such pawn moves should at any cost be avoided as do not contribute to the mobilisation of the pieces.  Castles, P—Q Kt 3, B—Kt 2, and Q Kt—Q 2 was the proper course.

### 7. B × Kt

This is better than to withdraw the Bishop ; Black's last move was clearly loss of time.

|     |          |          |
|-----|----------|----------|
| 7.  | ........ | B × B    |
| 8.  | B × P    | Kt—Q 2   |
| 9.  | Castles  | Castles  |

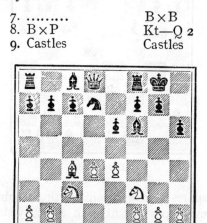

Diag. 149.

There seems to be nothing alarming about the position, yet on closer investigation a number of vital failings can be discerned in Black's camp.  The absence of a pawn in the centre and

the unsatisfactory development have a far-reaching influence.
White will be able to bring his forces to the King's side by way
of K 4, which is made accessible by the disappearance of
Black's Q P, before Black has time to bring his Q B to bear
on White's K 4 by P—Q Kt 3 and B—Kt 2. White's immediate threat (after P—K 5) is Q—K 2—K 4 and B—Q 3.
If Black does not wish to risk P—K Kt 3, he must defend himself with R—K 1, Kt—B 1. In the meantime White can play
R—Q 1 and threaten P—Q 5, opening the Queen's file. This
again necessitates P—B 3, which postpones the efficiency of
the Q B at Kt 2 until White's Q Kt and Q R have been brought
up for the attack. The game develops on these lines, and provides an excellent example of the advantage of the command
of the centre.

|  |  |  |
|---|---|---|
| 10. | P—K 5 | B—K 2 |
| 11. | Q—K 2 | R—K 1 |
| 12. | Q R—Q 1 | P—Q B 3 |
| 13. | Q—K 4 | Q—B 2 |

preparing P—Q Kt 3.

|  |  |  |
|---|---|---|
| 14. | K R—K 1 | Kt—B 1 |
| 15. | Q—Kt 4 | P—Q Kt 3 |
| 16. | Q—R 5 | B—Kt 2 |
| 17. | R—K 4 | B—Kt 5 |

Black cannot yet play P—Q B 4, as R—B 4 is threatened
with an attack on K B 7. The Bishop which obstructs the
Q would have no move, save the sorry retreat to Q 1, and
White would win speedily : 17...P—Q B 4 ; 18 R—B 4, B—Q 1 ;
19 P—Q 5, P×P ; 20 Kt×P, B×Kt ; 21 B×B, attacking
R and P.

|  |  |  |
|---|---|---|
| 18. | R—Kt 4 | B × Kt |
| 19. | P × B | K—R 1 |

Q × P was threatened.

|  |  |  |
|---|---|---|
| 20. | Kt—Kt 5 | R—K 2 |
| 21. | Kt—K 4 | |

Even the Knight is brought in via K4.

|  |  |  |
|---|---|---|
| 21. | ......... | R—Q 1 |
| 22. | R—Q 3 | P—Q B 4 |
| 23. | Kt—B 6 | |

threatening Q×P ch and R—Kt 8 mate. Black cannot capture the Kt because of Q×P ch and mate at Kt 7. But the mate cannot be delayed much longer in view of the concentration of superior forces for the attack.

| 23. ......... | Kt—Kt 3 |
| 24. R—R 3 | Resigns. |

There is no answer to Q—Kt 5 and R×P.

## GAME No. 37

White : Marshall.　　　Black : Capablanca.
Queen's Gambit Declined (see p. 52).

| 1. P—Q 4 | P—Q 4 |
| 2. P—Q B 4 | P—K 3 |
| 3. Kt—Q B 3 | Kt—K B 3 |
| 4. B—Kt 5 | B—K 2 |
| 5. P—K 3 | Kt—K 5 |

Diag. 150.

Lasker has played this move successfully in his match against Marshall; but it has not come into general use. White should get the better game by 6 B×B, Q×B; 7 Q—B 2, Kt×Kt; 8 Q×Kt or 7 P×P, Kt×Kt; 8 P×Kt, P×P; 9 Q—Kt 3, in the first case because the Black Q B is out of play, in the second case because of the open Kt file. 7 Kt × Kt is bad, because P × Kt prevents the natural development of the K Kt at B 3, and Black can obtain an attack after castling by P—K B 4-5.

|       |             |            |
|-------|-------------|------------|
| 6.    | B × B       | Q × B      |
| 7.    | B—Q 3       |            |

This also is a good move, as it furthers development.

|       |             |            |
|-------|-------------|------------|
| 7.    | .........   | Kt × Kt    |
| 8.    | P × Kt      | P × P      |

Giving up the centre pawn in this case is not against the spirit of the opening, as it opens the only diagonal on which the Black Q B can operate.

|       |             |            |
|-------|-------------|------------|
| 9.    | B × P       | P—Q Kt 3   |
| 10.   | Q—B 3       | P—Q B 3    |
| 11.   | Kt—K 2      | B—Kt 2     |
| 12.   | Castles K R | Castles    |
| 13.   | P—Q R 4     |            |

This move can only be good if White intends to operate on the Queen's side, possibly by K R—Kt 1 and P—R 5. But the position of the White Queen makes the adoption of a different plan compulsory. For one thing, it is rational to concentrate forces where the Queen can take her share, therefore, in this case, on the King's side. On the other hand, the manœuvre referred to could not be put into execution here because Black can prevent P—R 5 by P—Q B 4 and Kt—B 3. A fairly obvious course was to play P—K 4, taking possession of the centre. P—Q B 4 would then be answered by P—Q 5, after which the White Rooks would be very effective at Q 1 and K 1. In this game White does initiate a King's side attack subsequently, and thus 13...P—Q R 4 is clearly a lost move.

|       |             |            |
|-------|-------------|------------|
| 13.   | .........   | P—Q B 4    |
| 14.   | Q—Kt 3      | Kt—B 3     |
| 15.   | Kt—B 4      | Q R—B 1    |

The tempting move of P—K 4 cannot be played because of 16 Kt—Q 5, Q—Q 1; 17 P × B P, Kt—R 4; 18 K R—Q 1. The move in the text threatens P × P, Kt × P and R × B.

|       |             |            |
|-------|-------------|------------|
| 16.   | B—R 2       | K R—Q 1    |
| 17.   | K R—K 1     | Kt—R 4     |

This threatens B—B 3 attacking the R P. White decides to yield the same at once, thinking quite rightly that a direct attack must have good chances, as Black gets two pieces out of play in capturing the pawn.

|     |          |       |
| --- | -------- | ----- |
| 18. | Q R—Q 1  | B—B 3 |
| 19. | Q—Kt 4   |       |

Black cannot take the pawn yet, because of Kt×P and B×P ch.

|     |          |       |
| --- | -------- | ----- |
| 19. | ........ | P—B 5 |
| 20. | P—Q 5 ?  |       |

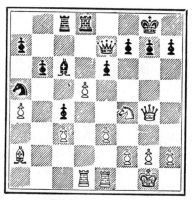

Diag. 151.

There is no need to play for violent complications. The logical course was to open the way to the King's side for the Rooks by P—K 4. The continuation could have been: 20 P—K 4, B×R P ; 21 Kt—R 5, P—Kt 3 ; 22 P—K 5, B×R ; 23 R×B followed by Kt—B 6, with a strong attack; also after 21...P—B 3, 22 R—Q 2, White's attacking chances are good. After the move in the text, Black could get an advantage by simply exchanging : 20...P×P ; 21 Kt×P, B×Kt ; 22 R×B, R×R ; 23 Q×R ch, R—Q 1 ; 24 Q—K B 5, P—Kt 3 ; 25 Q—B 2, Q—R 6. In taking the R P, however, Black incurs grave risks.

|     |          |        |
| --- | -------- | ------ |
| 20. | ........ | B×R P  |
| 21. | R—Q 2    | P—K 4  |
| 22. | Kt—R 5   | P—Kt 3 |
| 23. | P—Q 6    | Q—K 3  |
| 24. | Q—Kt 5   | K—R 1  |

Black finds the weaknesses at his K B 3 and K R 3 very troublesome. R×P would lose at once, because of 25 R×R, Q×R ; 26 Q—R 6 !

25. Kt—B 6          R×P
26. R×R            Q×R
27. B—Kt 1

Q—R 4 would have been answered by K—Kt 2.

27. .........       Kt—B 3

Black must try to bring back his minor pieces for the defence. If he succeeds in doing that in time, the end-game is easily won on the Queen's side.

28. B—B 5          R—Q 1

Not P×B because of Q—R 6.

29. P—K R 4

White's attacking resources seem inexhaustible. By ex- changing Queens he could have got his pawn back in this way : 29 B—Q 7, Q—B 1 (R×B ?, 30 Q—R 6) ; 30 B×Kt, B×B ; 31 Q×Q P, Q—Q 3 ; 32 Kt—Q 7, Q×Q ; 33 Kt×Q, B—K 1 ; 34 Kt×Q B P. But even then Black would maintain a superiority in the end-game owing to the freedom of his passed pawn, and because he can post his Rook at the seventh after P—Q Kt 4. This explains why Marshall prefers not to win back his pawn, but to enter upon a violent attack with a doubtful issue. However, Capablanca finds the right move in all the ensuing complications, and finally wins the game.

Diag. 152.

|       |         |        |
|-------|---------|--------|
| 29.   | .........| Kt—K 2 |
| 30.   | Kt—K 4  | Q—B 2  |
| 31.   | Q—B 6 ch | K—Kt 1 |
| 32.   | B—K 6   |        |

This is now compulsory. If White loses time in withdraw-
ing the B, Black consolidates his position by : Kt—Q 4 and
Q—K 2.

|       |         |        |
|-------|---------|--------|
| 32.   | .........| P×B    |

R—B 1 is refuted by 33 Kt—Kt 5 !, P×B ; 34 Q×R, etc.

|       |            |
|-------|------------|
| 33.   | Q×K P ch   |

Better than Kt—Kt 5, for after Kt—Q 4, 34 Q×P ch,
the Black King finds a safe retreat at Kt 2.

|       |         |        |
|-------|---------|--------|
| 33.   | .........| K—B 1  |
| 34.   | Kt—Kt 5 | Kt—Kt 1 |
| 35.   | P—B 4   |        |

in order to open the file for the Rook.

|       |         |        |
|-------|---------|--------|
| 35.   | .........| R—K 1  |
| 36.   | P×P     | R—K 2  |
| 37.   | R—B 1 ch | K—Kt 2 |
| 38.   | P—R 5   | B—K 1  |
| 39.   | P—R 6 ch | K—R 1  |

Kt×P fails on account of Q—B 6 ch.

|       |         |
|-------|---------|
| 40.   | Q—Q 6   |

White takes all possible advantage from the position, but
cannot bring home his attack, as Black has concentrated his
forces for the defence. Black must still be careful to avoid a
mate, *e.g.* Q×Q? ; 41 P×Q, R×P ; 42 R—B 7 or 41...R—Q 2 ;
42 R—B 8.

|       |         |        |
|-------|---------|--------|
| 40.   | .........| Q—B 4  |
| 41.   | Q—Q 4   |        |

Here White could have tried Q×Q and R—B 8. There was
then a permanent threat of R×B, *e.g.* 41 Q×Q, P×Q ;
42 R—B 8, R×P ; 43 Kt—B 3, R—K 2 ; 44 Kt—Kt 5, etc.
It seems as if Black would have to give up the piece again by
43...R—R 4 in order to win. White, however, would then have
drawing chances, which would have been a fitting conclusion
to this wonderful game.

41. .........          R × P
42. Q—Q 7          R—K 2
    Resigns.

### GAME No. 38
White : Rotlewi.          Black : Teichmann.
#### Queen's Gambit Declined.

|   |              |            |
|---|--------------|------------|
| 1. | P—Q 4        | P—Q 4      |
| 2. | Kt—K B 3     | Kt—K B 3   |
| 3. | P—B 4        | P—K 3      |
| 4. | Kt—B 3       | Q Kt—Q 2   |
| 5. | B—Kt 5       | B—K 2      |

Capablanca tried 5...B—Kt 5 ; against Ed. Lasker in New York, 1915.  The continuation was : 6 P—K 3, P—B 4 ; 7 B—Q 3, Q—R 4 ; 8 Q—Kt 3.

The correct move is here 8 Castles.  If Black wins the pawn by B × Kt ; 9 P × B, Q P × P ; 10 B × P, Q × B P, White obtains a strong attack, e.g., 11 R—B 1, Q—R 4 ; 12 B × Kt, P × B (Kt × B ; 13 P × P) ;  13 P—Q 5, with this possible continuation 13......Kt—Kt 3, 14 P × P, P × P ; 15 Q—Q 6, with a strong attack.

|   |          |          |
|---|----------|----------|
| 6. | P—K 3    | Castles  |
| 7. | Q—B 2    | P—B 4    |

White intends to castle on the Queen's side, and to follow this up with a storm by the King's side pawns.  Although Rubinstein has on many occasions been successful with this form of attack, it is open to criticism.  For, where Kings have castled on different wings, the attack on the King which has castled on the Q side should be more successful.

Diag. 153.

This is much stronger than P—Q Kt 3 and B—Kt 2, as then the Black Queen cannot participate in the attack quickly enough. As pointed out before, speed is the first consideration for the attack, whenever the Kings have castled on different wings. An interesting counterpart to the present game is found in a game won by Rubinstein from Teichmann (Match, Vienna, 1908) 7...P—Q Kt 3; 8 P×P, P×P; 9 B—Q 3, B—Kt 2; 10 Castles Q R, P—B 4; 11 P—K R 4, P—B 5? (the only hope lay in the opening of the Q B file); 12 B—B 5, R—K 1; 13 B×K Kt, Kt×B; 14 P—K Kt 4, B—Q 3; 15 P—Kt 5, Kt—K 5; 16 P—R 5, Q—K 2; 17 Q R—Kt 1, P—Q R 3; 18 B×P ch !, K×B; 19 P—Kt 6 ch, K—Kt 1; 20 Kt×Kt, P×Kt; 21 P—R 6, P—B 3; 22 P×P, P×Kt; 23 R—R 8 ch, K×P; 24 R—R 7 ch, and Black resigned a few moves later.

| | | |
|---|---|---|
| 8. Castles | | Q—R 4 |
| 9. P×Q P | | |

White loses time in the centre. It was imperative to proceed at once with P—K Kt 4 followed by B × Kt, P—Kt 5 and P—K R 4.

| | | |
|---|---|---|
| 9. ......... | | K P×P |
| 10. P×P | | Kt×P |
| 11. Kt—Q 4 | | B—K 3 |
| 12. K—Kt 1 | | |

It would be too risky to leave both King and Queen on the Q B file.

| | | |
|---|---|---|
| 12. ......... | | Q R—B 1 |
| 13. B—Q 3 | | P—K R 3 |

The threat was : B×Kt and B×P ch. Had White played P—K Kt 4 and P—K R 4 instead of effecting exchanges in the centre, Black would not have been able to afford this weakening move. But now Black wins the game on the other wing, before White is able to make use of the weakness thus created.

| | | |
|---|---|---|
| 14. B×Kt | | B×B |
| 15. B—B 5 | | K R—Q 1 |
| 16. B×B | | P×B |
| 17. Q—Kt 6 | | |

The Queen must leave the Q B file without delay, as Kt—K 5 is threatened.  Black's game is already superior ;  with the exception of the Queen, White has no piece available for the attack on the opposing King.

| | |
|---|---|
| 17. ......... | R—Q 3 |
| 18. R—Q B 1 | R—R 3 |

Now White must again provide against Black's Kt—K 5, as White's Q Kt is needed for the defence of Q R 2.

| | |
|---|---|
| 19. P—B 3 | R—Q 1 |

Black intends to move his B and then to advance his K P with an attack on the Queen.  The object of the text move is to prevent White from saving himself by an attack on the Rook (Q—B 5).

| | |
|---|---|
| 20. R—B 2 | B × Kt |

By this exchange Black achieves his object of driving off the Knight by P—Q 5, but White has time to give his R P further protection by P—Q Kt 3.  This, Black would have prevented by playing B—Kt 4 instead of the text move, *e.g.* 21 P—B 4, P—K 4 ;  22 Q—B 5, P × Kt ;  23 P × P, B—B 3 ; 24 P × Kt, P—Q 5, etc.

| | |
|---|---|
| 21. P × B | P—K 4 |
| 22. Q—Kt 4 | P × P |
| 23. Q × P | Kt—K 3 |
| 24. Q—K 5 | |

This delays the fatal advance of the Q P for one move.

| | |
|---|---|
| 24. ......... | P—Q Kt 4 |
| 25. P—Q Kt 3 | P—Q 5 |
| 26. Kt—K 4 | P—Q 6 |
| 27. R—Q 2 | Kt—Q 5 |
| 28. R—Q B 1 | Kt—B 7 |
| 29. Q—Kt 2 | Kt—R 6 ch |
| 30. K—R 1 | Kt—B 7 ch |

|         |            |            |
|---------|------------|------------|
| 31. | K—Kt 1 | Kt—R 6 ch |
| 32. | K—R 1  | Kt—B 7 ch |
| 33. | K—Kt 1 |            |

Diag. 154.

Black does not play for a draw, but only wishes to gain time.

33. .........          R—Q B 3

The intention is to double Rooks and to force an entry at B 7.  P—Kt 5 would not be good.  The White Rook would no longer be attacked, and the Knight could attack the Q P.

34. R (B 1)—Q 1        K R—Q B 1

Now that the White Rook has left the Q B file, one Rook would be sufficient to force an entry at B 7, and Kt—R 6 ch followed by P—Kt 5 could have been played at once, *e.g.* 34... Kt—R 6 ch ; 35 K—R 1, P—Kt 5 (preventing P—Q Kt 4) ; 36 Kt—B 2, R—B 7 ; 37 R×R, P×R ; 38 R—Q B 1, Q—Kt 3 ; 39 Kt—K 4, R—Q 8 followed by R×R ch, Q—Q 5 ch and P—B 8 mate.

|     |          |            |
|-----|----------|------------|
| 35. | R×P      | Kt—R 6 ch |
| 36. | K—R 1    | P—Kt 5     |
| 37. | R—Q 7    | Q—K 4 ! ! |

If Q×Q, Black mates in three.

|     |            |          |
|-----|------------|----------|
| 38. | R—Q 8 ch   | R×R      |
| 39. | R×R ch     | K—R 2    |
| 40. | R—Q 1      | Q×Q ch   |

Curiously enough there is nothing better. Q—B 2 only leads to the exchange of Queens and the same end-game, which, however, is an easy win for Black, as the permanent mating threat keeps the White Rook tied to the first rank, whilst the Black King threatens to capture all the White pawns.

If Q—B 2 White forces the exchange of Queens with the following combination : 41 Q—Q 2, R—B 7 ; 42 Q—Q 3, R—B 8 ch ; 43 K—Kt 2, with a threat of Kt—B 6 ch and Q—R 7 mate. Black therefore would have to play Q—B 7 ch, etc., as in the game.

| | | |
|---|---|---|
| 41. | K×Q | R—B 7 ch |
| 42. | K—R 1 | R×P |
| 43. | R—R 1 | P—Kt 4 |
| 44. | Kt—B 6 ch | K—Kt 2 |
| 45. | Kt—K 4 | K—Kt 3 |
| 46. | Kt—Q 6 | P—Q R 4 |

We have now a position with a forced move. If the White Knight moves, there follows K—B 4—B 5, etc. Therefore White gives up his R P voluntarily.

| | | |
|---|---|---|
| 47. | R—Q B 1 | R×P |
| 48. | Kt—B 4 | Kt—Kt 4 |

Now Kt—B 6 and R×P mate are threatened.

| | | |
|---|---|---|
| 49. | Kt—K 5 ch | K—Kt 2 |
| 50. | Kt—Kt 4 | R—K 7 |
| 51. | R—B 5 | R—K 8 ch |
| 52. | K—Kt 2 | Kt—R 6 |
| 53. | R—B 7 ch | K—B 1 |
| 54. | R—B 1 | R—K 7 ch |
| 55. | K—R 1 | Kt—B 7 ch |
| 56. | K—Kt 1 | Kt—R 6 ch |

Black again appears to be short of time.

| | | |
|---|---|---|
| 57. | K—R 1 | Kt—Kt 4 |
| 58. | R—B 5 | R—K 8 ch |
| 59. | K—Kt 2 | Kt—R 6 |
| 60. | R—B 1 | R—K 7 ch |

Now, after the sixtieth move Black has again plenty of time, and can prepare the final combination at leisure.

| 61. K—R 1 | R—K 3 |
|---|---|
| 62. R—R 1 | K—Kt 2 |
| 63. R—Q B 1 | K—Kt 3 |
| 64. R—B 6 | R×R |
| 65. Kt—K 5 ch | K—B 4 |
| 66. Kt×R | P--R 4 |
| 67. Kt—Q 4 ch | K—K 4 |
| 68. Kt—K 2 | Kt—B 7 ch |
| 69. K—Kt 2 | Kt—Q 5 |
| Resigns. | |

## GAME No. 39.

White : Rotlewi.     Black : Rubinstein
Queen's Gambit Declined.

| 1. P—Q 4 | P—Q 4 |
|---|---|
| 2. Kt—K B 3 | P—K 3 |
| 3. P—K 3 | P—Q B 4 |
| 4. P—B 4 | Kt—Q B 3 |
| 5. Kt—B 3 | Kt—B 3 |
| 6. Q P×P | B×P |
| 7. P—Q R 3 | P—Q R 3 |
| 8. P—Q Kt 4 | B—Q 3 |
| 9. B—Kt 2 | Castles |

Diag. 155.

10. Q—Q 2

White cannot win the Q P by 10 P×P, P×P ; 11 Kt×P, Kt×Kt ; 12 Q×Kt, because B×P ch wins the Queen. The text move is played with the intention of bringing up the Q R for the attack on the Q P.   However, it would have been more correct to fix the object of attack first by P×P, as Black could now cross White's intentions by playing P×P, after which he would sooner or later gain a move by occupying the Q file with a Rook, and forcing the White Queen to retreat.

10. .........       Q—K 2 !

Black offers to give up his Queen's Pawn.   If White accepts the sacrifice, Black's attack on the Queen's file will become deadly, as White must lose a move in bringing his Queen out of the line of action of the hostile Rook.   The White King has then no time to get into safety, *e.g.* 11 P×P, P×P ; 12 Kt×P, Kt×Kt ; 13 Q×Kt, R—Q 1 ; 14 Q—Kt 3, B—K 3 followed by Kt×P, etc.

11. B—Q 3 ?

Here again P×P (followed by B—K 2, R—Q 1, Castles) would have avoided the loss of a move, as indicated in my note to move 10.   Now White loses yet another move, as Black exchanges pawns and the Bishop has taken two moves to reach B 4, as against one only in the case of the Black K B. The loss of two moves in the opening stages should be fatal, and of this Rubinstein gives a striking example in the present game.

| | |
|---|---|
| 11. ......... | P×P |
| 12. B×P | P—Q Kt 4 |
| 13. B—Q 3 | R—Q 1 |
| 14. Q—K 2 | B—Kt 2 |
| 15. Castles K R | Kt—K 4 |

The advantage which Black obtains by his last move is generally gained by White in this opening (compare Diag. 36). But in the game White has lost two moves and Black has assumed the offensive, having moreover a Rook acting on the Q file.

| | |
|---|---|
| 16. Kt×Kt | B×Kt |
| 17. P—B 4 | |

Black's threat was : B×P ch followed by Q—Q 3 ch and
Q×B. If White replies : 17 K R—Q 1 the answer is Q—B 2
attacking both the R P and the Kt. The text move is
unsatisfactory, as it will be necessary to advance the K P to
K 4 or K 5, where it will block the diagonal of one of the
Bishops.

| 17. ......... | B—B 2 |
| 18. P—K 4 | Q R—B 1 |
| 19. P—K 5 | B—Kt 3 ch |
| 20. K—R 1 | Kt—Kt 5 ! ! |

Diag. 156.

The beginning of magnificent sacrifices. 21 Q × Kt cannot be
played because of R × B and R—Q 7, etc.

| 21. B—K 4 | Q—R 5 |
| 22. P—Kt 3 | |

After P—R 3 Black wins also in fine style : R × Kt ! ! ;
23 Q × Kt, Q × Q ; 24 P × Q, B × B ; 25 B × R, R—Q 6 threatening R—R 6 mate ; or, 23 B × R, B × B ; 24 Q × B, Q—Kt 6 ;
25 P × Kt, Q—R 5 mate.

| 22 ......... | R × Kt ! ! |
| 23. P × Q | R—Q 7 ! ! |
| 24. Q × R | B × B ch |
| 25. Q—Kt 2 | R—R 6 |

and mate at R 7.

## GAME NO. 40

White : Rubinstein.          Black : Capablanca.
Queen's Gambit Declined.

| | | |
|---|---|---|
| 1. | P—Q 4 | P—Q 4 |
| 2. | Kt—K B 3 | P—Q B 4 |
| 3. | P—B 4 | P—K 3 |
| 4. | P×Q P | K P×P |
| 5. | Kt—B 3 | Kt—Q B 3 |
| 6. | P—K Kt 3 | B—K 3 |
| 7. | B—Kt 2 | B—K 2 |
| 8. | Castles | R—B 1 |

This move is not satisfactory at this juncture. It rather
helps a combination which is frequently resorted to in similar
positions, namely, the exchange of the Black Q B and subsequent pressure on the K P by the White K B on the diagonal
K R 3—Q B 8. 8...Kt—B 3 should have been played, after

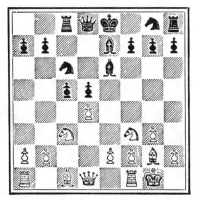

Diag. 157.

which White could hardly be said to possess any advantage, e.g.
9 B—Kt 5, Kt—K 5, or 9 B—K 3, Kt—K Kt 5, or 9 P—Q R 3,
or 9 P×P, B×P; 10 B—Kt 5, B—K 2. After 9 P×P, however, it would be weak to recapture with the Queen. In a

game E. Cohn—Ed. Lasker (match 1909) there followed: 9...
Q—R 4; 10 Kt—K Kt 5, Q×P; 11 B—K 3, Q—R 4; 12
Q—Kt 3, after which Black had to give up a pawn already:
Castles Q R; 13 Kt×B, P×Kt; 14 B—R 3, etc.

|  |  |  |
|---|---|---|
| 9. | P×P | B×P |
| 10. | Kt—K Kt 5 | Kt—B 3 |
| 11. | Kt×B | P×Kt |
| 12. | B—R 3 | Q—K 2 |
| 13. | B—Kt 5 | |

P—K 4 is stronger here, in order to play B—Kt 5 after
P×P. 13...P—Q 5 would then be refuted by Kt—Q 5.

|  |  |  |
|---|---|---|
| 13. | ......... | Castles |
| 14. | B×Kt | Q×B |

After this White gains a pawn by a complicated and well-
timed combination. Capablanca did not consider the subtle
reply on Rubinstein's seventeenth move. Otherwise he would
have recaptured with the pawn. However, in that case too,
White's chances are good in the end-game which ensues after:
15 Kt×P, P×Kt; 16 Q×P ch, K—R 1; 17 B×R. The
Rooks would soon become effective in view of the open K side.

|  |  |  |
|---|---|---|
| 15. | Kt×P | Q—R 3 |

B×P ch fails because of 16 K—Kt 2, Q—B 2; 17 Kt—B 4!

|  |  |  |
|---|---|---|
| 16. | K—Kt 2 | Q R—Q 1 |
| 17. | Q—B 1 | |

Diag. 158.

17. .........        P × Kt

If R × Kt, White exchanges Queens and plays B × P ch.

|  |  |  |
|---|---|---|
| 18. | Q × B | Q—Q 7 |
| 19. | Q—Kt 5 | Kt—Q 5 |
| 20. | Q—Q 3 |  |

With an extra pawn White forces the exchange of Queens. Black cannot prevent it, as 20...Q × Kt P loses the Knight on account of 21 K R—Kt 1, and 20...Q—Kt 5 loses the Q P by 21 K R—Q 1 and B—K 6 ch.

|  |  |  |
|---|---|---|
| 20. | ......... | Q × Q |
| 21. | P × Q | K R—K 1 |
| 22. | B—Kt 4 |  |

K R—K 1 would not prevent the entry of the Black Rook : Kt—B 7 ; 23 R × R ch, R × R ; 24 R—Q B 1, R—K 7 ; 25 B—Kt 4, R—Q 7. Black would win the pawn back and might even succeed in the end-game with a Knight against a Bishop.

|  |  |  |
|---|---|---|
| 22. | ......... | R—Q 3 |
| 23. | K R—K 1 | R × R |
| 24. | R × R | R—Q Kt 3 |

Black should first play his King to K B 3, and keep the Rook away from his K 5. Not that the Q P is of paramount importance ; the Q Kt P fully makes up for its loss. But as played the Knight is driven from his dominating position, and the badly placed Bishop gets into play. No doubt even after the text move the ending is most difficult, and it requires Rubinstein's full powers to bring it to a successful issue.

|  |  |  |
|---|---|---|
| 25. | R—K 5 | R × P |
| 26. | R × P | Kt—B 3 |
| 27. | B—K 6 ch | K—B 1 |
| 28. | R—B 5 ch | K—K 1 |
| 29. | B—B 7 ch | K—Q 2 |
| 30. | B—B 4 | P—Q R 3 |

Black's only chance is his extra pawn on the Q side. To exchange the Kt for the B by 30...K—Q 3 ; 31 R—B 7, Kt—K 4 ; 32 R × K Kt P, Kt × B would take too much time where time is all-important. White would clear the K side in the meantime, push on his K R P, and ultimately give up his R for Black's remaining P, as soon as the latter runs into Queen, after which the three passed pawns win easily against the Rook.  Generally speaking it is wise, in R endings like the present one, to advance pawns on the side where there is an extra pawn, in order to get a passed pawn as soon as possible. Then the hostile Rook has to look after that pawn lest it should queen, and the greater mobility of one's own Rook often saves the game even when opposed by a preponderance of pawns.

| | | |
|---|---|---|
| 31. | R—B 7 ch | K—Q 3 |
| 32. | R × K Kt P | P—Kt 4 |
| 33. | B—Kt 8 | P—Q R 4 |
| 34. | R × P | P—R 5 |
| 35. | P—R 4 | P—Kt 5 |
| 36. | R—R 6 ch | K—B 4 |
| 37. | R—R 5 ch | K—Kt 3 |
| 38. | B—Q 5 | P—Kt 6 |

R × P is tempting but unavailing, as White plays B—B 4 followed by R—Kt 5 ch and P—R 5–6, etc.  After the text move White has a problem-like continuation, which he has worked out with great accuracy.

| | | |
|---|---|---|
| 39. | P × P | P—R 6 |
| 40. | B × Kt | |

If now P—R 7, White simply plays 41 R—Kt 5 ch, K—R3 ; 42 R—Kt 8—R 8.

| | | |
|---|---|---|
| 40. | ......... | R × Kt P |
| 41. | B—Q 5 | P—R 7 |
| 42. | R—R 6 ch | Resigns. |

As the R holds the R P, *e.g.* K—R 4 ; 43 B—B 4 followed by R—R 6 ch or 42...K—R 2 ; 43 R—R 8, etc.

## GAME No. 41

White : Niemzowitsch.        Black : Tarrasch.
Queen's Gambit Declined.

| | | |
|---|---|---|
| 1. | P—Q 4 | P—Q 4 |
| 2. | Kt—K B 3 | P—Q B 4 |

| | |
|---|---|
| 3. P—B 4 | P—K 3 |
| 4. P—K 3 | Kt—K B 3 |
| 5. B—Q 3 | Kt—B 3 |
| 6. Castles | B—Q 3 |
| 7. P—Q Kt 3 | Castles |
| 8. B—Kt 2 | P—Q Kt 3 |
| 9. Q Kt—Q 2 | B—Kt 2 |
| 10. R—B 1 | Q—K 2 |
| 11. P×Q P | |

The most natural move to which the development of the Q Kt at Q 2 instead of B 3 would seem to lead is Kt—K 5 followed by P—B 4. After 11 Kt—K 5 Black could not yet attempt 11...P×Q P; 12 K P×P, B—R 6, weakening the Q P, because of 13 B×B, Q×B; 14 P×P, Kt×Kt; 15 P×Kt, Kt×P; 16 Kt—B 4 and Kt—Q 6.

| | |
|---|---|
| 11. ......... | K P×P |
| 12. Kt—R 4 | |

In order to provoke Black's weakening move : P—Kt 3, which might give White chances of attack on the long diagonal Q R 1—K R 8, White gives up two clear moves. Black is able to get considerably ahead in his development, much to White's disadvantage.

| | |
|---|---|
| 12. ......... | P—Kt 3 |
| 13. K Kt—B 3 | Q R—Q sq |

Not Kt—K 5 yet, on account of 14 P×P, P×P?; 15 B×Kt, P×B; 16 Kt×P.

| | |
|---|---|
| 14. P×P | |

White's position is uncomfortable, and a satisfactory continuation is hard to find. Possibly passive resistance might have been the best plan, thus : Q—K 2, K R—Q 1, Kt—B 1— Kt 3. The text move is a preliminary to operations on the Queen's side, but allows Black too much scope in the centre.

| | |
|---|---|
| 14. ......... | P×P |
| 15. B—Kt 5 | |

White wishes to get rid of the Black Knight which supports the advance of P—Q 5.

| 15. ......... | Kt—K 5 |
| 16. B×Kt | B×B |
| 17. Q—B 2 | |

White has no idea of the threatened disaster, or he would have played P—K Kt 3. Even then, however, Black has the better game with two Bishops, and the Q and Kt better placed.

| 17. ......... | Kt×Kt |

The beginning of a brilliant mating combination.

| 18. Kt×Kt | P—Q 5 ! |

Black would have played the same move if White had retaken with the Queen.

| 19. P×P | |

P—K 4 was comparatively the best move, although Black's attack would have become overwhelming after P—B 4, *e.g.* 20 P—B 3, B—B 5, etc.

Diag. 159.

| 19. ......... | B×P ch ! ! |
| 20. K×B | Q—R 5 ch |
| 21. K—Kt 1 | B×P ! |

Emanuel Lasker won a celebrated game from Bauer (Amsterdam, 1889) with a similar sacrifice of two Bishops, and very likely this is the reason why Tarrasch's beautiful game only earned him the second brilliancy prize at Petrograd (1914).

22. P—B 3

If K×B, then Q—Kt 5 ch ; 23 K—R 1, R—Q 4 ; 24 Q×P, R—R 4 ch ; 25 Q×R, Q×Q ch ; 26 K—Kt 2, Q—Kt 4 ch and Q×Kt.

| 22. ......... | K R—K 1 |

Not Q—Kt 6, because of Kt—K 4.

| 23. Kt—K 4 | Q—R 8 ch |
| 24. K—B 2 | B×R |
| 25. P—Q 5 | P—B 4 |
| 26. Q—B 3 | Q—Kt 7 ch |
| 27. K—K 3 | R×Kt ch ! |
| 28. P×R | P—B 5 ch |

With Q—Kt 6 ch Black mates two moves earlier.

| 29. K×P | R—B 1 ch |
| 30. K—K 5 | Q—R 7 ch |
| 31. K—K 6 | R—K 1 ch |
| Resigns. | |

If K—Q 7, B—Kt 4 mate, if K—B 6, Q—R 5 mate.[1]

## GAME NO. 42

White : Capablanca.　　　Black : Aljechin.
Queen's Gambit Declined (see pp. 57 and 58).

| 1. P—Q 4 | P—Q 4 |
| 2. P—Q B 4 | P—Q B 3 |
| 3. P—K 3 | Kt—B 3 |
| 4. Kt—K B 3 | P—K 3 |
| 5. Q Kt—Q 2 | Q Kt—Q 2 |

[1] Emanuel Lasker-Bauer: 1 P—K B 4, P—Q 4; 2 P—K 3, Kt—K B 3; 3 P—Q Kt 3, P—K 3; 4 B—Kt 2, B—K 2; 5 B—Q 3, P—Q Kt 3; 6 Kt—Q B 3, B—Kt 2; 7 Kt—B 3, Q Kt—Q 2; 8 Castles, Castles: 9 Kt—K 2, P—B 4; 10 Kt—Kt 3, Q—B 2; 11 Kt—K 5, Kt×Kt; 12 B×Kt, Q—B 3; 13 Q—K 2, P—Q R 3; 14 Kt—R 5, Kt×Kt; 15 B×P ch !!, K×B; 16 Q×Kt ch, K—Kt 1; 17 B ×P !, K×B; 18 Q—Kt 4 ch, K—R 2; 19 R—B 3, P—K 4; 20 R—R 3 ch, Q—R 3; 21 R×Q, K×R; 22 Q—Q 7, and White won.

| | |
|---|---|
| 6. B—Q 3 | B—K 2 |
| 7. Castles | Castles |
| 8. Q—B 2 | |

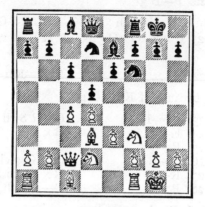

Diag. 160.

Black's difficulty is the development of his Q B, particularly after White's last move, which prevents P—K 4. If
now Q—B 2 White plays 9 P—K 4 and either the Queen or
the Knight bear on K 5, *e.g.* 9...P×K P; 10 Kt×P, P—K 4;
11 Q Kt—Kt 5, B—Q 3 ; 12 P—B 5, etc.

Black therefore must develop his Q B at Kt 2 with P—
Q Kt 3, B—Kt 2 and P—B 4. Having moved the Q B P twice,
Black is a move behind the development usual in this opening.
However, it would have been the lesser evil. In the present
game the Bishop does not get into play in time.

| | |
|---|---|
| 8. ......... | P×P |
| 9. Kt×P | P—B 4 |
| 10. Q Kt—K 5 | P×P |
| 11. P×P | Kt—Kt 3 |
| 12. Kt—Kt 5 | |

If Black captures the pawn, White gains time by threatening the Queen, and brings all his forces into play, whilst the Black
Queen's side remains undeveloped, *e.g.* : 12...Q×P; 13 R—
Q 1, Q—B 4 ; 14 Kt—Kt 4, P—Kt 3 ; 15 B—K 3, Q—R 4 ;
16 R—B 1, with a strong attack. Black of course need not
take the pawn, but the move in the text is a valuable one

nevertheless, as the threat Q—B 3—R 3 provokes a weakening pawn move.

| | |
|---|---|
| 12. ......... | P—Kt 3 |
| 13. K Kt—B 3 | K—Kt 2 |

preventing the entry of the B at R 6.

| | |
|---|---|
| 14. B—K Kt 5 | Q Kt—Q 4 |
| 15. Q R—B 1 | B—Q 2 |
| 16. Q—Q 2 | Kt—Kt 1 |

It should be noted how the weakness at K R 3 acts to the detriment of Black's game. The text move covers the weak square, but at the same time brings the Kt out of play. White in consequence gets the upper-hand on the Queen's side, and the Knight cannot return in time.

| | |
|---|---|
| 17. B×B | Q×B |

It would be no use taking with the K Kt, as the threat Kt—Kt 4 and Q—R 6 must be guarded against. If the other Kt captures there follows : 18 B—K 4, R—Kt 1 ; 19 R—B 3 and K R—B 1.

| | |
|---|---|
| 18. B—K 4 | B—Kt 4 |

This drives the Rook to a better square, but already now there is no satisfactory move. It would perhaps have been best to parry the threat of B×Kt and R—B 7 by playing Q—Q 3, although the pawn would have to recapture after 19 B×Kt, because of 20 R—B 5 and K R—B 1. The chance of bearing on the Q P through the open file, which was probably Black's intention all along, would then be lost. After the text move, however, White takes possession of the seventh rank, and Black's game collapses quickly.

| | |
|---|---|
| 19. K R—K 1 | Q—Q 3 |
| 20. B×Kt | P×B |
| 21. Q—R 5 | P—Q R 3 |
| 22. Q—B 7 | Q×Q |
| 23. R×Q | P—R 3 |

Kt—Kt 5 and Kt—K 6 ch was threatened.

| | |
|---|---|
| 24. R×P | Q R—B 1 |
| 25. P—Q Kt 3 | R—B 7 |
| 26. P—Q R 4 | B—K 7 |
| 27. Kt—R 4 ! | P—K R 4 |

The Kt P cannot be saved.

| | | |
|---|---|---|
| 28. | K Kt × P | R—K 1 |
| 29. | R × P ch | Resigns. |

### GAME No. 43

White : Capablanca.  Black : Bernstein.
Queen's Gambit Declined.

| | | |
|---|---|---|
| 1. | P—Q 4 | P—Q 4 |
| 2. | Kt—K B 3 | Kt—K B 3 |
| 3. | P—B 4 | P—K 3 |
| 4. | Kt—B 3 | Q Kt—Q 2 |
| 5. | B—Kt 5 | B—K 2 |
| 6. | P—K 3 | P—B 3 |
| 7. | B—Q 3 | P × P |

Before initiating this manœuvre, which aims at the development of the Queen's wing, Black should castle, as otherwise the King is exposed to dangerous and immediate attacks in the centre.

| | | |
|---|---|---|
| 8. | B × B P | P—Kt 4 |
| 9. | B—Q 3 | P—Q R 3 |

The system of opening chosen by Black has been tried frequently of late. It seems to be somewhat artificial, as the Q B Pawn takes two moves to get to his fourth. On the other hand the pawn formation at Q R 3, Q Kt 4, and Q B 4 is attained, whilst it can be prevented in other variations, *e.g.* 6...Castles ; 7 B—Q 3, P × P ; 8 B × P, P—Q R 3 ; 9 P—Q R 4.

| | | |
|---|---|---|
| 10. | P—K 4 | P—K 4 |

Diag. 161.

Black's only plausible move here seems to be P—B 4, and

many critics have remarked that after 11 P—K 5, P×P!; 12 Kt—K 4 (if P×Kt, P×Kt) Kt × Kt; 13 B × Kt, R—Q Kt 1; 14 B × B, Q × B; 15 Q × P, Q—B 4; the game would have been even. However, this is not the case, for on the 15th move White does not capture the pawn with the Q but with the Kt and Black has no satisfactory continuation. If he had castled he could play 15...B—Kt 2 which now is not available because of: 16 Kt—B 6, B × Kt; 17 B × B, with an overwhelming advantage in position for White. White's refutation of the text move is above criticism.

   11. P×P      Kt—Kt 5    12. B—K B 4    B—B 4

If Q—B 2, White would play R—B 1, after which Black could not recapture the K P yet, as the Q B P is *en prise*.

   13...K Kt × P; 14 Kt × Kt, Kt × Kt; 15 Kt—Q 5, Q—Q 3; 16 B × Kt, Q × B; 19 R × P, etc.

      13. Castles        Q—B 2
      14. R—B 1        P—B 3

Again Kt × P is not feasible on account of the loss of the Q B P, as can be easily seen.

      15. B—Kt 3        P×P

Black's game cannot be saved. If 15...Kt (Kt 5) × K P there follows 16 Kt × Kt, Kt × Kt; 17 Kt—Q 5, Q—Q 3; 18 B × Kt, P × B; 19 R ×B, or 16...P×Kt; 17 Q—R 5 ch, P—Kt 3, 18 Q—R 6.

      16. P—Kt 4!

Now White initiates a brilliant attack, driving it home without giving Black a moment's rest. If Black takes the pawn, White plays Kt—Q 4, with many threats, *e.g.* P—B 4; 18 Kt—Q 5, Q—Q 3; 19 Kt—K 6, or 17...Kt (Kt 5)—B 3; 18 Kt—K 6, etc.

   16. .........      B—R 2      17. B×Kt P

The sacrifice is fairly obvious, as White obtains three pawns for the piece, and moreover drives the King into the field of battle. However, this does not detract from the beauty of the game, which is full of brilliant phases.

   17. .........        R P × B
   18. Kt×Kt P        Q—Q 1

Or Q—Kt 3 ; 19 Kt—Q 6 ch, K—K 2 ; 20 Kt—B 5 ch, followed by Q—Q 6.

| | | |
|---|---|---|
| 19. | Kt—Q 6 ch | K—B 1 |
| 20. | R×P | Kt—Kt 3 |

The threat was : 21 Q—Q 5, Kt—R 3 ; 22 Kt×B, R×Kt ; 23 R—Q 6, etc. 20...Kt (Q 2)—B 3 is of no avail because of 21 Q—Kt 3, Kt—R 3 ; 22 Kt×P, or 21...Q—Q 2 ; 22 K R—B 1, etc.

| | | |
|---|---|---|
| 21. | B—R 4 | Q—Q 2 |
| 22. | Kt×B ! | Q×R |

Not R×Kt because of 23 Q×Q. Now Black is a whole Rook ahead. But it is as much out of play as his Queen's side pieces. The King is driven into a mating net by the concentration of superior White forces, and only escapes by giving up the extra piece.

| | | |
|---|---|---|
| 23. | Q—Q 8 ch | Q—K 1 |
| 24. | B—K 7 ch | K—B 2 |
| 25. | Kt—Q 6 ch | K—Kt 3 |
| 26. | Kt—R 4 ch | K—R 4 |

If K—R 3 there follows mate in three by 27 Kt (Q 6)—B 5 ch ; 28 Kt—Kt 3 ch ; 29 B—Kt 5 mate.

| | | |
|---|---|---|
| 27. | Kt×Q | R×Q |
| 28. | Kt×P ch | K—R 3 |
| 29. | Kt (Kt 7)—B 5 ch | K—R 4 |
| 30. | P—K R 3 ! | |

This threatens 31 P×Kt ch, K×P ; 32 P—B 3 ch, followed by P—Kt 3 or Kt 4 mate. If Black plays 30 Q R—K Kt 1, White wins as follows: 31 P×Ktch, R×P ; 32 P—B 3, Kt—B 1 ch ; 33 K—R 2, Kt×B ; 34 P×R ch, K×P ; 35 Kt×Kt, K×Kt ; 36 R—B 7. If 30...Kt—R 3 ; 31 Kt—Kt 7 mate.

| | | |
|---|---|---|
| 30. | ......... | Kt—B 1 |
| 31. | P×Kt ch | K×P |
| 32. | B×R | R×B |
| 33. | P—Kt 3 | R—Q 7 |
| 34. | K—Kt 2 | R—K 7 |
| 35. | P—R 4 | Kt—Kt 3 |

| | |
|---|---|
| 36. Kt—K 3 ch | K—R 4 |
| 37. P—R 5 | Kt—Q 2 |
| 38. Kt (R 4)—B 5 | Kt—B 3 |
| 39. P—Kt 5 | B—Q 5 |
| 40.. K—B 3 | R—R 7 |
| 41. P—R 6 | B—R 2 |
| 42. R—B 1 | R—Kt 7 |
| 43. P—Kt 4 ch | K—Kt 4 |
| 44. R—B 7 | R×P ch |
| 45. K×R | Kt×Kt P ch |
| 46. K—B 3 | Resigns. |

## GAME No. 44

White : Dus Chotimirski.      Black : Vidmar.

Queen's Pawn Game.

| | |
|---|---|
| 1. P—Q 4 | P—Q 4 |
| 2. Kt—K B 3 | P—Q B 4 |
| 3. P—B 3 | P—K 3 |
| 4. B—B 4 | |

We have seen on page 55 that Black can hardly develop his Q B without disadvantage. White, however, has no difficulty in doing so, as his Q P is protected, and after Black's Q—Kt 3 he has only to look after his Kt P. He could play Q—B 1, which might bring the Q into effective action on the diagonal to R 6.

The aim of the text move is the early occupation of K 5. But, as the present game shows, this cannot be effected. Black must not waste time with Q—Kt 3, but play B—Q 3 at once.

| | |
|---|---|
| 4. ......... | Kt—Q B 3 |
| 5. P—K 3 | Kt—B 3 |
| 6. Q Kt—Q 2 | B—Q 3 |
| 7. B—Kt 3 | Castles |
| 8. Kt—K 5 | B×Kt ! |
| 9. P×B | Kt—Q 2 |

Now White has no means of maintaining his centre.

Whether he supports the pawn with Kt—B 3 or P—K B 4, Black forces matters with P—B 3.

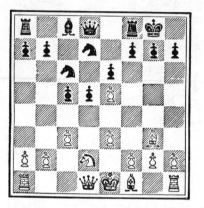

Diag. 162.

Now that the idea underlying White's opening strategy has proved impracticable, he has difficulty in formulating a plan. Making the best of a bad job, he abandons his K P in exchange for Black's K R P. But Black obtains a powerful pawn centre, a telling advantage.

| | | |
|---|---|---|
| 10. | B—Q 3 | K Kt × P |
| 11. | B × Kt | Kt × B |
| 12. | B × P ch | K × B |
| 13. | Q—R 5 ch | K—Kt 1 |
| 14. | Q × Kt | P—B 3 |
| 15. | Q—R 5 | Q—Kt 3 |

Black wishes to provoke the advance of the Q Kt P and Q B P in order to obtain a passed pawn (16 P—Q Kt 3, P—K 4; 17 Castles K R, Q—R 4; 18 P—Q B 4, P—Q 5). In order to avoid this continuation, White takes his chance of castling on the Queen's side. This turns out to Black's advantage. Indeed it is a foregone conclusion. In the ensuing double assault by pawns, Black is several moves ahead, as the White pawns concerned in the attack are still on their original squares.

|     |                |              |
|-----|----------------|--------------|
| 16. | Castles Q R    | P—K 4        |
| 17. | P—K Kt 4       | P—Q 5        |
| 18. | P—Q B 4        | B—Q 2        |
| 19. | P—Kt 5         | P×Kt P       |
| 20. | Q×P            | R×P          |
| 21. | P×P            | B P×P !      |

Finely played.  Black gives up his K P in order to get his
Q R into play with the gain of a move.

|     |           |             |
|-----|-----------|-------------|
| 22. | Q×P       | R—K 1       |
| 23. | Q—Kt 3    | Q R—K 7     |
| 24. | K R—K 1   |             |

K R—Kt 1 would also be of no avail because of Q—K R 3,
25 Q—Q 3, Q—K B 3 threatening B—B 4.  The move in the
text puts an end to the agony.

|     |            |          |
|-----|------------|----------|
| 24. | ………       | R×Kt ! !  |
|     | Resigns.   |          |

For after 25 R×R, R×R ; 26 K×R, Q×P ch ; 27 K—Q 3,
B—B 4 ch ; 28 R—K 4, Q—B 6 ch ; 29 K—K 2, Q×Q ;
Black remains with an extra piece.

## GAME No. 45

White : Rubinstein.          Black : Spielmann.
Irregular Opening.

|    |         |          |
|----|---------|----------|
| 1. | P—Q 4   | P—Q B 4  |

With this move Black tries to avoid well-trodden paths of
tournament practice.  White can, at will, lead into a peaceful
Queen's Gambit by 2 P—K 3 or into a Sicilian Defence by
P—K 4.  It is more usual, however, to play P—Q 5, which
blocks up the Black centre to some extent.

If 2 P×P, Black regains his pawn after P—K 3 without
any disadvantage.

|    |           |        |
|----|-----------|--------|
| 2. | P—Q 5     | P—Q 3  |
| 3. | P—Q B 4   |        |

Coupled with 4 P—K 4, this move is of doubtful value, as Black gains command of White's Q 4. It is advisable to keep the Q B P back, thus retaining the option of driving off a hostile piece from Q 4 by P—Q B 3. Moreover, the White K B is hemmed in by the pawn at Q B 4.

| | |
|---|---|
| 3. ......... | P—K Kt 3 |
| 4. P—K 4 | B—Kt 2 |
| 5. B—Q 3 | P—K 3 |

The development of the K Kt is not desirable at B 3, where it would block the long diagonal. From K 2, however, it commands K B 4, where it can take up a strong position after the exchange of pawns in the centre, or else it can support the advance of the K B P.

| | |
|---|---|
| 6. Kt—Q B 3 | Kt—K 2 |
| 7. K Kt—K 2 | |

Kt—B 3 would have been slightly better, because the Black Q Kt might play to his K 4.

| | |
|---|---|
| 7. ......... | P × P |
| 8. K P × P | Kt—Q 2 |
| 9. P—B 4 | |

This move weakens the King's position, and would be justified only if there was a possibility of opening the file for the Rook by P—B 5. But Black has too strong a hold on his K B 4. The text move aims at preventing the exchange of White's K B through Black's Kt—K 4. It would have been better to withdraw the B to B 2.

| | |
|---|---|
| 9. ......... | Kt—K B 3 |
| 10. Kt—Kt 3 | P—K R 4 ! |

Now White cannot enforce P—B 5, as Black can attack the Knight by P—R 5. White cannot prevent this with P—K R 4, as the Black Knight would take up a commanding position at Kt 5. Black's game is superior. He can concen-

trate all his minor pieces on the King's wing, while White's
Q B is ineffective on account of the ill-considered advance of
the K B P.

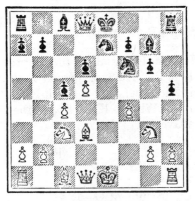

Diag. 163.

| | |
|---|---|
| 11. Castles | P—R 5 |
| 12. K Kt—K 4 | Kt × Kt |
| 13. B × Kt | |

White has to capture with the B, in order to exchange the
Black Knight if it should play to B 4. After 13 Kt × Kt,
B—Q 5 ch ; 14 K—R 1, Kt—B 4 ; White's Knight would not
be able to move from K 4 on account of the threat : Kt—Kt 6
ch. Sooner or later, Black would get a deciding advantage
by enforcing the exchange of White's Knight, *e.g.* 15 Q—K 1,
Q—K 2 ; 16 R—Q Kt 1, B—Q 2 ; 17 P—Q Kt 3, Castles Q R ;
18 B—Kt 2, Q × Kt ; 19 B × Q, Kt—Kt 6 ch ; 20 Q × Kt,
P × Q ; 21 P—K R 3, B × P ; 22 P × B, R × P ch ; 23 K—Kt 2,
R—R 7 ch ; 24 K × P, R × B ; or 21 B × B, R × P ch, followed
by P × B and Q R—R 1.

| | |
|---|---|
| 13. ......... | B—Q 5 ch |
| 14. K—R 1 | Kt—B 4 |
| 15. B × Kt | B × B |

White is helpless against the two powerful Bishops.

| | |
|---|---|
| 16. R—K 1 ch | K—B 1 |

Black forfeits his chance of castling, not a great loss under the circumstances. In any case his K R is needed on the Rook's file, and Black would only have castled on the Queen's side if at all.

### 17. Q—B 3

Here P—K R 3 was essential in order to prevent the further advance of the K R P. The weakness at Kt 3 would not have been so serious in the absence of a Black Knight. Now Black forces the advance of White's K Kt P, and the Bishops become immediately effective.

|  |  |
|---|---|
| 17. ......... | P—R 6 |
| 18. P—K Kt 3 | |

not P—K Kt 4 on account of Q—R 5.

|  |  |
|---|---|
| 18. ......... | Q—Q 2 |
| 19. B—Q 2 | B—Kt 5 |
| 20. Q—B 1 | |

If Q—Q 3, Black plays Q—B 4 and White cannot exchange Queens because of B—B 6 mate.

|  |  |
|---|---|
| 20. ......... | Q—B 4 |

threatening Q—B 7.

|  |  |
|---|---|
| 21. Q R—B 1 | K—Kt 2 |
| 22. B—K 3 | B—B 3 |

Black must not exchange his valuable Bishop.

|  |  |
|---|---|
| 23. P—Kt 3 | K R—K 1 |
| 24. B—B 2 | |

There is no answer to Black's threat of doubling the Rooks on the K file. If White plays Q—B 2, Black's Queen effects an entry at Q 6, after which he would double his Rooks, and White's Bishop cannot be defended. After the text move, Black forces the exchange of his two Rooks for the Queen.

Generally speaking, this is no disadvantage, but in consequence of the exposed position of the White King, it means a speedy loss for White.

| 24. ......... | B—B 6 ch |
| 25. K—Kt 1 | B—Kt 7 |
| 26. R×R | B×Q |
| 27. R×R | Q—Q 6 ! |

If now R×B Black plays Q—B 6.

28. R—K 8

In order to play R—K 3 if Black plays B×Kt.

| 28. ......... | Q—B 6 ! |
| 29. K×B | Q—R 8 ch |
| 30. B—Kt 1 | Q—Kt 7 ch |
| 31. K—K 1 | Q×B ch |
| 32. K—Q 2 | Q×P ch |
| Resigns | |

for the pawn queens.

## GAME No. 46

White : G. A. Thomas.    Black : Ed. Lasker.
Irregular Opening (compare Game No. 45).

| 1. P—Q 4 | P—Q B 4 |
| 2. P—Q 5 | P—Q 3 |
| 3. P—Q B 4 | P—K Kt 3 |
| 4. Kt—Q B 3 | B—Kt 2 |
| 5. B—Q 2 | |

This is not necessary. Black could hardly exchange his B for the Kt ; the weakness at his K B 3 and K R 3 would become too serious a disadvantage.

| 5. ......... | P—K 3 |
| 6. P—K 4 | P×P |
| 7. Kt×P ! | |

In view of the fact that Black's position after B P or
K P × P would be very promising, as all his pieces would be
easy to bring into play, White decides upon the sacrifice of a
pawn, in order to further his own development.

| | |
|---|---|
| 7. ......... | B × P |
| 8. R—Kt 1 | B—Kt 2 |
| 9. Q—R 4 ch | Kt—B 3 |
| 10. K Kt—B 3 | |

Kt—Kt 6, R—Kt sq ; 11 B—R 5 leads to nothing, as Black
plays 12 Q K 2.

| | |
|---|---|
| 10. ......... | P—K R 3 |

If Black plays K Kt—K 2 at once, his position becomes
somewhat cramped after 11 B—Kt 5. Castles ; 12 Kt—B 6 ch,
K—R 1 ; 13 Q—Q 1.

| | |
|---|---|
| 11. B—Q 3 | Kt—K 2 |
| 12. Castles | Castles |
| 13. Q—B 2 | P—Kt 3 |

This allows the development of the Q B.

| | |
|---|---|
| 14. B—B 3 | Kt × Kt |
| 15. K P × Kt | Kt—K 4 |

Diag. 164.

Kt—K 2 should have been played here in order to play
B×B; 17 Q×B, B—Kt 5 with Kt—B 4, in answer to 16 Q—
Kt 2. Black is still open to attack in consequence of his
broken King's side, but there is no demonstrable advantage
for White. The text move is a mistake, and gives White
chances of a decisive attack.

|     |         |        |
| --- | ------- | ------ |
| 16. | Kt×Kt   | B×Kt   |
| 17. | B×B     | P×B    |
| 18. | B×P !   | Q—Kt 4 |

Of course not P×B, on account of 19 Q×P ch, K—R 1 ;
20 Q×P ch, K—Kt 1 ; 21 R—Kt 3, etc. 18...P—B 4 fails
because of 19 R—Kt 3.

|     |          |       |
| --- | -------- | ----- |
| 19. | B—K 4    | P—B 4 |
| 20. | P—B 4 !! |       |

This elegant continuation decides the game. If P×P,
White simply plays 21 B—Q 3, and Black can hardly hope to
save the end-game, as his pawns are broken up.   If the Queen
retreats, however, there follows :  21 P×P, and White obtains
two passed pawns for the B and has the superior position.

|     |          |          |
| --- | -------- | -------- |
| 20. | ......... | Q—Kt 2   |
| 21. | P×P      | P×B      |
| 22. | R×R ch   | Q×R      |
| 23. | R—K B 1  | Q—Kt 2   |
| 24. | Q×P      | Q—Kt 5   |
| 25. | R—B 4    | Q—Q 8 ch |
| 26. | K—B 2    | Q—Q 5 ch |
| 27. | Q×Q      | P×Q      |
| 28. | P—K 6    | B—R 3    |
| 29. | R×P      | R—B 1 ch |

If K—B 1, 30 P—Q 6.

|     |       |          |
| --- | ----- | -------- |
| 30. | K—K 3 | R—B 3    |
| 31. | K—K 4 | R—B 7    |
| 32. | P—Q 6 | R—K 7 ch |

He might play K—Q 5, after which B—Kt 2 ch has points.

|     |       |         |
| --- | ----- | ------- |
| 33. | K—Q 3 | Resigns. |

## Game No. 47

White : Tartakower.          Black : Asztalos.

Dutch Opening.

1. P—K B 4          P—Q 4

It has been tried to refute White's non-developing first move by a pawn sacrifice : 1...P—K 4; which leads to a rapid mobilisation of the Black forces after 2 P×P, P—Q 3 ; 3 P×P, B×P. But this attack—called the From Gambit—does not seem to prevail against the best defence. In a match game, Tartakower-Spielmann (Vienna, 1913), White won as follows :
4 Kt—K B 3, P—K Kt 4 ; 5 P—Q 4, P—Kt 5 ; 6 Kt—K 5, Kt—Q B 3 ; 7 Kt×Kt, P×Kt ; 8 P—K Kt 3, P—K R 4 ; 9 B—Kt 2, P—R 5 ; 10 Q—Q 3, B—Q 2 ; 11 Kt—B 3, R—Kt 1; 12 Castles, P×P ; 13 P×P, P—Q B 4 ; 14 B—B 4, B×B ; 15 R×B, Q—Kt 4 ; 16 Kt—K 4, Q—R 3 ; 17 Kt×P, Kt—B 3 ; 18 Kt×B, Kt×Kt ; 19 Q—K 4 ch, K—Q 1 ; 20 R×B P, R—K 1 ; 21 Q×P, Q—K 6 ch ; 22 K—B 1, Resigns.

When Black plays P—K B 4 in answer to 1 P—Q 4 we have the Dutch Defence. After 1 P—Q 4, P—K B 4, White can also sacrifice a pawn by 2 P—K 4, and thereby obtain a far more favourable position than Black does in From's gambit, as he is a move to the good, having already advanced his Q P, e.g. 2 P—K 4, P×P ; 3 Kt—Q B 3, Kt—K B 3 ; 4 P—B 3 or 4 B—Kt 5 and then P—B 3. If Black captures the K B P, White obtains a powerful attack. A drastic example is found in the following little game, played by two students in an academic tournament at Petrograd : 4 P—B 3, P×P ; 5 Kt×P, P—K 3 ; 6 B—K Kt 5, B—K 2 ; 7 B—Q 3, Castles ; 8 Castles, P—Q Kt 3 ; 9 Kt—K 5, B—Kt 2 ; 10 B× Kt, B×B ; 11 B×P ch, K×B ; 12 Q—R 5 ch, K—Kt 1 ; 13 Kt—Kt 6, R—K 1 ; 14 Q—R 8 ch, K—B 2 ; 15 Kt—K 5 ch, K—K 2 ; 16 Q×P ch ! !, B×Q ; 17 R—B 7 ch, K—Q 3 ; 18 Kt—Kt 5 ch, K—Q 4 ; 19 P—B 4 ch, K—K 5 ; 20 R—K 1 mate.

Black's best answer is to play P—Q 4 after White's 4 P—K B 3 (5 B—Kt 5, B—B 4). If 4 B—Kt 5, it is not yet possible to play P—Q 4 because of the threat : B×Kt, Q—R 5 ch, and

Q×Q P. In that case Black must first play P—Q B 3, after which White again obtains a strong attack by P—K B 3.

Black can avoid the attacks which follow after 1 P—Q 4, P—K B 4 ; 2 P—K 4, by playing P—K 3 on his first move, and then lead into the Dutch defence with P—K B 4 on his second move. He must, however, reckon with having to play the French defence which White can bring about with 2 P—K 4.

| | | |
|---|---|---|
| 2. | P—K 3 | P—K 3 |
| 3. | Kt—K B 3 | P—Q B 4 |
| 4. | P—Q Kt 3 | Kt—Q B 3 |
| 5. | B—Kt 5 | Kt—B 3 |

Black should have played B—Q 2 here, as White can exchange at B 6, leaving Black with a doubled pawn. This in itself is not a drawback, but in the present position it is serious, as Black will have difficulty in finding a place for his Q B. For there is no prospect of enforcing P—K 4, as White commands that square in sufficient force.

| | | |
|---|---|---|
| 6. | B—Kt 2 | B—K 2 |
| 7. | Castles | Castles |
| 8. | B×Q Kt | P×B |
| 9. | Kt—K 5 | Q—B 2 |
| 10. | P—Q 3 | P—Q R 4 |

Black's attempt of capturing his K 4 by playing Kt—Q 2 and P—B 3, White would cross at once with Q—Kt 4. With the text move Black begins operations on the Q side, which is quite correct, as White has the upper hand on the other wing.

11. Q—K 2

White should have prevented the further advance of the Black R P by 11 P—Q R 4. This would have been sound policy in any case, as the R file could not have been forced open for the Black Rooks.

| | | |
|---|---|---|
| 11. | ......... | P—R 5 |
| 12. | Kt—Q 2 | P×P |

Premature. The capture is only of value if the file can be held. To that end it is first necessary to play B—Kt 2 and to occupy the R file with Rooks and Queen. After the exchange

of Rooks, Black is at a disadvantage for the end-game because
of the inefficiency of the Q B.

Diag. 165.

If instead of the text move Black had driven off the Bishop
to B 1 with P—R 6 (13 B—B 3 ?, P—Q 5 ! ; 14 P×P, Kt—Q 4)
he could have enforced his P—K 4, but in the long run White
would have captured the Q R P, and remained with a passed
pawn on the R file, a powerful weapon for the end-game, *e.g.*
12...P—R 6 ; 13 B—B 1, Kt—Q 2 ; 14 Kt×Kt, B×Kt ;
15 P—K 4, P—K B 3 ; 16 P—B 4, followed by Kt—Kt 1.

|        |         |
|--------|---------|
| 13. R P×P | R×R |
| 14. R×R | B—Kt 2 |
| 15. P—K Kt 4 | |

The Black pieces being cut off from the K side, White is
free to attack.

|        |         |
|--------|---------|
| 15. ......... | R—R 1 |
| 16. R×R ch | B×R |
| 17. P—Kt 5 | Kt—Q 2 |
| 18. Q Kt—B 3 | Kt×Kt |
| 19. B×Kt | Q—R 4 |
| 20. P—B 4 | |

in order to prevent the release of the B by the pawn sacrifice
P—B 5 and P—B 4.

|        |         |
|--------|---------|
| 20. ......... | B—Kt 2 |
| 21. K—B 2 | K—B 1 |

| 22. P—R 4 | B—R 3 |
| 23. P—R 5 | B—Kt 2 |
| 24. P—R 6 | P—Kt 3 |

By advancing his R P White has weakened Black's K B 3, with the constant threat of establishing his Kt there and of capturing the R P.

25. K—B 1

This move is superfluous and probably dictated by time pressure. The proper plan is : Q—Q Kt 2 with the threat of B—B 7 or Kt 8 and Q—R 8 ch.

| 25. ......... | Q—R 6 |
| 26. Q—Q Kt 2 | |

The end-game is a clear win for White. He plays his Kt to K Kt 4, threatening to reach B 6 or K 5. The effect is twofold.

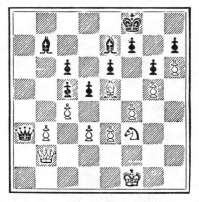

Diag. 166.

Black must keep his B at K 2 and his K must remain near the K B P. White's King marches to Q Kt 6 and captures the Q B pawns, queening his Q Kt P. Black cannot prevent the White King from doing this by B—Q 1, as White, by attacking Black's Q B 4 with his B, could at any time force the B back to his K 2. The remainder of the game needs no comment.

| 26. ......... | Q×Q |
| 27. B×Q | B—Q 3 |
| 28. Kt—R 2 | K—K 1 |

| | |
|---|---|
| 29. Kt—Kt 4 | B—K 2 |
| 30. B—K 5 | K—Q 2 |
| 31. K—K 2 | K—K 1 |
| 32. K—Q 2 | K—Q 2 |
| 33. K—B 2 | K—K 1 |
| 34. K—Kt 2 | K—Q 2 |
| 35. K—R 3 | K—K 1 |
| 36. K—R 4 | K—Q 2 |
| 37. B—Kt 8 | K—B 1 |
| 38. B—R 7 | K—Q 2 |
| 39. B—Kt 6 | P—Q 5 |
| 40. P—K 4 | K—K 1 |
| 41. P—K 5 | K—Q 2 |
| 42. Kt—B 2 | Resigns. |

because there follows Kt—K 4 and B × P.

## GAME No. 48

White : Blackburne.  Black : Niemzowitsch.
Irregular Opening.

1. P—K 3  P—Q 3

It is due to this reply of Black's that the opening is irregular. For had he played P—Q 4 a peaceful Q P game would have resulted, or after White's 2 P—K B 4 a Dutch opening.

2. P—K B 4  P—K 4
3. P × P  P × P

Black has the superior position ; he has a pawn in the centre and his pieces are more free.

4. Kt—Q B 3  B—Q 3

As was seen on a former occasion, it is a shade better to develop the Knights before the Bishops, as the choice of moves for the latter is less limited. The alternative might have been 5 Kt—B 3, B—K Kt 5 ; 6 B—K 2, Kt—B 3.

5. P—K 4

Now White has also a pawn in the centre, but he is a move behind in his development.

| | | |
|---|---|---|
| 5. | ......... | B—K 3 |
| 6. | Kt—B 3 | P—K B 3 |
| 7. | P—Q 3 | Kt—K 2 |
| 8. | B—K 3 | P—Q B 4 |
| 9. | Q—Q 2 | Q Kt—B 3 |
| 10. | B—K 2 | Kt—Q 5 |
| 11. | Castles K R | Castles |
| 12. | Kt—Q 1 | K Kt—B 3 |
| 13. | P—B 3 | |

Now Black has gained an advantage from the command of his Q 5. The advance of White's Q B P, which was necessitated by the dominating position of the Black Knight, has left White with a " backward " pawn at Q 3.

| | | |
|---|---|---|
| 13. | ......... | Kt × B ch |
| 14. | Q × Kt | R—K 1 |

If now a general exchange takes place after P—Q 4, the K P is lost through B—Q 4.

|  |  |
|---|---|
| 15. | Kt—R 4 |

White's counter attack on the King's side becomes threatening, and Black must continue his operations on the Queen's wing with the greatest care, as he may be called upon at any time to concentrate his pieces for the defence of the King's wing.

| | | |
|---|---|---|
| 15. | ......... | B—K B 1 |
| 16. | Kt—B 5 | K—R 1 |
| 17. | P—K Kt 4 | Q—Q 2 |
| 18. | Kt—B 2 | P—Q R 4 |

Black wishes to open up files on the Queen's side.

|  |  |
|---|---|
| 19. | P—Q R 3 |

Freeing the Q R.

| | | |
|---|---|---|
| 19. | ......... | P—Q Kt 4 |
| 20. | Q R—Q 1 | Q R—Kt 1 |
| 21. | R—Q 2 | P—Kt 5 |
| 22. | R P × P | R P × P |
| 23. | P—B 4 | R—R 1 |
| 24. | Q—B 3 | R—R 7 |

Before trying to push home his advantage on the Queen's side, which is made possible by the weakness of White's Q P,

Black should look after his King's side, where White has col-
lected an alarming array of forces.   After the text move the
Rook is quite out of play.

| 25. P—Kt 5 | P—Kt 3 ? |
|---|---|

Diag. 167.

Black should simply play P × P with the following continuation :  26 B × P, Kt—Q 5 ;  27 Kt × Kt, Q × Kt ;  28 B—K 3,
Q—Q 3.   After the move in the text, White's attack is overwhelming.

26. Kt—Kt 4 !

White obtains a Rook and two pawns for his two Knights ;
this is in itself an equivalent of material.   In the present instance the exchange is of decisive advantage for White, as
Black must lose several moves to bring up his Rook for the
defence of his unguarded King.

| 26. ......... | P × Kt |
|---|---|
| 27. Kt × B P | Kt—Q 5 |

If P × P, White wins by 28 Q—R 5, Q—B 2 ; 29 P—Kt 6,
Q × P ch ; 30 Q × Q and Kt × R.

| 28. Q—B 2 | Q—B 3 |
|---|---|
| 29. Kt × R | Q × Kt |
| 30. B × Kt | K P × B |
| 31. P × P | B—Q 2 |
| 32. R—K 1 | Q—B 2 |
| 33. Q—R 4 ! | R—R 1 |

Not B×P because of 34 R—K B 2, followed by K R—K B sq.

|  | |
|---|---|
| 34. R—K B 2 | B—B 3 |
| 35. Q—Kt 4 | |

The threat is to open the Rook's file by P—Kt 6 with an attack on the King by the Rooks.

|  | |
|---|---|
| 35. ......... | R—K 1 |
| 36. R×R | Q×R |

B×R in order to play Q—R 4 might be better. With the Queens off the board, Black has winning chances on account of his two Bishops. But then White might evade the exchange and proceed to seize the King's file with the Rook after 37 Q—B 4.

|  | |
|---|---|
| 37. R—K 2 | Q—Q 2 |
| 38. R—K 6 | B—R 1 |

in order to play Q—Q Kt 2 or R 2.

|  | |
|---|---|
| 39. P—Kt 6 ! | P×P |

If Q—Q Kt 2, 40 R—K 8 !, if Q—R 2, 40 Q—R 4. White wins in either case.

|  | |
|---|---|
| 40. R×P | Q—K R 2 |
| 41. Q—Kt 3 | |

Threatens Q—K 5 ch.

|  | |
|---|---|
| 41. ......... | Q—R 4 |
| 42. R—Kt 4 ! | Resigns. |

# TABLE OF OPENINGS

## A. KING'S PAWN GAMES

## B. QUEEN'S PAWN GAMES

# INDEX

# A CATALOGUE OF SELECTED DOVER BOOKS
## IN ALL FIELDS OF INTEREST

# A CATALOGUE OF SELECTED DOVER BOOKS
## IN ALL FIELDS OF INTEREST

AMERICA'S OLD MASTERS, James T. Flexner. Four men emerged unexpectedly from provincial 18th century America to leadership in European art: Benjamin West, J. S. Copley, C. R. Peale, Gilbert Stuart. Brilliant coverage of lives and contributions. Revised, 1967 edition. 69 plates. 365pp. of text.

21806-6 Paperbound $3.00

FIRST FLOWERS OF OUR WILDERNESS: AMERICAN PAINTING, THE COLONIAL PERIOD, James T. Flexner. Painters, and regional painting traditions from earliest Colonial times up to the emergence of Copley, West and Peale Sr., Foster, Gustavus Hesselius, Feke, John Smibert and many anonymous painters in the primitive manner. Engaging presentation, with 162 illustrations. xxii + 368pp.

22180-6 Paperbound $3.50

THE LIGHT OF DISTANT SKIES: AMERICAN PAINTING, 1760-1835, James T. Flexner. The great generation of early American painters goes to Europe to learn and to teach: West, Copley, Gilbert Stuart and others. Allston, Trumbull, Morse; also contemporary American painters—primitives, derivatives, academics—who remained in America. 102 illustrations. xiii + 306pp.

22179-2 Paperbound $3.00

A HISTORY OF THE RISE AND PROGRESS OF THE ARTS OF DESIGN IN THE UNITED STATES, William Dunlap. Much the richest mine of information on early American painters, sculptors, architects, engravers, miniaturists, etc. The only source of information for scores of artists, the major primary source for many others. Unabridged reprint of rare original 1834 edition, with new introduction by James T. Flexner, and 394 new illustrations. Edited by Rita Weiss. 6⅜ x 9⅝.

21695-0, 21696-9, 21697-7 Three volumes, Paperbound $13.50

EPOCHS OF CHINESE AND JAPANESE ART, Ernest F. Fenollosa. From primitive Chinese art to the 20th century, thorough history, explanation of every important art period and form, including Japanese woodcuts; main stress on China and Japan, but Tibet, Korea also included. Still unexcelled for its detailed, rich coverage of cultural background, aesthetic elements, diffusion studies, particularly of the historical period. 2nd, 1913 edition. 242 illustrations. lii + 439pp. of text.

20364-6, 20365-4 Two volumes, Paperbound $6.00

THE GENTLE ART OF MAKING ENEMIES, James A. M. Whistler. Greatest wit of his day deflates Oscar Wilde, Ruskin, Swinburne; strikes back at inane critics, exhibitions, art journalism; aesthetics of impressionist revolution in most striking form. Highly readable classic by great painter. Reproduction of edition designed by Whistler. Introduction by Alfred Werner. xxxvi + 334pp.

21875-9 Paperbound $2.50

LAPLACE TRANSFORMS AND THEIR APPLICATIONS TO DIFFERENTIAL EQUATIONS, N. W. McLachlan. Introduction to modern operational calculus, applying it to ordinary and partial differential equations. Laplace transform, theorems of operational calculus, solution of equations with constant coefficients, evaluation of integrals, derivation of transforms, of various functions, etc. For physics, engineering students. Formerly *Modern Operational Calculus*. xiv + 218pp.

60192-7 Paperbound $2.50

PARTIAL DIFFERENTIAL EQUATIONS OF MATHEMATICAL PHYSICS, Arthur G. Webster. Introduction to basic method and theory of partial differential equations, with full treatment of their applications to virtually every field. Full, clear chapters on Fourier series, integral and elliptic equations, spherical, cylindrical and ellipsoidal harmonics, Cauchy's method, boundary problems, method of Riemann-Volterra, many other basic topics. Edited by Samuel J. Plimpton. 97 figures. vii + 446pp.

60263-X Paperbound $2.75

PRINCIPLES OF STELLAR DYNAMICS, Subrahmanyan Chandrasekhar. Theory of stellar dynamics as a branch of classical dynamics; stellar encounter in terms of 2-body problem, Liouville's theorem and equations of continuity. Also two additional papers. 50 illustrations. x + 313pp. $5\frac{5}{8}$ x $8\frac{3}{8}$.

60659-7 Paperbound $3.00

CELESTIAL OBJECTS FOR COMMON TELESCOPES, T. W. Webb. The most used book in amateur astronomy: inestimable aid for locating and identifying hundreds of celestial objects. Volume 1 covers operation of telescope, telescope photography, precise information on sun, moon, planets, asteroids, meteor swarms, etc.; Volume 2, stars, constellations, double stars, clusters, variables, nebulae, etc. Nearly 4,000 objects noted. New edition edited, updated by Margaret W. Mayall. 77 illustrations. Total of xxxix + 606pp.

20917-2, 20918-0 Two volumes, Paperbound $5.00

A SHORT HISTORY OF ASTRONOMY, Arthur Berry. Earliest times through the 19th century. Individual chapters on Copernicus, Tycho Brahe, Galileo, Kepler, Newton, etc. Non-technical, but precise, thorough, and as useful to specialist as layman. 104 illustrations, 9 portraits, xxxi + 440 pp.

20210-0 Paperbound $3.00

ORDINARY DIFFERENTIAL EQUATIONS, Edward L. Ince. Explains and analyzes theory of ordinary differential equations in real and complex domains: elementary methods of integration, existence and nature of solutions, continuous transformation groups, linear differential equations, equations of first order, non-linear equations of higher order, oscillation theorems, etc. "Highly recommended," *Electronics Industries*. 18 figures. viii + 558pp.

60349-0 Paperbound $3.50

DICTIONARY OF CONFORMAL REPRESENTATIONS, H. Kober. Laplace's equation in two dimensions for many boundary conditions; scores of geometric forms and transformations for electrical engineers, Joukowski aerofoil for aerodynamists, Schwarz-Christoffel transformations, transcendental functions, etc. Twin diagrams for most transformations. 447 diagrams. xvi + 208pp. $6\frac{1}{8}$ x $9\frac{1}{4}$.

60160-9 Paperbound $2.50

INCIDENTS OF TRAVEL IN YUCATAN, John L. Stephens. Classic (1843) exploration of jungles of Yucatan, looking for evidences of Maya civilization. Stephens found many ruins; comments on travel adventures, Mexican and Indian culture. 127 striking illustrations by F. Catherwood. Total of 669 pp.
20926-1, 20927-X Two volumes, Paperbound $5.00

INCIDENTS OF TRAVEL IN CENTRAL AMERICA, CHIAPAS, AND YUCATAN, John L. Stephens. An exciting travel journal and an important classic of archeology. Narrative relates his almost single-handed discovery of the Mayan culture, and exploration of the ruined cities of Copan, Palenque, Utatlan and others; the monuments they dug from the earth, the temples buried in the jungle, the customs of poverty-stricken Indians living a stone's throw from the ruined palaces. 115 drawings by F. Catherwood. Portrait of Stephens. xii + 812pp.
22404-X, 22405-8 Two volumes, Paperbound $6.00

A NEW VOYAGE ROUND THE WORLD, William Dampier. Late 17-century naturalist joined the pirates of the Spanish Main to gather information; remarkably vivid account of buccaneers, pirates; detailed, accurate account of botany, zoology, ethnography of lands visited. Probably the most important early English voyage, enormous implications for British exploration, trade, colonial policy. Also most interesting reading. Argonaut edition, introduction by Sir Albert Gray. New introduction by Percy Adams. 6 plates, 7 illustrations. xlvii + 376pp. 6½ x 9¼.
21900-3 Paperbound $3.00

INTERNATIONAL AIRLINE PHRASE BOOK IN SIX LANGUAGES, Joseph W. Bátor. Important phrases and sentences in English paralleled with French, German, Portuguese, Italian, Spanish equivalents, covering all possible airport-travel situations; created for airline personnel as well as tourist by Language Chief, Pan American Airlines. xiv + 204pp.
22017-6 Paperbound $2.00

STAGE COACH AND TAVERN DAYS, Alice Morse Earle. Detailed, lively account of the early days of taverns; their uses and importance in the social, political and military life; furnishings and decorations; locations; food and drink; tavern signs, etc. Second half covers every aspect of early travel; the roads, coaches, drivers, etc. Nostalgic, charming, packed with fascinating material. 157 illustrations, mostly photographs. xiv + 449pp.
22518-6 Paperbound $4.00

NORSE DISCOVERIES AND EXPLORATIONS IN NORTH AMERICA, Hjalmar R. Holand. The perplexing Kensington Stone, found in Minnesota at the end of the 19th century. Is it a record of a Scandinavian expedition to North America in the 14th century? Or is it one of the most successful hoaxes in history. A scientific detective investigation. Formerly *Westward from Vinland*. 31 photographs, 17 figures. x + 354pp.
22014-1 Paperbound $2.75

A BOOK OF OLD MAPS, compiled and edited by Emerson D. Fite and Archibald Freeman. 74 old maps offer an unusual survey of the discovery, settlement and growth of America down to the close of the Revolutionary war: maps showing Norse settlements in Greenland, the explorations of Columbus, Verrazano, Cabot, Champlain, Joliet, Drake, Hudson, etc., campaigns of Revolutionary war battles, and much more. Each map is accompanied by a brief historical essay. xvi + 299pp. 11 x 13¾.
22084-2 Paperbound $6.00

ADVENTURES OF AN AFRICAN SLAVER, Theodore Canot. Edited by Brantz Mayer. A detailed portrayal of slavery and the slave trade, 1820-1840. Canot, an established trader along the African coast, describes the slave economy of the African kingdoms, the treatment of captured negroes, the extensive journeys in the interior to gather slaves, slave revolts and their suppression, harems, bribes, and much more. Full and unabridged republication of 1854 edition. Introduction by Malcom Cowley. 16 illustrations. xvii + 448pp. 22456-2 Paperbound $3.50

MY BONDAGE AND MY FREEDOM, Frederick Douglass. Born and brought up in slavery, Douglass witnessed its horrors and experienced its cruelties, but went on to become one of the most outspoken forces in the American anti-slavery movement. Considered the best of his autobiographies, this book graphically describes the in-human treatment of slaves, its effects on slave owners and slave families, and how Douglass's determination led him to a new life. Unaltered reprint of 1st (1855) edition. xxxii + 464pp. 22457-0 Paperbound $2.50

THE INDIANS' BOOK, recorded and edited by Natalie Curtis. Lore, music, narratives, dozens of drawings by Indians themselves from an authoritative and important survey of native culture among Plains, Southwestern, Lake and Pueblo Indians. Standard work in popular ethnomusicology. 149 songs in full notation. 23 draw-ings, 23 photos. xxxi + 584pp. 6⅝ x 9⅜. 21939-9 Paperbound $4.50

DICTIONARY OF AMERICAN PORTRAITS, edited by Hayward and Blanche Cirker. 4024 portraits of 4000 most important Americans, colonial days to 1905 (with a few important categories, like Presidents, to present). Pioneers, explorers, colonial figures, U. S. officials, politicians, writers, military and naval men, scientists, inven-tors, manufacturers, jurists, actors, historians, educators, notorious figures, Indian chiefs, etc. All authentic contemporary likenesses. The only work of its kind in existence; supplements all biographical sources for libraries. Indispensable to any-one working with American history. 8,000-item classified index, finding lists, other aids. xiv + 756pp. 9¼ x 12¾. 21823-6 Clothbound $30.00

TRITTON'S GUIDE TO BETTER WINE AND BEER MAKING FOR BEGINNERS, S. M. Tritton. All you need to know to make family-sized quantities of over 100 types of grape, fruit, herb and vegetable wines; as well as beers, mead, cider, etc. Com-plete recipes, advice as to equipment, procedures such as fermenting, bottling, and storing wines. Recipes given in British, U. S., and metric measures. Accompanying booklet lists sources in U. S. A. where ingredients may be bought, and additional information. 11 illustrations. 157pp. 5⅝ x 8⅛. (USO) 22090-7 Clothbound $3.50

GARDENING WITH HERBS FOR FLAVOR AND FRAGRANCE, Helen M. Fox. How to grow herbs in your own garden, how to use them in your cooking (over 55 recipes included), legends and myths associated with each species, uses in medicine, per-fumes, etc.—these are elements of one of the few books written especially for Amer-ican herb fanciers. Guides you step-by-step from soil preparation to harvesting and storage for each type of herb. 12 drawings by Louise Mansfield. xiv + 334pp. 22540-2 Paperbound $2.50

THE PHILOSOPHY OF THE UPANISHADS, Paul Deussen. Clear, detailed statement of upanishadic system of thought, generally considered among best available. History of these works, full exposition of system emergent from them, parallel concepts in the West. Translated by A. S. Geden. xiv + 429pp.

21616-0 Paperbound $3.00

LANGUAGE, TRUTH AND LOGIC, Alfred J. Ayer. Famous, remarkably clear introduction to the Vienna and Cambridge schools of Logical Positivism; function of philosophy, elimination of metaphysical thought, nature of analysis, similar topics. "Wish I had written it myself," Bertrand Russell. 2nd, 1946 edition. 160pp.

20010-8 Paperbound $1.35

THE GUIDE FOR THE PERPLEXED, Moses Maimonides. Great classic of medieval Judaism, major attempt to reconcile revealed religion (Pentateuch, commentaries) and Aristotelian philosophy. Enormously important in all Western thought. Unabridged Friedländer translation. 50-page introduction. lix + 414pp.

(USO) 20351-4 Paperbound $2.50

OCCULT AND SUPERNATURAL PHENOMENA, D. H. Rawcliffe. Full, serious study of the most persistent delusions of mankind: crystal gazing, mediumistic trance, stigmata, lycanthropy, fire walking, dowsing, telepathy, ghosts, ESP, etc., and their relation to common forms of abnormal psychology. Formerly *Illusions and Delusions of the Supernatural and the Occult.* iii + 551pp. 20503-7 Paperbound $3.50

THE EGYPTIAN BOOK OF THE DEAD: THE PAPYRUS OF ANI, E. A. Wallis Budge. Full hieroglyphic text, interlinear transliteration of sounds, word for word translation, then smooth, connected translation; Theban recension. Basic work in Ancient Egyptian civilization; now even more significant than ever for historical importance, dilation of consciousness, etc. clvi + 377pp. 6½ x 9¼.

21866-X Paperbound $3.95

PSYCHOLOGY OF MUSIC, Carl E. Seashore. Basic, thorough survey of everything known about psychology of music up to 1940's; essential reading for psychologists, musicologists. Physical acoustics; auditory apparatus; relationship of physical sound to perceived sound; role of the mind in sorting, altering, suppressing, creating sound sensations; musical learning, testing for ability, absolute pitch, other topics. Records of Caruso, Menuhin analyzed. 88 figures. xix + 408pp.

21851-1 Paperbound $2.75

THE I CHING (THE BOOK OF CHANGES), translated by James Legge. Complete translated text plus appendices by Confucius, of perhaps the most penetrating divination book ever compiled. Indispensable to all study of early Oriental civilizations. 3 plates. xxiii + 448pp. 21062-6 Paperbound $3.00

THE UPANISHADS, translated by Max Müller. Twelve classical upanishads: Chandogya, Kena, Aitareya, Kaushitaki, Isa, Katha, Mundaka, Taittiriyaka, Brhadaranyaka, Svetasvatara, Prasna, Maitriyana. 160-page introduction, analysis by Prof. Müller. Total of 826pp. 20398-0, 20399-9 Two volumes, Paperbound $5.00

JIM WHITEWOLF: THE LIFE OF A KIOWA APACHE INDIAN, Charles S. Brant, editor. Spans transition between native life and acculturation period, 1880 on. Kiowa culture, personal life pattern, religion and the supernatural, the Ghost Dance, breakdown in the White Man's world, similar material. 1 map. xii + 144pp.
22015-X Paperbound $1.75

THE NATIVE TRIBES OF CENTRAL AUSTRALIA, Baldwin Spencer and F. J. Gillen. Basic book in anthropology, devoted to full coverage of the Arunta and Warramunga tribes; the source for knowledge about kinship systems, material and social culture, religion, etc. Still unsurpassed. 121 photographs, 89 drawings. xviii + 669pp.
21775-2 Paperbound $5.00

MALAY MAGIC, Walter W. Skeat. Classic (1900); still the definitive work on the folklore and popular religion of the Malay peninsula. Describes marriage rites, birth spirits and ceremonies, medicine, dances, games, war and weapons, etc. Extensive quotes from original sources, many magic charms translated into English. 35 illustrations. Preface by Charles Otto Blagden. xxiv + 685pp.
21760-4 Paperbound $4.00

HEAVENS ON EARTH: UTOPIAN COMMUNITIES IN AMERICA, 1680-1880, Mark Holloway. The finest nontechnical account of American utopias, from the early Woman in the Wilderness, Ephrata, Rappites to the enormous mid 19th-century efflorescence; Shakers, New Harmony, Equity Stores, Fourier's Phalanxes, Oneida, Amana, Fruitlands, etc. "Entertaining and very instructive." *Times Literary Supplement*. 15 illustrations. 246pp.
21593-8 Paperbound $2.00

LONDON LABOUR AND THE LONDON POOR, Henry Mayhew. Earliest (c. 1850) sociological study in English, describing myriad subcultures of London poor. Particularly remarkable for the thousands of pages of direct testimony taken from the lips of London prostitutes, thieves, beggars, street sellers, chimney-sweepers, street-musicians, "mudlarks," "pure-finders," rag-gatherers, "running-patterers," dock laborers, cab-men, and hundreds of others, quoted directly in this massive work. An extraordinarily vital picture of London emerges. 110 illustrations. Total of lxxvi + 1951pp. 6⅝ x 10.
21934-8, 21935-6, 21936-4, 21937-2 Four volumes, Paperbound $14.00

HISTORY OF THE LATER ROMAN EMPIRE, J. B. Bury. Eloquent, detailed reconstruction of Western and Byzantine Roman Empire by a major historian, from the death of Theodosius I (395 A.D.) to the death of Justinian (565). Extensive quotations from contemporary sources; full coverage of important Roman and foreign figures of the time. xxxiv + 965pp. 21829-5 Record, book, album. Monaural. $3.50

AN INTELLECTUAL AND CULTURAL HISTORY OF THE WESTERN WORLD, Harry Elmer Barnes. Monumental study, tracing the development of the accomplishments that make up human culture. Every aspect of man's achievement surveyed from its origins in the Paleolithic to the present day (1964); social structures, ideas, economic systems, art, literature, technology, mathematics, the sciences, medicine, religion, jurisprudence, etc. Evaluations of the contributions of scores of great men. 1964 edition, revised and edited by scholars in the many fields represented. Total of xxix + 1381pp. 21275-0, 21276-9, 21277-7 Three volumes, Paperbound $7.75

AMERICAN FOOD AND GAME FISHES, David S. Jordan and Barton W. Evermann. Definitive source of information, detailed and accurate enough to enable the sportsman and nature lover to identify conclusively some 1,000 species and sub-species of North American fish, sought for food or sport. Coverage of range, physiology, habits, life history, food value. Best methods of capture, interest to the angler, advice on bait, fly-fishing, etc. 338 drawings and photographs. 1 + 574pp. 6⅝ x 9⅜.

22383-1 Paperbound $4.50

THE FROG BOOK, Mary C. Dickerson. Complete with extensive finding keys, over 300 photographs, and an introduction to the general biology of frogs and toads, this is the classic non-technical study of Northeastern and Central species. 58 species; 290 photographs and 16 color plates. xvii + 253pp.

21973-9 Paperbound $4.00

THE MOTH BOOK: A GUIDE TO THE MOTHS OF NORTH AMERICA, William J. Holland. Classical study, eagerly sought after and used for the past 60 years. Clear identification manual to more than 2,000 different moths, largest manual in existence. General information about moths, capturing, mounting, classifying, etc., followed by species by species descriptions. 263 illustrations plus 48 color plates show almost every species, full size. 1968 edition, preface, nomenclature changes by A. E. Brower. xxiv + 479pp. of text. 6½ x 9¼.

21948-8 Paperbound $5.00

THE SEA-BEACH AT EBB-TIDE, Augusta Foote Arnold. Interested amateur can identify hundreds of marine plants and animals on coasts of North America; marine algae; seaweeds; squids; hermit crabs; horse shoe crabs; shrimps; corals; sea anemones; etc. Species descriptions cover: structure; food; reproductive cycle; size; shape; color; habitat; etc. Over 600 drawings. 85 plates. xii + 490pp.

21949-6 Paperbound $3.50

COMMON BIRD SONGS, Donald J. Borror. 33⅓ 12-inch record presents songs of 60 important birds of the eastern United States. A thorough, serious record which provides several examples for each bird, showing different types of song, individual variations, etc. Inestimable identification aid for birdwatcher. 32-page booklet gives text about birds and songs, with illustration for each bird.

21829-5 Record, book, album. Monaural. $2.75

FADS AND FALLACIES IN THE NAME OF SCIENCE, Martin Gardner. Fair, witty appraisal of cranks and quacks of science: Atlantis, Lemuria, hollow earth, flat earth, Velikovsky, orgone energy, Dianetics, flying saucers, Bridey Murphy, food fads, medical fads, perpetual motion, etc. Formerly "In the Name of Science." x + 363pp.

20394-8 Paperbound $2.00

HOAXES, Curtis D. MacDougall. Exhaustive, unbelievably rich account of great hoaxes: Locke's moon hoax, Shakespearean forgeries, sea serpents, Loch Ness monster, Cardiff giant, John Wilkes Booth's mummy, Disumbrationist school of art, dozens more; also journalism, psychology of hoaxing. 54 illustrations. xi + 338pp.

20465-0 Paperbound $2.75

PLANETS, STARS AND GALAXIES: DESCRIPTIVE ASTRONOMY FOR BEGINNERS, A. E. Fanning. Comprehensive introductory survey of astronomy: the sun, solar system, stars, galaxies, universe, cosmology; up-to-date, including quasars, radio stars, etc. Preface by Prof. Donald Menzel. 24pp. of photographs. 189pp. 5¼ x 8¼.
21680-2 Paperbound $1.50

TEACH YOURSELF CALCULUS, P. Abbott. With a good background in algebra and trig, you can teach yourself calculus with this book. Simple, straightforward introduction to functions of all kinds, integration, differentiation, series, etc. "Students who are beginning to study calculus method will derive great help from this book." Faraday House Journal. 308pp.
20683-1 Clothbound $2.00

TEACH YOURSELF TRIGONOMETRY, P. Abbott. Geometrical foundations, indices and logarithms, ratios, angles, circular measure, etc. are presented in this sound, easy-to-use text. Excellent for the beginner or as a brush up, this text carries the student through the solution of triangles. 204pp.
20682-3 Clothbound $2.00

TEACH YOURSELF ANATOMY, David LeVay. Accurate, inclusive, profusely illustrated account of structure, skeleton, abdomen, muscles, nervous system, glands, brain, reproductive organs, evolution. "Quite the best and most readable account,' *Medical Officer.* 12 color plates. 164 figures. 311pp. 4¾ x 7.
21651-9 Clothbound $2.50

TEACH YOURSELF PHYSIOLOGY, David LeVay. Anatomical, biochemical bases; digestive, nervous, endocrine systems; metabolism; respiration; muscle; excretion; temperature control; reproduction. "Good elementary exposition," *The Lancet.* 6 color plates. 44 illustrations. 208pp. 4¼ x 7. 21658-6 Clothbound $2.50

THE FRIENDLY STARS, Martha Evans Martin. Classic has taught naked-eye observation of stars, planets to hundreds of thousands, still not surpassed for charm, lucidity, adequacy. Completely updated by Professor Donald H. Menzel, Harvard Observatory. 25 illustrations. 16 x 30 chart. x + 147pp. 21099-5 Paperbound $1.25

MUSIC OF THE SPHERES: THE MATERIAL UNIVERSE FROM ATOM TO QUASAR, SIMPLY EXPLAINED, Guy Murchie. Extremely broad, brilliantly written popular account begins with the solar system and reaches to dividing line between matter and nonmatter; latest understandings presented with exceptional clarity. Volume One: Planets, stars, galaxies, cosmology, geology, celestial mechanics, latest astronomical discoveries; Volume Two: Matter, atoms, waves, radiation, relativity, chemical action, heat, nuclear energy, quantum theory, music, light, color, probability, antimatter, antigravity, and similar topics. 319 figures. 1967 (second) edition. Total of xx + 644pp. 21809-0, 21810-4 Two volumes, Paperbound $5.00

OLD-TIME SCHOOLS AND SCHOOL BOOKS, Clifton Johnson. Illustrations and rhymes from early primers, abundant quotations from early textbooks, many anecdotes of school life enliven this study of elementary schools from Puritans to middle 19th century. Introduction by Carl Withers. 234 illustrations. xxxiii + 381pp.
21031-6 Paperbound $2.50

TWO LITTLE SAVAGES; BEING THE ADVENTURES OF TWO BOYS WHO LIVED AS INDIANS AND WHAT THEY LEARNED, Ernest Thompson Seton. Great classic of nature and boyhood provides a vast range of woodlore in most palatable form, a genuinely entertaining story. Two farm boys build a teepee in woods and live in it for a month, working out Indian solutions to living problems, star lore, birds and animals, plants, etc. 293 illustrations. vii + 286pp.

20985-7 Paperbound $2.50

PETER PIPER'S PRACTICAL PRINCIPLES OF PLAIN & PERFECT PRONUNCIATION. Alliterative jingles and tongue-twisters of surprising charm, that made their first appearance in America about 1830. Republished in full with the spirited woodcut illustrations from this earliest American edition. 32pp. $4\frac{1}{2}$ x $6\frac{3}{8}$.

22560-7 Paperbound $1.00

SCIENCE EXPERIMENTS AND AMUSEMENTS FOR CHILDREN, Charles Vivian. 73 easy experiments, requiring only materials found at home or easily available, such as candles, coins, steel wool, etc.; illustrate basic phenomena like vacuum, simple chemical reaction, etc. All safe. Modern, well-planned. Formerly *Science Games for Children*. 102 photos, numerous drawings. 96pp. $6\frac{1}{8}$ x $9\frac{1}{4}$.

21856-2 Paperbound $1.25

AN INTRODUCTION TO CHESS MOVES AND TACTICS SIMPLY EXPLAINED, Leonard Barden. Informal intermediate introduction, quite strong in explaining reasons for moves. Covers basic material, tactics, important openings, traps, positional play in middle game, end game. Attempts to isolate patterns and recurrent configurations. Formerly *Chess*. 58 figures. 102pp. (USO) 21210-6 Paperbound $1.25

LASKER'S MANUAL OF CHESS, Dr. Emanuel Lasker. Lasker was not only one of the five great World Champions, he was also one of the ablest expositors, theorists, and analysts. In many ways, his Manual, permeated with his philosophy of battle, filled with keen insights, is one of the greatest works ever written on chess. Filled with analyzed games by the great players. A single-volume library that will profit almost any chess player, beginner or master. 308 diagrams. xli x 349pp.

20640-8 Paperbound $2.75

THE MASTER BOOK OF MATHEMATICAL RECREATIONS, Fred Schuh. In opinion of many the finest work ever prepared on mathematical puzzles, stunts, recreations; exhaustively thorough explanations of mathematics involved, analysis of effects, citation of puzzles and games. Mathematics involved is elementary. Translated by F. Göbel. 194 figures. xxiv + 430pp.

22134-2 Paperbound $3.00

MATHEMATICS, MAGIC AND MYSTERY, Martin Gardner. Puzzle editor for Scientific American explains mathematics behind various mystifying tricks: card tricks, stage "mind reading," coin and match tricks, counting out games, geometric dissections, etc. Probability sets, theory of numbers clearly explained. Also provides more than 400 tricks, guaranteed to work, that you can do. 135 illustrations. xii + 176pp.

20338-2 Paperbound $1.50

MATHEMATICAL PUZZLES FOR BEGINNERS AND ENTHUSIASTS, Geoffrey Mott-Smith. 189 puzzles from easy to difficult—involving arithmetic, logic, algebra, properties of digits, probability, etc.—for enjoyment and mental stimulus. Explanation of mathematical principles behind the puzzles. 135 illustrations. viii + 248pp.

20198-8 Paperbound $1.25

PAPER FOLDING FOR BEGINNERS, William D. Murray and Francis J. Rigney. Easiest book on the market, clearest instructions on making interesting, beautiful origami. Sail boats, cups, roosters, frogs that move legs, bonbon boxes, standing birds, etc. 40 projects; more than 275 diagrams and photographs. 94pp.

20713-7 Paperbound $1.00

TRICKS AND GAMES ON THE POOL TABLE, Fred Herrmann. 79 tricks and games—some solitaires, some for two or more players, some competitive games—to entertain you between formal games. Mystifying shots and throws, unusual caroms, tricks involving such props as cork, coins, a hat, etc. Formerly *Fun on the Pool Table*. 77 figures. 95pp.

21814-7 Paperbound $1.00

HAND SHADOWS TO BE THROWN UPON THE WALL: A SERIES OF NOVEL AND AMUSING FIGURES FORMED BY THE HAND, Henry Bursill. Delightful picturebook from great-grandfather's day shows how to make 18 different hand shadows: a bird that flies, duck that quacks, dog that wags his tail, camel, goose, deer, boy, turtle, etc. Only book of its sort. vi + 33pp. 6½ x 9¼. 21779-5 Paperbound $1.00

WHITTLING AND WOODCARVING, E. J. Tangerman. 18th printing of best book on market. "If you can cut a potato you can carve" toys and puzzles, chains, chessmen, caricatures, masks, frames, woodcut blocks, surface patterns, much more. Information on tools, woods, techniques. Also goes into serious wood sculpture from Middle Ages to present, East and West. 464 photos, figures. x + 293pp.

20965-2 Paperbound $2.00

HISTORY OF PHILOSOPHY, Julián Marias. Possibly the clearest, most easily followed, best planned, most useful one-volume history of philosophy on the market; neither skimpy nor overfull. Full details on system of every major philosopher and dozens of less important thinkers from pre-Socratics up to Existentialism and later. Strong on many European figures usually omitted. Has gone through dozens of editions in Europe. 1966 edition, translated by Stanley Appelbaum and Clarence Strowbridge. xviii + 505pp. 21739-6 Paperbound $3.00

YOGA: A SCIENTIFIC EVALUATION, Kovoor T. Behanan. Scientific but non-technical study of physiological results of yoga exercises; done under auspices of Yale U. Relations to Indian thought, to psychoanalysis, etc. 16 photos. xxiii + 270pp.

20505-3 Paperbound $2.50

*Prices subject to change without notice.*
Available at your book dealer or write for free catalogue to Dept. GI, Dover Publications, Inc., 180 Varick St., N. Y., N. Y. 10014. Dover publishes more than 150 books each year on science, elementary and advanced mathematics, biology, music, art, literary history, social sciences and other areas.

EAST O' THE SUN AND WEST O' THE MOON, George W. Dasent. Considered the best of all translations of these Norwegian folk tales, this collection has been enjoyed by generations of children (and folklorists too). Includes True and Untrue, Why the Sea is Salt, East O' the Sun and West O' the Moon, Why the Bear is Stumpy-Tailed, Boots and the Troll, The Cock and the Hen, Rich Peter the Pedlar, and 52 more. The only edition with all 59 tales. 77 illustrations by Erik Werenskiold and Theodor Kittelsen. xv + 418pp.  22521-6 Paperbound $3.00

GOOPS AND HOW TO BE THEM, Gelett Burgess. Classic of tongue-in-cheek humor, masquerading as etiquette book. 87 verses, twice as many cartoons, show mischievous Goops as they demonstrate to children virtues of table manners, neatness, courtesy, etc. Favorite for generations. viii + 88pp. 6½ x 9¼.
22233-0 Paperbound $1.25

ALICE'S ADVENTURES UNDER GROUND, Lewis Carroll. The first version, quite different from the final Alice in Wonderland, printed out by Carroll himself with his own illustrations. Complete facsimile of the "million dollar" manuscript Carroll gave to Alice Liddell in 1864. Introduction by Martin Gardner. viii + 96pp. Title and dedication pages in color.  21482-6 Paperbound $1.25

THE BROWNIES, THEIR BOOK, Palmer Cox. Small as mice, cunning as foxes, exuberant and full of mischief, the Brownies go to the zoo, toy shop, seashore, circus, etc., in 24 verse adventures and 266 illustrations. Long a favorite, since their first appearance in St. Nicholas Magazine. xi + 144pp. 6⅝ x 9¼.
21265-3 Paperbound $1.75

SONGS OF CHILDHOOD, Walter De La Mare. Published (under the pseudonym Walter Ramal) when De La Mare was only 29, this charming collection has long been a favorite children's book. A facsimile of the first edition in paper, the 47 poems capture the simplicity of the nursery rhyme and the ballad, including such lyrics as I Met Eve, Tartary, The Silver Penny. vii + 106pp. 21972-0 Paperbound $1.25

THE COMPLETE NONSENSE OF EDWARD LEAR, Edward Lear. The finest 19th-century humorist-cartoonist in full: all nonsense limericks, zany alphabets, Owl and Pussycat, songs, nonsense botany, and more than 500 illustrations by Lear himself. Edited by Holbrook Jackson. xxix + 287pp.  (USO) 20167-8 Paperbound $2.00

BILLY WHISKERS: THE AUTOBIOGRAPHY OF A GOAT, Frances Trego Montgomery. A favorite of children since the early 20th century, here are the escapades of that rambunctious, irresistible and mischievous goat—Billy Whiskers. Much in the spirit of Peck's Bad Boy, this is a book that children never tire of reading or hearing. All the original familiar illustrations by W. H. Fry are included: 6 color plates, 18 black and white drawings. 159pp.  22345-0 Paperbound $2.00

MOTHER GOOSE MELODIES. Faithful republication of the fabulously rare Munroe and Francis "copyright 1833" Boston edition—the most important Mother Goose collection, usually referred to as the "original." Familiar rhymes plus many rare ones, with wonderful old woodcut illustrations. Edited by E. F. Bleiler. 128pp. 4½ x 6⅜.  22577-1 Paperbound $1.25

THE RED FAIRY BOOK, Andrew Lang. Lang's color fairy books have long been children's favorites. This volume includes Rapunzel, Jack and the Bean-stalk and 35 other stories, familiar and unfamiliar. 4 plates, 93 illustrations x + 367pp.
21673-X Paperbound $2.50

THE BLUE FAIRY BOOK, Andrew Lang. Lang's tales come from all countries and all times. Here are 37 tales from Grimm, the Arabian Nights, Greek Mythology, and other fascinating sources. 8 plates, 130 illustrations. xi + 390pp.
21437-0 Paperbound $2.50

HOUSEHOLD STORIES BY THE BROTHERS GRIMM. Classic English-language edition of the well-known tales — Rumpelstiltskin, Snow White, Hansel and Gretel, The Twelve Brothers, Faithful John, Rapunzel, Tom Thumb (52 stories in all). Translated into simple, straightforward English by Lucy Crane. Ornamented with headpieces, vignettes, elaborate decorative initials and a dozen full-page illustrations by Walter Crane. x + 269pp.
21080-4 Paperbound $2.50

THE MERRY ADVENTURES OF ROBIN HOOD, Howard Pyle. The finest modern versions of the traditional ballads and tales about the great English outlaw. Howard Pyle's complete prose version, with every word, every illustration of the first edition. Do not confuse this facsimile of the original (1883) with modern editions that change text or illustrations. 23 plates plus many page decorations. xxii + 296pp.
22043-5 Paperbound $2.50

THE STORY OF KING ARTHUR AND HIS KNIGHTS, Howard Pyle. The finest children's version of the life of King Arthur; brilliantly retold by Pyle, with 48 of his most imaginative illustrations. xviii + 313pp. 6⅛ x 9¼.
21445-1 Paperbound $2.50

THE WONDERFUL WIZARD OF OZ, L. Frank Baum. America's finest children's book in facsimile of first edition with all Denslow illustrations in full color. The edition a child should have. Introduction by Martin Gardner. 23 color plates, scores of drawings. iv + 267pp.
20691-2 Paperbound $2.25

THE MARVELOUS LAND OF OZ, L. Frank Baum. The second Oz book, every bit as imaginative as the Wizard. The hero is a boy named Tip, but the Scarecrow and the Tin Woodman are back, as is the Oz magic. 16 color plates, 120 drawings by John R. Neill. 287pp.
20692-0 Paperbound $2.50

THE MAGICAL MONARCH OF MO, L. Frank Baum. Remarkable adventures in a land even stranger than Oz. The best of Baum's books not in the Oz series. 15 color plates and dozens of drawings by Frank Verbeck. xviii + 237pp.
21892-9 Paperbound $2.00

THE BAD CHILD'S BOOK OF BEASTS, MORE BEASTS FOR WORSE CHILDREN, A MORAL ALPHABET, Hilaire Belloc. Three complete humor classics in one volume. Be kind to the frog, and do not call him names . . . and 28 other whimsical animals. Familiar favorites and some not so well known. Illustrated by Basil Blackwell. 156pp.
(USO) 20749-8 Paperbound $1.25

LAST AND FIRST MEN AND STAR MAKER, TWO SCIENCE FICTION NOVELS, Olaf Stapledon. Greatest future histories in science fiction. In the first, human intelligence is the "hero," through strange paths of evolution, interplanetary invasions, incredible technologies, near extinctions and reemergences. Star Maker describes the quest of a band of star rovers for intelligence itself, through time and space: weird inhuman civilizations, crustacean minds, symbiotic worlds, etc. Complete, unabridged. v + 438pp. 21962-3 Paperbound $2.50

THREE PROPHETIC NOVELS, H. G. WELLS. Stages of a consistently planned future for mankind. When the Sleeper Wakes, and A Story of the Days to Come, anticipate Brave New World and 1984, in the 21st Century; The Time Machine, only complete version in print, shows farther future and the end of mankind. All show Wells's greatest gifts as storyteller and novelist. Edited by E. F. Bleiler. x + 335pp. (USO) 20605-X Paperbound $2.25

THE DEVIL'S DICTIONARY, Ambrose Bierce. America's own Oscar Wilde—Ambrose Bierce—offers his barbed iconoclastic wisdom in over 1,000 definitions hailed by H. L. Mencken as "some of the most gorgeous witticisms in the English language." 145pp. 20487-1 Paperbound $1.25

MAX AND MORITZ, Wilhelm Busch. Great children's classic, father of comic strip, of two bad boys, Max and Moritz. Also Ker and Plunk (Plisch und Plumm), Cat and Mouse, Deceitful Henry, Ice-Peter, The Boy and the Pipe, and five other pieces. Original German, with English translation. Edited by H. Arthur Klein; translations by various hands and H. Arthur Klein. vi + 216pp. 20181-3 Paperbound $2.00

PIGS IS PIGS AND OTHER FAVORITES, Ellis Parker Butler. The title story is one of the best humor short stories, as Mike Flannery obfuscates biology and English. Also included, That Pup of Murchison's, The Great American Pie Company, and Perkins of Portland. 14 illustrations. v + 109pp. 21532-6 Paperbound $1.00

THE PETERKIN PAPERS, Lucretia P. Hale. It takes genius to be as stupidly mad as the Peterkins, as they decide to become wise, celebrate the "Fourth," keep a cow, and otherwise strain the resources of the Lady from Philadelphia. Basic book of American humor. 153 illustrations. 219pp. 20794-3 Paperbound $1.50

PERRAULT'S FAIRY TALES, translated by A. E. Johnson and S. R. Littlewood, with 34 full-page illustrations by Gustave Doré. All the original Perrault stories—Cinderella, Sleeping Beauty, Bluebeard, Little Red Riding Hood, Puss in Boots, Tom Thumb, etc.—with their witty verse morals and the magnificent illustrations of Doré. One of the five or six great books of European fairy tales. viii + 117pp. 8⅛ x 11. 22311-6 Paperbound $2.00

OLD HUNGARIAN FAIRY TALES, Baroness Orczy. Favorites translated and adapted by author of the Scarlet Pimpernel. Eight fairy tales include "The Suitors of Princess Fire-Fly," "The Twin Hunchbacks," "Mr. Cuttlefish's Love Story," and "The Enchanted Cat." This little volume of magic and adventure will captivate children as it has for generations. 90 drawings by Montagu Barstow. 96pp. (USO) 22293-4 Paperbound $1.95

POEMS OF ANNE BRADSTREET, edited with an introduction by Robert Hutchinson. A new selection of poems by America's first poet and perhaps the first significant woman poet in the English language. 48 poems display her development in works of considerable variety—love poems, domestic poems, religious meditations, formal elegies, "quaternions," etc. Notes, bibliography. viii + 222pp.
22160-1 Paperbound $2.00

THREE GOTHIC NOVELS: THE CASTLE OF OTRANTO BY HORACE WALPOLE; VATHEK BY WILLIAM BECKFORD; THE VAMPYRE BY JOHN POLIDORI, WITH FRAGMENT OF A NOVEL BY LORD BYRON, edited by E. F. Bleiler. The first Gothic novel, by Walpole; the finest Oriental tale in English, by Beckford; powerful Romantic supernatural story in versions by Polidori and Byron. All extremely important in history of literature; all still exciting, packed with supernatural thrills, ghosts, haunted castles, magic, etc. xl + 291pp.
21232-7 Paperbound $2.00

THE BEST TALES OF HOFFMANN, E. T. A. Hoffmann. 10 of Hoffmann's most important stories, in modern re-editings of standard translations: Nutcracker and the King of Mice, Signor Formica, Automata, The Sandman, Rath Krespel, The Golden Flowerpot, Master Martin the Cooper, The Mines of Falun, The King's Betrothed, A New Year's Eve Adventure. 7 illustrations by Hoffmann. Edited by E. F. Bleiler. xxxix + 419pp.
21793-0 Paperbound $2.50

GHOST AND HORROR STORIES OF AMBROSE BIERCE, Ambrose Bierce. 23 strikingly modern stories of the horrors latent in the human mind: The Eyes of the Panther, The Damned Thing, An Occurrence at Owl Creek Bridge, An Inhabitant of Carcosa, etc., plus the dream-essay, Visions of the Night. Edited by E. F. Bleiler. xxii + 199pp.
20767-6 Paperbound $1.50

BEST GHOST STORIES OF J. S. LEFANU, J. Sheridan LeFanu. Finest stories by Victorian master often considered greatest supernatural writer of all. Carmilla, Green Tea, The Haunted Baronet, The Familiar, and 12 others. Most never before available in the U. S. A. Edited by E. F. Bleiler. 8 illustrations from Victorian publications. xvii + 467pp.
20415-4 Paperbound $3.00

THE TIME STREAM, THE GREATEST ADVENTURE, AND THE PURPLE SAPPHIRE— THREE SCIENCE FICTION NOVELS, John Taine (Eric Temple Bell). Great American mathematician was also foremost science fiction novelist of the 1920's. *The Time Stream*, one of all-time classics, uses concepts of circular time; *The Greatest Adventure*, incredibly ancient biological experiments from Antarctica threaten to escape; The *Purple Sapphire*, superscience, lost races in Central Tibet, survivors of the Great Race. 4 illustrations by Frank R. Paul. v + 532pp.
21180-0 Paperbound $3.00

SEVEN SCIENCE FICTION NOVELS, H. G. Wells. The standard collection of the great novels. Complete, unabridged. *First Men in the Moon, Island of Dr. Moreau, War of the Worlds, Food of the Gods, Invisible Man, Time Machine, In the Days of the Comet.* Not only science fiction fans, but every educated person owes it to himself to read these novels. 1015pp.
20264-X Clothbound $5.00

AGAINST THE GRAIN (A REBOURS), Joris K. Huysmans. Filled with weird images, evidences of a bizarre imagination, exotic experiments with hallucinatory drugs, rich tastes and smells and the diversions of its sybarite hero Duc Jean des Esseintes, this classic novel pushed 19th-century literary decadence to its limits. Full unabridged edition. Do not confuse this with abridged editions generally sold. Introduction by Havelock Ellis. xlix + 206pp.      22190-3 Paperbound $2.00

VARIORUM SHAKESPEARE: HAMLET. Edited by Horace H. Furness; a landmark of American scholarship. Exhaustive footnotes and appendices treat all doubtful words and phrases, as well as suggested critical emendations throughout the play's history. First volume contains editor's own text, collated with all Quartos and Folios. Second volume contains full first Quarto, translations of Shakespeare's sources (Belleforest, and Saxo Grammaticus), Der Bestrafte Brudermord, and many essays on critical and historical points of interest by major authorities of past and present. Includes details of staging and costuming over the years. By far the best edition available for serious students of Shakespeare. Total of xx + 905pp.
21004-9, 21005-7, 2 volumes, Paperbound $7.00

A LIFE OF WILLIAM SHAKESPEARE, Sir Sidney Lee. This is the standard life of Shakespeare, summarizing everything known about Shakespeare and his plays. Incredibly rich in material, broad in coverage, clear and judicious, it has served thousands as the best introduction to Shakespeare. 1931 edition. 9 plates. xxix + 792pp.      (USO) 21967-4 Paperbound $3.75

MASTERS OF THE DRAMA, John Gassner. Most comprehensive history of the drama in print, covering every tradition from Greeks to modern Europe and America, including India, Far East, etc. Covers more than 800 dramatists, 2000 plays, with biographical material, plot summaries, theatre history, criticism, etc. "Best of its kind in English," New Republic. 77 illustrations. xxii + 890pp.
20100-7 Clothbound $8.50

THE EVOLUTION OF THE ENGLISH LANGUAGE, George McKnight. The growth of English, from the 14th century to the present. Unusual, non-technical account presents basic information in very interesting form: sound shifts, change in grammar and syntax, vocabulary growth, similar topics. Abundantly illustrated with quotations. Formerly Modern English in the Making. xii + 590pp.
21932-1 Paperbound $3.50

AN ETYMOLOGICAL DICTIONARY OF MODERN ENGLISH, Ernest Weekley. Fullest, richest work of its sort, by foremost British lexicographer. Detailed word histories, including many colloquial and archaic words; extensive quotations. Do not confuse this with the Concise Etymological Dictionary, which is much abridged. Total of xxvii + 830pp. 6½ x 9¼.
21873-2, 21874-0 Two volumes, Paperbound $6.00

FLATLAND: A ROMANCE OF MANY DIMENSIONS, E. A. Abbott. Classic of science-fiction explores ramifications of life in a two-dimensional world, and what happens when a three-dimensional being intrudes. Amusing reading, but also useful as introduction to thought about hyperspace. Introduction by Banesh Hoffmann. 16 illustrations. xx + 103pp.      20001-9 Paperbound $1.00

JOHANN SEBASTIAN BACH, Philipp Spitta. One of the great classics of musicology, this definitive analysis of Bach's music (and life) has never been surpassed. Lucid, nontechnical analyses of hundreds of pieces (30 pages devoted to St. Matthew Passion, 26 to B Minor Mass). Also includes major analysis of 18th-century music. 450 musical examples. 40-page musical supplement. Total of xx + 1799pp.
(EUK) 22278-0, 22279-9 Two volumes, Clothbound $15.00

MOZART AND HIS PIANO CONCERTOS, Cuthbert Girdlestone. The only full-length study of an important area of Mozart's creativity. Provides detailed analyses of all 23 concertos, traces inspirational sources. 417 musical examples. Second edition. 509pp. (USO) 21271-8 Paperbound $3.50

THE PERFECT WAGNERITE: A COMMENTARY ON THE NIBLUNG'S RING, George Bernard Shaw. Brilliant and still relevant criticism in remarkable essays on Wagner's Ring cycle, Shaw's ideas on political and social ideology behind the plots, role of Leitmotifs, vocal requisites, etc. Prefaces. xxi + 136pp.
21707-8 Paperbound $1.50

DON GIOVANNI, W. A. Mozart. Complete libretto, modern English translation; biographies of composer and librettist; accounts of early performances and critical reaction. Lavishly illustrated. All the material you need to understand and appreciate this great work. Dover Opera Guide and Libretto Series; translated and introduced by Ellen Bleiler. 92 illustrations. 209pp.
21134-7 Paperbound $1.50

HIGH FIDELITY SYSTEMS: A LAYMAN'S GUIDE, Roy F. Allison. All the basic information you need for setting up your own audio system: high fidelity and stereo record players, tape records, F.M. Connections, adjusting tone arm, cartridge, checking needle alignment, positioning speakers, phasing speakers, adjusting hums, trouble-shooting, maintenance, and similar topics. Enlarged 1965 edition. More than 50 charts, diagrams, photos. iv + 91pp. 21514-8 Paperbound $1.25

REPRODUCTION OF SOUND, Edgar Villchur. Thorough coverage for laymen of high fidelity systems, reproducing systems in general, needles, amplifiers, preamps, loudspeakers, feedback, explaining physical background. "A rare talent for making technicalities vividly comprehensible," R. Darrell, *High Fidelity*. 69 figures. iv + 92pp. 21515-6 Paperbound $1.00

HEAR ME TALKIN' TO YA: THE STORY OF JAZZ AS TOLD BY THE MEN WHO MADE IT, Nat Shapiro and Nat Hentoff. Louis Armstrong, Fats Waller, Jo Jones, Clarence Williams, Billy Holiday, Duke Ellington, Jelly Roll Morton and dozens of other jazz greats tell how it was in Chicago's South Side, New Orleans, depression Harlem and the modern West Coast as jazz was born and grew. xvi + 429pp.
21726-4 Paperbound $2.50

FABLES OF AESOP, translated by Sir Roger L'Estrange. A reproduction of the very rare 1931 Paris edition; a selection of the most interesting fables, together with 50 imaginative drawings by Alexander Calder. v + 128pp. 6½x9¼.
21780-9 Paperbound $1.25

THE ARCHITECTURE OF COUNTRY HOUSES, Andrew J. Downing. Together with Vaux's *Villas and Cottages* this is the basic book for Hudson River Gothic architecture of the middle Victorian period. Full, sound discussions of general aspects of housing, architecture, style, decoration, furnishing, together with scores of detailed house plans, illustrations of specific buildings, accompanied by full text. Perhaps the most influential single American architectural book. 1850 edition. Introduction by J. Stewart Johnson. 321 figures, 34 architectural designs. xvi + 560pp.

22003-6 Paperbound $4.00

LOST EXAMPLES OF COLONIAL ARCHITECTURE, John Mead Howells. Full-page photographs of buildings that have disappeared or been so alteied as to be denatured, including many designed by major early American architects. 245 plates. xvii + 248pp. 7⅞ x 10¾.

21143-6 Paperbound $3.00

DOMESTIC ARCHITECTURE OF THE AMERICAN COLONIES AND OF THE EARLY REPUBLIC, Fiske Kimball. Foremost architect and restorer of Williamsburg and Monticello covers nearly 200 homes between 1620-1825. Architectural details, construction, style features, special fixtures, floor plans, etc. Generally considered finest work in its area. 219 illustrations of houses, doorways, windows, capital mantels. xx + 314pp. 7⅞ x 10¾.

21743-4 Paperbound $3.50

EARLY AMERICAN ROOMS: 1650-1858, edited by Russell Hawes Kettell. Tour of 12 rooms, each representative of a different era in American history and each furnished, decorated, designed and occupied in the style of the era. 72 plans and elevations, 8-page color section, etc., show fabrics, wall papers, arrangements, etc. Full descriptive text. xvii + 200pp. of text. 8⅜ x 11¼.

21633-0 Paperbound $5.00

THE FITZWILLIAM VIRGINAL BOOK, edited by J. Fuller Maitland and W. B. Squire. Full modern printing of famous early 17th-century ms. volume of 300 works by Morley, Byrd, Bull, Gibbons, etc. For piano or other modern keyboard instrument; easy to read format. xxxvi + 938pp. 8⅜ x 11.

21068-5, 21069-3 Two volumes, Paperbound $8.00

HARPSICHORD MUSIC, Johann Sebastian Bach. Bach Gesellschaft edition. A rich selection of Bach's masterpieces for the harpsichord: the six English Suites, six French Suites, the six Partitas (Clavierübung part I), the Goldberg Variations (Clavierübung part IV), the fifteen Two-Part Inventions and the fifteen Three-Part Sinfonias. Clearly reproduced on large sheets with ample margins; eminently playable. vi + 312pp. 8⅛ x 11.

22360-4 Paperbound $5.00

THE MUSIC OF BACH: AN INTRODUCTION, Charles Sanford Terry. A fine, nontechnical introduction to Bach's music, both instrumental and vocal. Covers organ music, chamber music, passion music, other types. Analyzes themes, developments, innovations. x + 114pp.

21075-8 Paperbound $1.25

BEETHOVEN AND HIS NINE SYMPHONIES, Sir George Grove. Noted British musicologist provides best history, analysis, commentary on symphonies. Very thorough, rigorously accurate; necessary to both advanced student and amateur music lover. 436 musical passages. vii + 407 pp.

20334-4 Paperbound $2.25

DESIGN BY ACCIDENT; A BOOK OF "ACCIDENTAL EFFECTS" FOR ARTISTS AND DESIGNERS, James F. O'Brien. Create your own unique, striking, imaginative effects by "controlled accident" interaction of materials: paints and lacquers, oil and water based paints, splatter, crackling materials, shatter, similar items. Everything you do will be different; first book on this limitless art, so useful to both fine artist and commercial artist. Full instructions. 192 plates showing "accidents," 8 in color. viii + 215pp. 8⅜ x 11¼. 21942-9 Paperbound $3.50

THE BOOK OF SIGNS, Rudolf Koch. Famed German type designer draws 493 beautiful symbols: religious, mystical, alchemical, imperial, property marks, runes, etc. Remarkable fusion of traditional and modern. Good for suggestions of timelessness, smartness, modernity. Text. vi + 104pp. 6⅛ x 9¼.
20162-7 Paperbound $1.25

HISTORY OF INDIAN AND INDONESIAN ART, Ananda K. Coomaraswamy. An unabridged republication of one of the finest books by a great scholar in Eastern art. Rich in descriptive material, history, social backgrounds; Sunga reliefs, Rajput paintings, Gupta temples, Burmese frescoes, textiles, jewelry, sculpture, etc. 400 photos. viii + 423pp. 6⅜ x 9¾. 21436-2 Paperbound $4.00

PRIMITIVE ART, Franz Boas. America's foremost anthropologist surveys textiles, ceramics, woodcarving, basketry, metalwork, etc.; patterns, technology, creation of symbols, style origins. All areas of world, but very full on Northwest Coast Indians. More than 350 illustrations of baskets, boxes, totem poles, weapons, etc. 378 pp.
20025-6 Paperbound $3.00

THE GENTLEMAN AND CABINET MAKER'S DIRECTOR, Thomas Chippendale. Full reprint (third edition, 1762) of most influential furniture book of all time, by master cabinetmaker. 200 plates, illustrating chairs, sofas, mirrors, tables, cabinets, plus 24 photographs of surviving pieces. Biographical introduction by N. Bienenstock. vi + 249pp. 9⅞ x 12¾. 21601-2 Paperbound $4.00

AMERICAN ANTIQUE FURNITURE, Edgar G. Miller, Jr. The basic coverage of all American furniture before 1840. Individual chapters cover type of furniture—clocks, tables, sideboards, etc.—chronologically, with inexhaustible wealth of data. More than 2100 photographs, all identified, commented on. Essential to all early American collectors. Introduction by H. E. Keyes. vi + 1106pp. 7⅞ x 10¾.
21599-7, 21600-4 Two volumes, Paperbound $11.00

PENNSYLVANIA DUTCH AMERICAN FOLK ART, Henry J. Kauffman. 279 photos, 28 drawings of tulipware, Fraktur script, painted tinware, toys, flowered furniture, quilts, samplers, hex signs, house interiors, etc. Full descriptive text. Excellent for tourist, rewarding for designer, collector. Map. 146pp. 7⅞ x 10¾.
21205-X Paperbound $2.50

EARLY NEW ENGLAND GRAVESTONE RUBBINGS, Edmund V. Gillon, Jr. 43 photographs, 226 carefully reproduced rubbings show heavily symbolic, sometimes macabre early gravestones, up to early 19th century. Remarkable early American primitive art, occasionally strikingly beautiful; always powerful. Text. xxvi + 207pp. 8⅜ x 11¼. 21380-3 Paperbound $3.50

ALPHABETS AND ORNAMENTS, Ernst Lehner. Well-known pictorial source for decorative alphabets, script examples, cartouches, frames, decorative title pages, calligraphic initials, borders, similar material. 14th to 19th century, mostly European. Useful in almost any graphic arts designing, varied styles. 750 illustrations. 256pp. 7 x 10.                                            21905-4 Paperbound $4.00

PAINTING: A CREATIVE APPROACH, Norman Colquhoun. For the beginner simple guide provides an instructive approach to painting: major stumbling blocks for beginner; overcoming them, technical points; paints and pigments; oil painting; watercolor and other media and color. New section on "plastic" paints. Glossary. Formerly *Paint Your Own Pictures*. 221pp.            22000-1 Paperbound $1.75

THE ENJOYMENT AND USE OF COLOR, Walter Sargent. Explanation of the relations between colors themselves and between colors in nature and art, including hundreds of little-known facts about color values, intensities, effects of high and low illumination, complementary colors. Many practical hints for painters, references to great masters. 7 color plates, 29 illustrations. x + 274pp.
20944-X Paperbound $2.50

THE NOTEBOOKS OF LEONARDO DA VINCI, compiled and edited by Jean Paul Richter. 1566 extracts from original manuscripts reveal the full range of Leonardo's versatile genius: all his writings on painting, sculpture, architecture, anatomy, astronomy, geography, topography, physiology, mining, music, etc., in both Italian and English, with 186 plates of manuscript pages and more than 500 additional drawings. Includes studies for the Last Supper, the lost Sforza monument, and other works. Total of xlvii + 866pp. 7⅞ x 10¾.
22572-0, 22573-9 Two volumes, Paperbound $10.00

MONTGOMERY WARD CATALOGUE OF 1895. Tea gowns, yards of flannel and pillow-case lace, stereoscopes, books of gospel hymns, the New Improved Singer Sewing Machine, side saddles, milk skimmers, straight-edged razors, high-button shoes, spittoons, and on and on . . . listing some 25,000 items, practically all illustrated. Essential to the shoppers of the 1890's, it is our truest record of the spirit of the period. Unaltered reprint of Issue No. 57, Spring and Summer 1895. Introduction by Boris Emmet. Innumerable illustrations. xiii + 624pp. 8½ x 11⅝.
22377-9 Paperbound $6.95

THE CRYSTAL PALACE EXHIBITION ILLUSTRATED CATALOGUE (LONDON, 1851). One of the wonders of the modern world—the Crystal Palace Exhibition in which all the nations of the civilized world exhibited their achievements in the arts and sciences—presented in an equally important illustrated catalogue. More than 1700 items pictured with accompanying text—ceramics, textiles, cast-iron work, carpets, pianos, sleds, razors, wall-papers, billiard tables, beehives, silverware and hundreds of other artifacts—represent the focal point of Victorian culture in the Western World. Probably the largest collection of Victorian decorative art ever assembled— indispensable for antiquarians and designers. Unabridged republication of the Art-Journal Catalogue of the Great Exhibition of 1851, with all terminal essays. New introduction by John Gloag, F.S.A. xxxiv + 426pp. 9 x 12.
22503-8 Paperbound $4.50

INTRODUCTION TO ASTROPHYSICS: THE STARS, Jean Dufay. Best guide to observational astrophysics in English. Bridges the gap between elementary popularizations and advanced technical monographs. Covers stellar photometry, stellar spectra and classification, Hertzsprung-Russell diagrams, Yerkes 2-dimensional classification, temperatures, diameters, masses and densities, evolution of the stars. Translated by Owen Gingerich. 51 figures, 11 tables. xii + 164pp.
(USCO) 60771-2 Paperbound $2.00

INTRODUCTION TO BESSEL FUNCTIONS, Frank Bowman. Full, clear introduction to properties and applications of Bessel functions. Covers Bessel functions of zero order, of any order; definite integrals; asymptotic expansions; Bessel's solution to Kepler's problem; circular membranes; etc. Math above calculus and fundamentals of differential equations developed within text. 636 problems. 28 figures. x + 135pp.
60462-4 Paperbound $1.75

DIFFERENTIAL AND INTEGRAL CALCULUS, Philip Franklin. A full and basic introduction, textbook for a two- or three-semester course, or self-study. Covers parametric functions, force components in polar coordinates, Duhamel's theorem, methods and applications of integration, infinite series, Taylor's series, vectors and surfaces in space, etc. Exercises follow each chapter with full solutions at back of the book. Index. xi + 679pp.
62520-6 Paperbound $4.00

THE EXACT SCIENCES IN ANTIQUITY, O. Neugebauer. Modern overview chiefly of mathematics and astronomy as developed by the Egyptians and Babylonians. Reveals startling advancement of Babylonian mathematics (tables for numerical computations, quadratic equations with two unknowns, implications that Pythagorean theorem was known 1000 years before Pythagoras), and sophisticated astronomy based on competent mathematics. Also covers transmission of this knowledge to Hellenistic world. 14 plates, 52 figures. xvii + 240pp.
22332-9 Paperbound $2.50

THE THIRTEEN BOOKS OF EUCLID'S ELEMENTS, translated with introduction and commentary by Sir Thomas Heath. Unabridged republication of definitive edition based on the text of Heiberg. Translator's notes discuss textual and linguistic matters, mathematical analysis, 2500 years of critical commentary on the Elements. Do not confuse with abridged school editions. Total of xvii + 1414pp.
60088-2, 60089-0, 60090-4 Three volumes, Paperbound $8.50

AN INTRODUCTION TO SYMBOLIC LOGIC, Susanne K. Langer. Well-known introduction, popular among readers with elementary mathematical background. Starts with simple symbols and conventions and teaches Boole-Schroeder and Russell-Whitehead systems. 367pp.
60164-1 Paperbound $2.25

*Prices subject to change without notice.*